# READ THE REVIEWS

"Contracts are the foundation of any business, and the average Global 1000 corporation maintains over 40,000 active contracts. Yet, for most companies, the word processor, circa 1976, was the last great innovation adopted for managing these strategic agreements. This presents an array of challenges, from lack of visibility into legal and financial risk—to maverick contracting and poor contract enforcement. The results are lost savings and revenue. Enterprise contract management can help companies actively manage their contracts with a direct impact on the bottom line, and this book by Anuj Saxena can show you how. I highly recommend it for anyone examining enterprise contract management."

**—Avner Schneur, Chief Executive Officer, Emptoris, Inc.**

"*Enterprise Contract Management: A Practical Guide to Successfully Implementing an ECM Solution* is the most readable and comprehensive guide to understanding and implementing an Enterprise Contract Management solution that I have read. It builds a compelling business case for ECM and provides step-by-step guidance for successfully developing and implementing this complex, neglected but critical application."

**—D. Paul Murphy, Former Principal, Ernst and Young Consulting**

"This is the best book that I've read on Enterprise Contract Management. Every CEO, CFO, CIO, and CPO who is interested in increasing shareholder value, reducing risk, and sustaining compliance via ECM solution implementation needs to read this book and make it required reading for his or her management and implementation teams."

**—Sue Levengood, Director, Corporate Sourcing, Westfield Insurance**

"This book is a must-read for any organization embarking on the journey to implement an Enterprise Contract Management solution. The concepts and theories presented in the book provide an excellent roadmap for successful ECM implementation. Save your company time and money—read the book!"

**—Kathleen Blount, Former Procurement Advisor, ConocoPhillips**

# READ THE REVIEWS

"Amazing is the word that immediately comes to mind after reading this book—finally a comprehensive resource. Every organization looking at deploying an ECM solution needs to read this book twice and reference it through every step of the deployment. I have no doubt that in doing so, your implementation will be much more successful and that you'll get a significantly faster return on investment! This book is a 'must-read' for executives, contract managers, project managers, and supply managers and a critical element for every practitioner, consultant, and solution provider in the ECM space."

**—Ashif Mawji, CEO, Upside Software, Inc.**

"This is the definitive book on the history and practical approach to implementing ECM. If you're considering or leading an ECM project, Saxena's book is a must-read. The time spent reading the book will return multiples in better decisions and increase business value."

**—Randy Jacops, President and CEO, Nextance**

"I highly recommend *Enterprise Contract Management: A Practical Guide to Successfully Implementing an ECM Solution* by Anuj Saxena to all organizations that are considering implementing an ECM solution and organizations that have implemented but want to harvest more value from the solution. Mr. Saxena provides comprehensive guidance on how to be successful with an initiative of this kind, and he presents in a structured manner how to maximize the value of implementing an ECM solution.

"The winners in today's global networked economy have the ability to make and manage commitments faster, more reliably, and more profitably than their competitors. Negotiation, contracts, and relationship management are rapidly becoming sources of competitive advantage. For the best performers, their aim is not only to be more efficient—meaning quicker decision-making, increased delegation, and improved controls—but also to become more effective. That means achieving superior outcomes from their negotiations and relationships, with the commercial staff the focus for making that happen. Whether within sales, legal, procurement, or finance, things are changing fast—and this means dramatic opportunities for growth in status, role, and contribution."

**—Tom-Inge Aas, CEO, CMA, Contiki**

# ENTERPRISE CONTRACT MANAGEMENT

## A Practical Guide to Successfully Implementing an ECM Solution

**Anuj Saxena**

J.ROSS PUBLISHING

IACCM
International Association for Contract
and Commercial Management

Copyright ©2008 by Anuj Saxena

ISBN-13: 978-1-932159-90-5

Printed and bound in the U.S.A. Printed on acid-free paper
10  9  8  7  6  5  4  3  2  1

**Library of Congress Cataloging-in-Publication Data**

Saxena, Anuj, 1971-
  Enterprise contract management : a practical guide to successfully
implementing an ECM solution / by Anuj Saxena.
        p. cm.
  Includes index.   7047817
  ISBN-13: 978-1-932159-90-5 (hbk. : alk. paper)
 1. Purchasing—Management. 2. Vendors and purchasers. 3.
Contracts—Management. 4. Commercial documents—Management. I. Title.
  HF5437.S29 2008
  658.7′23—dc22                                          2007052784

Phone: (954) 727-9333
Fax: (561) 892-0700
Web: www.jrosspub.com

# TABLE OF CONTENTS

# LIST OF TABLES

# LIST OF FIGURES

# FOREWORD

Today's business managers operate in globally networked markets. They face growing competition and complexity as shifts in economic power coincide with an era of increased governance and regulatory oversight. Many companies are struggling to achieve a balance between risk and opportunity. Many managers feel overwhelmed by workload and the uncertainty of how they—and their function or department—can demonstrate higher value.

In every world region, as businesses contend with these new economic realities, traditional relationships and organizational structures are breaking down. They confront an environment where any misstep is broadcast rapidly to a worldwide audience, where relative power is constantly shifting, and where trust and reputation have become global imperatives.

In such a world, the need to form and manage effective trading relationships, crossing new boundaries, has become critical to success—yet few corporations possess this competency. Without it, the weakness of internal decision-making processes and poor information flows soon becomes apparent and leaves a business exposed to transactional overload or unacceptable risks.

At the heart of this dilemma sits the process that is used to make and manage commitments and promises. The problem is that contracts are the vehicle through which commitments are typically established, and contracting is rarely a holistic process. Most corporate managers cannot point to a defined set of procedures, nor can they pinpoint anyone accountable for the quality or integrity of the contracting process. Commitments are managed through a range of stakeholder groups, resulting in a complex decision-making matrix. The result is either inflexibility or extended lead times, poor planning, and transactional decisions that suboptimize results.

Contracting frequently is viewed as a mechanism for control and for the allocation of risks. It is allowed to become a straitjacket where success is measured in narrow terms of compliance or cost savings, rather than added value, economic efficiency, or good governance. A sense of bureaucracy and confrontation typifies the view of the process; as one top executive recently commented: "We tell our clients that you can collaborate in spite of the contract." As we cross these boundaries of culture, and face a world of such rapid and dynamic change, can we afford such an anachronistic method of forming and managing the relationships on which our businesses depend?

To illustrate the point, recent years have seen an increase in the average cycle times for nonstandard contracts. They have witnessed high failure rates in many complex relationships, such as outsourcing. They have seen a continued shift to a services economy, where the contractual record is often the only tangible output of our engagement—and struggles to reflect our needs, aspirations, or intent.

So at the very time when a networked economy places a premium on our ability to shape and manage successful trading relationships, corporate capabilities are found wanting—and there is no evident point of leadership to fix the problem.

To sustain growth while ensuring compliance, companies must develop value-add market offerings that offer competitive difference and contribute to a sense of integrity and trust. This means that their commitment processes must be well tuned to market conditions, agile yet subject to appropriate review, flexible yet well aligned with business capabilities and needs.

Contracts are certainly not new; in fact, they are one of the oldest features of trading relationships and date back thousands of years. For most of that time, there was scarcely any change in the way that contracts were formed and managed. Now, in a fast-moving and increasingly competitive world, where transactions and negotiations are increasingly crossing traditional boundaries, the contracting process is becoming an obstacle, an impediment to trust and collaboration. One key reason for this is that although contracts are core assets and although they contain a wealth of critical business data, the process by which they are formed, recorded, monitored, and amended is one of the last areas of business automation. Another is that "the contract" is the bastion of one of the last nationally oriented professional groups—the attorneys. For many, "globalization" and "automation" represent a major threat to their knowledge and prestige. A courageous minority has grasped the need for change and is leading their profession into the networked world.

Without automation, managers lack a source of data and information to drive change and improvement. The complexity of transactional and manual activities lies hidden behind core issues such as cycle times, decision processes, business assurance, and customer/supplier satisfaction.

Farsighted executives understand that the contracting process, and the policies reflected in business terms and negotiation behaviors, has a direct connection to key attributes, such as ease of doing business and reputation for fairness and integrity. As they venture across new borders and wrestle with the complexity of networked organizations, the linkage offered by contractual relationships becomes critical to business performance and change management.

Top corporations want to know how to drive new approaches and methods in the way they form requirements, negotiate, and manage trading relationships. They see the connection with the contract, but it is often tough to define the reengineered process that will tie things together. Answers come when dynamic and enthusiastic individuals work together to design and implement the framework and systems that support this new world of networked trading relationships. They come also from following the practical guidance offered in this important book.

Few organizations have yet realized the value they can gain from a well-defined and managed contract management process. It is an opportunity waiting to be discovered—and as this book explains, it can yield savings, incremental revenue opportunities, potential competitive advantage—and improved management of risk.

*Tim Cummins*
*President & CEO*
*International Association for*
*Contract & Commercial Management*

# PREFACE

In today's rapidly changing and increasingly competitive global economy, bottom-line results are the focus at every level in virtually all organizations. The two core elements involved in bottom-line performance—increasing revenues and decreasing costs—are influenced to a great degree by how well an organization manages its relationships with its business partners. At the heart of every business relationship are contracts, the documents that memorialize and codify the essential elements of business transactions. Since contracts define and underpin all commercial relationships, they not only provide a platform for the profitable growth of an organization, but also determine the organization's future competitiveness in an ever-changing business and geoeconomic environment. Today, between 60 and 80% of all business-to-business transactions are governed by a formal trade agreement, with the typical Fortune 1000 company maintaining 20,000 to 40,000 active contracts at any given time.*

A number of factors have led to a significant rise in the importance, volume, and complexity of modern contractual agreements. These factors include the advent of global supply chains, increasing economic uncertainties, geopolitical instability, outsourcing, procurement and sales force automation, and new regulatory requirements. Yet, in spite of these recent profound changes in the business environment, many organizations still manage the contracting process in a fragmented, manual, and ad hoc manner, resulting in poor visibility into contracts, ineffective monitoring and management of contract compliance, and inadequate analysis of contract performance. The net result of such inefficient contract management is significantly higher costs, numerous revenue delays, customer dissatisfaction, overcharges, erroneous payments, performance glitches,

---

* Institute for Supply Management.

missed savings opportunities, regulatory violations, and increased risks. It is, therefore, not surprising that three studies conducted by the Aberdeen Group found that "enterprises rated contract management among the top business application investments prioritized for the next 24 months."*

## ENTERPRISE CONTRACT MANAGEMENT SOLUTIONS

The heightened interest in automation of contract management processes has put the spotlight on contract life cycle management—often referred to as Enterprise Contract Management (ECM)—solutions. The goal of an ECM solution is to automate and streamline all stages in the life cycle of a contract, enforce consistent and efficient contracting processes, institute organizational controls, gain visibility into an organization's risks and opportunities, and ensure compliance with regulatory and financial accountability requirements. Several research firms have provided estimates as to the prospective returns resulting from implementing an ECM solution. According to AMR Research, "ECM implementations take two to three months—and achieve a 150% to 200% payback within one year."** The Aberdeen Group has reported that "the ROI for an organization with $750 million in annual revenue and $200 million in annual spend from an ECM implementation is more than 3X in the first year!"* While the estimates will vary by organization and by industry, it is obvious that research groups and organizations agree that implementation of an ECM solution, if done correctly, can help reduce costs, maximize revenues, and minimize risks for any organization.

ECM solutions are a relatively new addition to the world of technology solutions. While a few existing books present the theory behind ECM, there is very little, if any, published material concerning ECM solutions. Given the limited familiarity of today's business leaders (from CEOs to project managers to contract authors and administrators) with the capabilities of current ECM solutions, it is not surprising that the prospect of implementing an ECM solution appears daunting to most organizations. This book was, therefore, written with the goal of introducing ECM solutions, their key functions and capabilities, and the benefits afforded to an organization by such a technology solution. It presents the theory behind ECM, followed by a discussion of how an ECM solution addresses the challenges, and satisfies the business require-

---

* The Contract Management Solution Selection Report, Aberdeen Group, Boston, June 2005.
** The Compelling ROI of Contract Management, AMR Research, Boston, February 2003.

ments, of an organization's contract management. Lastly, and perhaps most importantly, this book fills the void in current literature by linking the theoretical background of ECM and ECM solutions with the practical aspects of implementing these solutions.

This book is organized into two sections. The first section (Chapters 1 to 5) presents the basic concepts, fundamentals, and theory behind ECM. The second section of the book (Chapters 6 to 11) provides project managers, consultants, and senior managers tasked with the implementation of an ECM solution with the knowledge essential to ensure a successful implementation.

## SECTION I

Chapter 1 begins our journey toward gaining a basic understanding of contracts. During the past decade, contracts have undergone substantial transformations, in large part due to globalization, complex supply chains, outsourcing, advancements in technology, and ever-increasing compliance requirements. This chapter, therefore, begins with a discussion of the evolution of contracts. The phenomenal increase in the number of contracts as well as in the level of complexity of each contractual document has led to increased confusion concerning the exact definition of the term. A definition of the term "contract" is provided, followed by a detailed description of the key types of contracts and their different flavors.

Chapter 2 builds on the material presented about contracts in Chapter 1 by describing the key phases in the life cycle of a contract: contract conception and creation, contract collaboration, contract execution, contract administration, as well as contract closeout and analysis. This chapter also introduces the concept of ECM as the process of managing all phases in the life cycle of a contract with the goal of minimizing costs and risks, maximizing revenue, streamlining operations, and improving compliance with policies, procedures, regulations, and negotiated terms and conditions. Key pain points of most organizations in ECM are presented via discussions on the current state of ECM across organizations, the impact of poor ECM on individual organizations, and key challenges faced by most organizations in ECM.

As mentioned earlier, according to a recent Aberdeen Group study, many organizations have begun to seriously consider the implementation of a technology solution as one way to address some of the pain points associated with ECM. Such technology solutions are commonly known as ECM solutions and are the primary topic of discussion in the next chapter. Chapter 3 is a primer on ECM solutions and answers some of the key questions that senior executives and managers considering an ECM solution implementation would have, such as:

- What is an ECM solution?
- How does an ECM solution address the challenges in the contract life cycle?
- Is an ECM solution right for my organization?
- Which ECM solution is right for my organization?
- What are the current trends in the ECM solution market?
- Where will this ECM solution fit in my organization?
- What benefits can I expect from this ECM solution?

One of the key benefits (described in Chapter 3) of implementing an ECM solution is that it helps an organization in achieving compliance with regulations, with organizational policies and procedures, and with the existing contractual terms and conditions with business partners. Chapter 4 dives deeper into this particular topic and presents the intimate, complex, and potentially powerful relationship between ECM applications and compliance management. It outlines the three major domains—regulatory, contractual, and procedural—of compliance for an organization and discusses the interrelationships between these domains and the demands that these relationships place upon an organization, both internally and externally. These demands arise from the need to interact with the various agencies involved in establishing and monitoring compliance policies, the divisions within an organization that must work effectively to achieve sustained compliance, and the various vendors, customers, and business partners with which a company must interact in a compliance-friendly environment. The role of ECM in streamlining these relationships is emphasized, including the role of an ECM solution as a tool in contract creation, approval, execution, monitoring, and analysis, utilizing appropriate templates, reporting mechanisms, and notifications of compliance activities as they relate to predetermined standards. Finally, this chapter makes the case that by properly implementing an ECM solution in an organization's enterprise applications, policies, and procedures, ECM can become a valuable and proactive force in positioning the organization to deal effectively with the challenges of compliance, today and tomorrow. It can also increase the overall value of the organization for its stakeholders through instilling a compliance-friendly corporate culture.

Contracts play an unprecedented role in the present operation and in the future survival and success of today's large and complex organizations. Given this fact, only the most sophisticated and well-designed approach will enable such an organization to effectively evolve from its present state of ECM to the state of ongoing process and cultural evolution typified by excellence at all levels. This approach must involve a combination of vision, will, commitment, technology, and discipline that fully considers the dynamic nature of the organization and its contractual relationships with its business partners. Such an approach must take into account the very real fact that each organization—and each division within each organization—is at a unique stage of development, process maturity, and process capability. A tailored approach is, therefore, required to implement an effective and efficient ECM system and to ensure that permanent and positive improvements are made at all levels.

Chapter 5 addresses these issues by presenting an ECM Maturity Model and an ECM Maturity Appraisal Method. The ECM Maturity Model is a five-level evolutionary path by which an organization may ascend from a relatively low level of maturity in its ECM capabilities to the highest level possible: sustainable ECM excellence. It is a comprehensive model by which an organization might assess its current competence in contract management, benchmark its contracting processes against those of its competitors, develop a vision to ensure and enforce use of best-in-class contract management practices, and chart a road map to reach these goals. The overall objectives and scope of this model are described, followed by a detailed discussion of each evolutionary stage in the model.

The four key aspects common to each level in the ECM Maturity Model are described: people, process, technology, and risk/reward. Each of these aspects is contrasted and compared for the five evolutionary levels of the model. Since an ECM implementation or its improvement within the context of a maturity model is a process, the tools required to measure and monitor an organization's progress in ECM capabilities are provided in the ECM Maturity Appraisal Method. This method permits necessary baselines, benchmarks, and metrics to be employed in monitoring the process of migration from lower levels of ECM capability to higher levels. A case study is presented as an example, and key process areas and practices for each stage in the contract life cycle are discussed. The use of the appraisal method is demonstrated quantitatively, with specific scoring and ranking described and discussed. Chapter 5 concludes the first section of the book.

## SECTION II

The second section of the book (Chapters 6 to 11) presents practical considerations for ensuring the successful implementation of an ECM solution. This includes a review of project management methodologies, change management, and risk management considerations, as well as approaches to integrating an ECM solution within and beyond the organization.

The sheer depth and breadth of an ECM solution implementation suggest its power to bring about positive and lasting change within an organization. Many implementation methodologies have been utilized for ECM solution implementations in the past. Chapter 6 presents three proven implementation methodologies, including the Six Sigma methodology. Six Sigma is a proven, time-tested, and highly quantitative approach to process optimization that is based in metrics and analytics, but recognizes the human, intuitive, and philosophical elements critical to the success of any complex initiative. This chapter focuses specifically on those aspects of Six Sigma which are required for and optimally suited to a successful and sustained ECM solution implementation. The role of certain Six Sigma approaches, specifically DMAIC (Define, Measure, Analyze, Improve, and Control) and Design for Six Sigma (DFSS), is dealt with in considerable detail, as are the composition of the Six Sigma team and the roles of its members. This chapter presents a compelling case that the combination of the traditional Six Sigma DMAIC methodology and the relatively newer DFSS methodology offers the best prospects for maximizing the potential benefits of ECM solution implementation. In addition to the Six Sigma implementation methodology, the IDEAL^SM Model developed by the Software Engineering Institute and a generic ECM solution implementation methodology are also presented in detail.

The implementation of any technology solution, especially one as complex as an ECM solution, can never occur in a vacuum. Due to the very nature of the business processes included in such a technology solution, its implementation will inevitably involve large, heterogeneous, intra- and interorganizational groups of people. Thus it is not surprising to learn that some of the biggest challenges facing such an implementation are often behavioral rather than technical. Chapter 7, therefore, makes the case that by understanding the dynamics of organizational change, and by using these dynamics for maximum positive effect, lasting benefits may be derived from ECM solution implementation initiatives. This chapter identifies eight organizational change management elements, which, if considered proactively, permit the greatest value to be obtained from implementing an ECM solution both within and across organizations.

Even if the project management and organizational change management aspects of an ECM solution implementation are managed well, all technology implementation projects involve some level of real or perceived risks. Real risks, while for the most part known and quantifiable, must nonetheless be anticipated and minimized to the extent possible. Perceived risks, while in some cases nonexistent, can still represent a real impediment to the buy-in needed to build a coherent and forward-looking ECM implementation team. Early identification and continuing management of true, as well as perceived, risks are vital to a successful ECM solution implementation. Thus, Chapter 8 classifies the real and perceived risks associated with a typical ECM solution implementation into six risk types and presents a systematic process for addressing them.

Chapter 9 addresses one of the final stages of ECM solution implementation by focusing on its integration within, throughout, and beyond the organization. While stand-alone ECM solution implementations have been known to provide a high return on investment to organizations in the short term, only through the integration of an ECM solution within and beyond each organization can organizations fully expect to realize the maximum possible return on investment on an ongoing basis. The benefits of a well-designed, integrated ECM solution reach far beyond the surface elements of cost savings, speed, and accuracy—they have actually been proven to have a profound influence on the components of latency at critical stages in the life cycle of virtually all major business decisions within an organization. The net result of this benefit is to dramatically accelerate the value realization of an organization's business decisions as they migrate to tangible relationships and transactions in the world of commerce.

Chapter 9 outlines the many challenges facing the managers of today's mid-size to large enterprises in the context of the benefits made available through integrating an ECM solution, including:

- The impact of effective ECM solution integration on the extended enterprise
- The impact of such integration on an organization's agility in a competitive marketplace
- The role of ECM solution integration in a global business environment
- The impact of technology advances, outsourcing, and today's increasing era of compliance on the role that ECM solution integration can play in enhancing an organization's prospects for survival and success

This outline makes a compelling business case for integrating an ECM solution with other enterprise-wide applications and is followed by a description of the major integration approaches and steps that can be used to accomplish the vision of an integrated ECM solution.

While project management, change management, risk management, and integration considerations are all important in ensuring a successful ECM solution implementation, none of these tasks is as critical as measuring and ensuring the actual results and benefits of the ECM solution implemented on an ongoing basis. A combination of metrics and subjective surveys is essential in measuring the results of an ECM solution implementation, including the value added to the core contracting group, to business functions such as procurement and sales, and to the organization as a whole. By defining, quantifying, and measuring key elements in each of these areas, and coupling these results with subjective surveys to learn the human effect, an ECM solution implementation and rollout can routinely be evaluated for the value it adds to an organization. Toward that end, Chapter 10 begins with a generic discussion about metrics, specifically covering what metrics are, which metrics work best, how metrics should be used, when they should be used, and how a metrics-based program can be implemented. It then provides some key metrics that can be used by an organization before, during, and after ECM solution implementation.

The final chapter of this book, Chapter 11, summarizes the top ten success factors and pitfalls observed in past ECM solution implementations and closes with a discussion of how to sustain success and continuous improvement in ECM.

# ACKNOWLEDGMENTS

Researching and writing a book is a time-consuming process, especially if the book is on a new topic such as Enterprise Contract Management, for which there are very few knowledgeable and experienced resources. I would like to take this opportunity to acknowledge several individuals who were either directly or indirectly responsible for this book.

First and foremost, I would like to thank my parents, Dr. J.P. Saxena and Mrs. Rajesh Mobar, for inspiring and encouraging me to write this book, as well as for my dad's critical and honest feedback. I would also like to thank my wife and best friend, Deepali, who provided the emotional support and patience when I was tapping away at the computer instead of spending time with her. Additionally, she provided critical feedback on the content and graphics within the manuscript.

I would also like to thank the many clients for whom I have implemented an ECM solution. Specifically, I would like to thank my ConocoPhillips ECM team—Orv Wiens, Mark Sonnier, Paul Creech, Mike Tessman, and Kathy Blount—and my colleagues—Karthik Radhakrishnan and Brian Mueller—for providing the opportunity to both share with and learn from them. Such collective learning is the backbone of this book.

I would like to acknowledge the contribution of my friend and editor, Ernest Hubbard, not only for his excellent editing effort but also for his invaluable contributions to many chapters of this book based on his past experience with authoring and administering contracts.

I would also like to acknowledge the contributions made by IACCM in helping to frame this book and its recommendations. As the only professional association focused on commercial contract management, and with a worldwide membership, IACCM research and strategy is providing global leadership in raising the profile and understanding of contract management. This general acknowledgment is given in place of the many individual references that the author might have made to IACCM work and materials.

Last but not least, I would like to thank my long-time friend, Scott Webster, for his support and guidance with regard to this effort, as well for constantly motivating me to write this book.

I would certainly appreciate receiving any corrections, additions, or other comments in regard to the content of this work. Any such contributions that are used will be acknowledged in any future editions of this work. It is said that you can learn something from everyone. I have attempted to learn something from each person with whom I have worked and hope to share some of that knowledge through this book.

# ABOUT THE AUTHOR

 **Anuj Saxena** is an internationally known expert in the field of Enterprise Contract Management who has led over twenty-five ECM solution implementations in the United States and Europe, authored several journal articles, and speaks frequently at popular conferences throughout the United States. He has over ten years of experience in selling and delivering management consulting services to organizations in the oil and gas, chemicals, high-tech, automotive, and pharmaceutical industry sectors. His domain expertise includes supply chain management, materials management, sales and distribution, enterprise asset management, and master data management.

Mr. Saxena has a bachelor's degree in mechanical engineering and master's degrees in information systems and decision sciences and in industrial and manufacturing systems engineering. In addition to holding several vendor certifications, he is a Certified Purchasing Manager (CPM), Certified in Production & Inventory Management (CPIM), Certified Project Management Professional (PMP), Certified in Commercial and Contract Management (MCCM), and a Six Sigma Black Belt Professional. He is an active member of several professional organizations, including the International Association for Contract and Commercial Management and the National Contract Management Association.

# ABOUT IACCM

The International Association for Contract & Commercial Management (IACCM) is a nonprofit foundation recognized as the international authority on the role of contracting and commitment management in the global networked economy and as the global forum for innovation in trading relationships and practices. IACCM works with corporations and public and academic bodies to provide thought leadership and understanding of "best practice" contracting and relationship standards and to define organizational models and skills to ensure integrity, trust, and the collaborative trading relationships that are necessary to support the continued development of the global economy. Its membership is drawn from more than 1,600 corporations and public sector organizations in over 90 countries and represents a community of contract and commercial managers, attorneys, and supply management executives and professionals. IACCM's primary objectives are: to define and promote the role of contracts and negotiation professionals in industry and commerce; to provide the services, knowledge, education, and training required to enable organizational and professional excellence in contracting and commercial management; and to enhance employment opportunities for its members.

IACCM offers:

- Unique "on-demand" research and benchmarks on commercial contracting topics and organization and professional development
- Access to a worldwide community through over 50 different Communities of Interest
- A powerful collaborative forum that brings together sales contracting, legal, and strategic sourcing experts around the world

- Extensive training materials, classes, e-learning modules, and professional accreditation
- An IACCM Store that contains helpful reports, books, and DVDs and an Executive Library that contains thousands of valuable articles
- Free webcasts and audio calls featuring top authors, academics, and subject-matter experts
- Newsletters, a Commitment Matters blog, regular updates, and news on commercial contracting, supply chain, professional development and related subjects, and much more

IACCM provides insight into leading-edge contracting and commercial skills, policies, procedures, and methods fundamental to managing risk. This insight equips professionals and their leaders to implement best practice governance of contractual commitments and trading relationships. Through a worldwide presence and networked technology, IACCM members gain access to the thought leadership and practical tools that are essential for competitiveness in today's fiercely contested global markets.

To join IACCM, or for complete information on the many benefits and services of IACCM membership, go to www.iaccm.com or contact IACCM at 90 Grove Street, Ridgefield, CT 06877 or by phone at 203-431-8741.

Web
Added
Value™

*Free value-added materials available from*
*the Download Resource Center at www.jrosspub.com*

At J. Ross Publishing we are committed to providing today's professional with practical, hands-on tools that enhance the learning experience and give readers an opportunity to apply what they have learned. That is why we offer free ancillary materials available for download on this book and all participating Web Added Value™ publications. These online resources may include interactive versions of material that appears in the book or supplemental templates, worksheets, models, plans, case studies, proposals, spreadsheets and assessment tools, among other things. Whenever you see the WAV™ symbol in any of our publications, it means bonus materials accompany the book and are available from the Web Added Value Download Resource Center at www.jrosspub.com.

Downloads available for *Enterprise Contract Management: A Practical Guide to Successfully Implementing an ECM Solution* consist of best practices for implementing an ECM solution, a sample project plan and an RFP template, and other valuable resources.

# SECTION I.
# BASIC CONCEPTS,
# FUNDAMENTALS,
# AND THEORY

# CONTRACTS

## IN THIS CHAPTER:

- Evolution of Contracts
- Definition of a Contract
- Types of Contracts

## 1.1 OVERVIEW

In today's business world, the phrase "the document drives the deed" might be well regarded as the maxim—or perhaps "the document *should* drive the deed" would be more apropos. Today's modern organization is formed by, operates under, and is regulated by an enormous and complex universe of documents we generally refer to as "contracts"—a term whose simplicity belies the nearly incomprehensible array of variety and form that such documents can assume. From the simplest of transactions (e.g., paying the electric bill) to the most complex transactions imaginable involving billions of dollars, scores of enterprises, and governmental agencies—both domestic and foreign, the single fact stands that success in today's world of commerce depends to a very great extent upon an organization's ability to effectively—and proactively—manage its contracts.

It is worthwhile to point out that in the past, the number of contractual agreements that any single organization had to manage was relatively low, and their level of complexity was not particularly daunting. As the cliché goes, "that was then." Today, it is not uncommon for there to be, at any point in time for a large organization, tens of thousands of legal agreements driving its operations, a situation several times more complex than in the past. At this level of complexity, one person, or even a skilled and experienced team, would find it nearly impossible to manage such a dynamic, complex, and critical population of documents without a set of sophisticated tools enabling an efficient implementation of contract life cycle management to the benefit of the organization. The first step in this process is to ensure that those involved have a clear understanding of the term *contract* itself.

Therefore, we begin by providing some background information and a high-level overview of the following topics in this chapter:

- History of the evolution of contracts
- Definition of the term contract
- Types of contracts commonly used in today's business environment

## 1.2  EVOLUTION OF CONTRACTS

Contracts have evolved over the centuries as a virtually universal method of forming lawfully binding relationships between two or more parties. The nature and scope of a contractual relationship can occur across a wide spectrum—from a small, temporary project to a full-scale corporate takeover or a treaty between nations. Generally, contracts are comprised of standardized tangible elements and codification and tend to be structured in accordance with the laws of the country in which they are written. While in some countries and cultures contracting parties elect to recognize verbal and handshake agreements that consist of informal promises or trades of goods and services, most contracts in modern commerce require documentation codified in legally binding language and terminology, consistent with all relevant statutes, regulations, policies, and laws, and duly signed and approved by the authorized parties concerned. Only then can a contract be considered valid and active, and even then it is subject to interpretation by the parties and the legal systems under which it is construed. Interpretation notwithstanding, contracts thus entered into by the parties involved are considered to be in full force and effect by their respective organizations.

As the needs of people, governments, and other institutions have become increasingly complex, contracts have evolved to reflect and codify these changing needs. During the past decade, contracts have undergone substantial transformations, in large part because of the use of computers and the Internet and the subsequent globalization of our economy. Add to this the increasing complexity of supply chains, outsourcing, and deregulation and the ever-increasing number and types of competitors. With all these changes, it's no wonder that agreements written a decade ago frequently seem simple and one dimensional compared with many agreements entered into by contemporary enterprises. This revolution in contract structure, content, and format has occurred within the broader context of the changing roles that contracts play in today's business world. What was once a relatively simple document designed to protect parties against worst-case scenarios has evolved into a dynamic and powerful tool with far-reaching implications for long-term business and personal relationships.

The rise in the sheer number of contracts under which a modern organization must operate was referred to above. As with any multiplicative process, this rise in number must be overlaid against the dimension of increased complexity of each individual contract in order to fully appreciate the new challenges that modern organizations must confront in their quest to remain compliant and competitive.

## 1.3  DEFINITION OF A CONTRACT

Given the rapid and dynamic evolution of contracts during the past several decades, it is not surprising that different experts and research organizations vary in their views and definitions of modern contracts. Gartner Research, for example, defines a contract as "the sum of all transactions and interactions that have taken place between the parties, both before and after the award of the contract."[*] While other authorities and authors define a contract in a variety of forms, some of which are quite limited, for the purpose of this book a contract may be defined as follows:

> A **contract** is a set of documents, governed and restricted by law, that clearly establish the boundaries, extent, and intent of the executing parties' relationship, along with the rights and responsibilities of the entities involved.

Purchasing agreements, sales agreements, service agreements, insurance policies, warranties, loans, mortgages, and rental leases are examples of contracts as

---

[*]  Six Keys to Better Procurement Contract Management, Gartner Research, Stamford, CT, October 2003.

defined for the purposes of this book. These may be priced agreements, but many contracts are not, examples of which are nondisclosure agreements, noncompete agreements, and teaming agreements. In the next section of this chapter, the different types of contracts that are commonly used in today's business environment are discussed.

## 1.4  TYPES OF CONTRACTS

There are a number of factors that influence the use of a specific type of contract on a particular job or project. Project scope, pricing, and scheduling would seem to be the "bottom line," but other factors are equally important over the project life cycle and must be addressed before deciding on contract type. Some of these factors include:

- Availability and accuracy of pricing data
- Accuracy in definition of project scope
- Flexibility allowed in delivery schedule
- Acceptable risk level for each participant
- Intensity of competition
- Relative strength of the buyer or the seller

The following are the main types of contracts in use in today's business environment:

- Fixed-price contracts
- Cost-reimbursable contracts
- Partially defined contracts
- Letter agreements

In the following sections of this chapter, a brief description of each of these types of contracts is provided.

### 1.4.1  Fixed-Price Contracts

Fixed-price contracts are usually favored by most buyers. Under such agreements, price does not vary from that agreed upon at the time of ordering, regardless of changing conditions. The seller assumes the risk involved and is, therefore, motivated to improve efficiency and minimize costs. There are several slight variations of the traditional fixed-price contract. These are:

■ **Firm fixed price:** These are sometimes referred to as "turnkey projects," where the buyer agrees to pay a specified amount upon the delivery of a service. Such contracts require minimum monitoring from the buyer's side as the financial risk is transferred to the seller. Such contracts are sometimes used when the buyer is unsure of the exact amount of raw materials or effort involved in the delivery of goods or equipment and wishes to transfer the risk involved to the seller. Sellers usually charge a premium for entering such agreements to cover the risks/uncertainty involved.

■ **Fixed price with adjustment:** Firm fixed-price contracts do not work very well in situations where the activity involved extends over a long period of time, during which labor or raw material rates may fluctuate considerably. Sellers also avoid firm fixed-price contracts in situations where the scope of the project may vary considerably once work is initiated. In such cases, an adjustment or escalation clause can be used, which provides protection to both buyers and sellers in the event of upward or downward pricing or rate changes over the duration of the project.

■ **Fixed price with redetermination:** These contracts are very similar to the adjustment contracts described above. Both types of contracts allow for upward or downward change in price after the contract is executed. The difference lies in the initial understanding of a project's required time, materials, and effort. In adjustment contracts, these factors are known with a degree of accuracy, but with redetermination contracts these essentials are unknown. Redetermination contracts are also typically used when project scope is not yet well defined. For example, in the case of several information technology implementation projects, the exact time required for the job is initially unknown. The total duration of individual tasks, and of the overall project, may vary significantly depending on a myriad of factors such as the functional and/or technology landscape of the organization, level of maturity and complexity of business processes and current systems, quantity and quality of data, and level of skill, knowledge, and abilities and availability of resources. In such situations, a temporary fixed price is used to execute the contract, and as the team gains a better understanding of the scope of work involved through an initial assessment, the price is redetermined and may be changed upward or downward as appropriate.

■ **Fixed price with downward price protection:** Downward price protection contracts are a variation of the adjustment contracts and provide maximum protection to the buyer since under such contracts price may be adjusted only in the downward direction.

■ **Fixed price with incentive**: As the name suggests, these contracts offer an incentive to the seller for accomplishing the awarded job within a preestablished target cost or ceiling price. Under such contracts, the buyer and seller share any savings at prenegotiated rates if the seller can keep the overall cost below the target cost. Such contracts are typically used in high-cost, long-lead-time projects, such as construction projects.

## 1.4.2 Cost-Reimbursable Contracts

With cost-reimbursable contracts, the buyer guarantees the seller a price that covers all, or an agreed-upon fraction, of the total costs, along with an agreed-upon fee, which may be a fixed fee, a fraction of the cost, or an award fee. The financial risk in most of these contracts falls on the buyer, and therefore such contracts require careful monitoring/administration.

One type of cost-reimbursable contract is the *cost-without-fee* contract. Cost-without-fee contracts are commonly used when financial profit is not the primary motive to enter into the contractual agreement and are, therefore, often used by such entities as nonprofit and research organizations.

Another type of cost-reimbursable contract is the *cost-sharing* contract. Under a cost-sharing contract, the buyer and seller share costs and benefits involved with the entire project. Such agreements are applicable in situations where the contracting parties are equal in strength and both parties stand to gain equally from the joint effort. For example, software vendors often team up with consulting firms to develop key functionality that ultimately becomes part of the end product that they sell. Software vendors gain from their consulting partners' subject matter expertise, adding critical functionality that may drive improved customer satisfaction and increased sales. On the other hand, involvement in such projects provides a competitive advantage to the consulting partners, since their resources gain knowledge and experience from implementing new functionality, which other consulting firms will not be able to offer to clients.

## 1.4.3 Partially Defined Contracts

Partially defined contracts are agreements where either the specific goods/services, the delivery schedule, or the quantity is unknown at the time of contract execution. The specification of required goods/services may be dependent on the production schedule or on the shutdown of equipment in a manufacturing environment. Manufacturing organizations often set up partially defined contracts such as *value contracts* (in which the maximum value of the contract is defined, but individual goods or services are unknown) or *quantity contracts* (in which the maximum quantity of goods or services to be procured is known). These are also referred to as *blanket arrangements* or *blanket purchase orders.*

*Time and material contracts* are examples of partially defined contracts. Such contracts only define the rate per hour for each type of service provided, but the exact quantity and/or schedule is usually unknown at the time of contract execution.

### 1.4.4 Letter Agreements

Letter agreements are sometimes used as a buyer's authorization for suppliers to begin work even before all details of the deal are finalized and before a formal contract has been executed. Such agreements are commonly used where the buyer and supplier have a preestablished working relationship from previous projects or where additional work is being assigned to a supplier that may already be working on a related project for the buyer at the time. The buyer should take care in such cases to clearly state liability limits in the event that the deal cannot be satisfactorily concluded and to assert the terms and conditions of the purchase.

## 1.5  SUMMARY

Over time, what is meant by the term contract has expanded from the quite simple handshake agreement to the multidimensional documents contracts have become today. The contemporary business organization often has a complex and ever-growing list of contractual goals and obligations that inform its activities and should therefore drive them. It is imperative that organizations manage the entire life cycle of their contracts in order to maximize contractual benefits, maintain compliance, and foster competitive advantage. Competitive advantage is particularly important when considering the number and types of contracts into which any organization might enter. As this chapter has illustrated, every type of contract requires a specific level of oversight in order to fully capitalize on the potential benefits.

It is obvious that for larger organizations, the burden of maintaining these contracts can be prohibitively complicated without the assistance of a more sophisticated system for managing all the stages in the life cycle of their contractual agreements. In the next chapter, we will discuss the different stages in the life cycle of a contract, the common challenges faced by organizations during these stages, and the impact of poor management of contracting processes within an organization.

# ENTERPRISE CONTRACT MANAGEMENT

## IN THIS CHAPTER:

- Definition of Enterprise Contract Management
- The Contract Life Cycle
- Challenges in the Contract Life Cycle
- Current State of Contract Management
- Impact of Poor Contract Management

## 2.1 OVERVIEW

In the previous chapter, we discussed the evolution of contracts. A definition of a contract was presented, along with examples of the different types of contracts that an organization may enter into in today's business environment.

The volume, type, importance, and complexity of modern contractual agreements have significantly risen across industry sectors and geographical regions. A number of factors, such as the advent of global supply chains, increasing economic uncertainties, geopolitical instability, outsourcing, procurement and sales force automation, and new regulatory requirements, have led to this rise in volume and complexity within contract management. Yet, in spite of these recent profound changes in the business environment, many organizations still manage the contracting process in a fragmented, manual, and ad hoc manner, resulting in poor visibility into contracts, ineffective monitoring and management of contract compliance, and inadequate analysis of contract performance. The net result of such inefficient contract management is significantly higher costs, numerous revenue recognition delays, customer dissatisfaction, overcharges, erroneous payments, performance glitches, missed savings opportunities, regulatory violations, and increased risk. It is, therefore, not surprising that three studies conducted by the Aberdeen Group found that "enterprises rated contract management among the top business application investments prioritized for the next 24 months."* However, before embarking on the discussion around contract management applications, we need to shed light on the topic of Enterprise Contract Management itself.

## 2.2  DEFINITION OF ENTERPRISE CONTRACT MANAGEMENT

In its broadest definition, Enterprise Contract Management (ECM) encompasses a wide spectrum of applications, protocols, and systems for managing an enterprise's contracts from A to Z. For the purposes of this book, ECM may be defined as follows:

> **ECM** is the process of managing all stages—such as conception and creation, collaboration, execution, administration, closeout, and analysis—in the life cycle of enterprise-wide contracts with the goal of minimizing costs and risks, maximizing revenues, streamlining operations, and improving compliance with policies, procedures, regulations, and negotiated terms and conditions.

## 2.3  THE CONTRACT LIFE CYCLE

Like many organizations and documents, contracts may be viewed in one context as resembling living organisms in a number of fundamental respects. Like living entities, contracts begin with conception, followed by phases of gestation, birth, maturation, and finally by either termination or renewal. The typical phases in the life cycle of a contract are shown in Figure 2.1. A detailed description of the contract life cycle phases is provided in the following sections.

---

* The Contract Management Solution Selection Report, Aberdeen Group, Boston, June 2005.

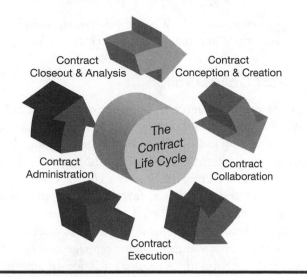

**FIGURE 2.1.  The Contract Life Cycle**

## 2.3.1  Contract Conception and Creation

Like living organisms, contracts are the fruits of conception—they do not arise out of the ether, but are the products of the goals and intentions of the contracting parties. Each party to a future contract has one or more goals in forming a relationship codified by the contract in question. A simple example would be a company's goal of having its facilities adequately well lit for safe operation and therefore entering into a contract with a local utility company to provide electrical service. The utility company, on the other hand, has the goal of offering high-quality electrical service in a financially beneficial manner. It is the convergence of these two goals that results in the formation of a contract whereby electricity is provided to the facility and through which the organization pays its power bill. Without such an agreement, there would be no basis for the deeds that permit both organizations to achieve their goals.

Once the conceptual basis for a contractual agreement has been established by both parties (often prememorialized in a letter of intent or memorandum of understanding), the actual process of creating the contract begins. This first step in the birth of a new contract is considered by many to be the most important phase in the life cycle of a contract. During contract creation, the document's author(s) must determine the purest and optimal wording to describe the relationship between the parties, including the nature and scope of products and/

or services to be exchanged and all other related aspects involved with the contemplated transactions and their consequences.

## 2.3.2  Contract Collaboration

During the contract drafting and negotiating processes, but before a contract is executed, it is customary—and in most cases essential—for a contract to be reviewed and approved by individuals within, as well as outside, the organization. Such internal and external review and authorization constitute the contract collaboration phase. During this phase, a contract is routed, based on an organization's policies and procedures, for review or approval to appropriate personnel in the organization's functional groups, such as legal, risk management, tax, audit, and insurance. Such routing of a contract within the organization may also include approval from senior management based on the dollar value of the contract, particularly if a contract is for an amount greater than the authority delegated to the contract author per the organization's policy. External collaboration during this phase of the contract life cycle includes one or more cycles of negotiations with suppliers, customers, or other business partners via fax, e-mail, or Web-based applications with the goal of reaching a mutually agreeable set of terms and conditions, which are documented in the contract.

## 2.3.3  Contract Execution

After all parties working toward establishment of the contract have reviewed and agreed upon its language, scope, and other contents, and after the contract has been thoroughly reviewed by all legal, regulatory, and compliance-related elements within the respective organizations, the contract may be executed. As with any birth, this formal execution of a contract operationally defines the effective start and end dates of the contractual relationship, duly enacted as evidenced by the signatures of authorized personnel from all parties involved. Moreover, execution of a contract formalizes and enables enforcement of mechanisms and procedures for amending the contract should such a need—or a dispute—arise.

## 2.3.4  Contract Administration

Once executed, a contract must be monitored and cared for, to ensure its proper enactment in light of the original goals of the contracting parties. Contract administration or contract monitoring includes the tracking and auditing of contract terms, including a sometimes dizzying array of issues such as pricing, rebates, service-level compliance, amendments, and performance. This phase of the cycle is made easier when the core mechanisms and procedures for contract administration are clearly set forth during the contract collaboration phase. The main goal of this phase of the contract life cycle is to ensure procedural, contractual, and regulatory compliance such that in the "outworking" of the contract, the organization actually achieves its original objectives and realizes the desired benefits and value hoped for when the contract was originally conceived, negotiated, and executed.

### 2.3.5 Contract Closeout and Analysis

As the saying goes, "It's more important how you say good-bye than how you say hello," and in this regard, the contract closeout and analysis phase is perhaps more critical than its place on the life cycle totem pole belies. While some analysis is conducted during ongoing administration of a contract, this particular phase specifically focuses on enforcing spend against budgets, balancing orders between preferred suppliers to optimize usage and returns, and assigning resources for the optimal management of the most profitable products and customers. In this phase, contract performance and attributes are also analyzed in order to determine the best methods to address future procurement, sales, budgeting, outsourcing, supplier management, and risk strategies. As a result of a well-executed analysis phase, the decision may be made to either close out or renew a contract. If a decision is made to terminate a contract, procedures and supporting documentation will have been put in place to adequately verify that all administrative matters involved in completing and settling the contract, as well as resolution of any open items, are available, in order, and ready for conclusion.

## 2.4 CHALLENGES IN THE CONTRACT LIFE CYCLE

In a perfect world, all contracts would be negotiated in good faith by all parties, contract wording would be clearly and consistently interpreted, and the relationship originally envisioned by the contracting parties would be fulfilled according to the original intent of the contract. Contractual relationships, however, do not always mirror this perfect world, nor are they always managed with optimal efficiency. It is, therefore, understandably in the best interests of an organization to preemptively identify those areas where problems in the contract life cycle might arise and to focus attention upon these areas, thereby minimizing the risk of negative outcomes and increasing the probability that the accuracy, integrity, and performance of every contract entered into will be achieved.

It is logical to ask for specifics in this regard. What are the major threats to successful execution of a contract? There are five major challenges to an organization in the successful enactment of a contract life cycle:

- **Fragmentation (disconnect) of critical procedures**: By definition, an organization's contracts can involve virtually every element of the organization, either in their development or their execution. Traditionally, contracting processes that span multiple organizational functional groups (such as procurement, sales, legal, and risk management) have been fragmented and subject to frequent miscommunications and disconnects during the processes of authoring, review, negotiation, and approval. These processes are not only complex in and of themselves, but they are also fraught with the constant risk of data entry errors.

- **Labor-intensive (expensive, time-consuming) processes**: Traditional contract management remains, for the most part, a highly manual process, in which frequent drafting, revision, printing, faxing, and storing of documents are required. These relatively unsophisticated processes add cost and time to the entire contract life cycle, resulting in missed revenue opportunities, diminished negotiating leverage, suboptimal compliance with regulations, and most importantly, an overall elevation of inefficiency and risk for the organization.

- **Poor visibility into contracts (lack of key intelligence)**: In today's large organizations, contracts are no longer held in central repositories that are accessible using simple authorization and document retrieval procedures. Instead, today's contracts often reside in multiple locations, in digital and hard-copy files, in archives, and in virtual systems that must be accessible at will by authorized individuals from both within and outside the organization's physical boundaries. Clearly, the issue of contract visibility is a paradoxical one, requiring constant management and monitoring of access and protection while ensuring accuracy of data and retention of file integrity. Simultaneously, an organization's contracts must be locked down from a data integrity and security standpoint, while being sufficiently accessible to be subject to periodic, ad hoc, and routine revision and modification by the appropriate parties. It is no great stretch to appreciate why, in a large organization with tens of thousands of contracts spread across scores of major divisions at hundreds of geographically disparate locations, the issue of contract visibility and security is beyond the scope of management by manual human protocols.

■ **Ineffective monitoring and management of compliance:** In many organizations, systems have not yet been implemented for routine monitoring of contract compliance, leading to what might best be referred to as rearview mirror reporting and brushfire management of compliance issues. The information most critical to compliance is virtually always maintained in contracts. Because of this, the processes that monitor and manage compliance during the contract life cycle are often suboptimal, ineffective, and inefficient. This leaves an organization ill-equipped to address the challenges and requirements of procedural, contractual, legal, and regulatory requirements. The degree to which an organization's inattentiveness in this area places it at risk cannot be overemphasized. In today's post-Enron/WorldCom world, the excuse that "I just didn't realize we were out of compliance" falls on deaf ears.

■ **Inadequate analysis of contract performance:** As the old saying goes, "If you don't know where you are going, you are almost sure to get there." Traditional approaches to contract performance analysis tend to be ad hoc and retrospective in nature, often adhering to the motto "if it isn't broken, don't fix it." This approach to contract performance analysis leads to an accumulation of under-the-radar problems, hidden costs, and liabilities, which can remain unobserved within an organization for years. Such time bombs can have far-reaching effects in reducing a company's profitability, unnecessarily adding to costs and inefficiencies and leaving it open to unsuspected disputes or, worse, litigation.

## 2.5 CURRENT STATE OF CONTRACT MANAGEMENT

Given the challenges facing the health of a contract during its life cycle, it is logical to ask: What can be done to manage the process? Of course, the field of contract management has been the subject of intense study for decades, heightened further by events in recent years which have elevated competitiveness and compliance to center stage. Having defined contracts, provided an overview of the contract life cycle, and identified the challenges faced by a typical organization at various stages of the contract life cycle, it is now appropriate to review the subject of contract management and in particular ECM as it has evolved and come to be practiced in most complex modern organizations.

In a recent study by the Institute for Supply Management, it was determined that between 60 and 80% of all business-to-business transactions are governed by a formal written agreement, with the typical Fortune 1000 company maintaining 20,000 to 40,000 active contracts at any given time. Given this statistic, it is difficult to believe that many organizations have yet to acquire or implement the efficient, effective controls and processes that would enable them to manage their contract portfolio with maximum efficiency and minimal risk. As discussed earlier, contract management in most organizations usually involves relying on manual, disjointed, and decentralized processes that result in limited visibility into contracts and their performance, missed revenue opportunities, inflated costs, diminished negotiation leverage, and poor compliance with regulations. A number of other factors—the advent of global supply chains, increasing economic uncertainties, geopolitical instability, outsourcing, procurement and sales force automation, and new regulatory requirements—have also added fuel to the fire, causing an increasing number of organizations to recognize the importance of an enterprise-level gestalt that employs procedures and systems to manage the contract life cycle.

During the past few decades, heightened interest in addressing the challenges faced during the contract life cycle has led to the rise in popularity of a new breed of technology solutions called ECM solutions. Contract life cycle management, a synonymous term for ECM, is also commonly used. ECM solutions have been specifically designed to automate and streamline all phases in the contract life cycle, thereby:

- Ensuring consistent and efficient contracting processes
- Instituting organizational controls
- Providing efficient and appropriate visibility into an organization's contractually based risks and opportunities
- Ensuring procedural, contractual, as well as regulatory compliance

As would be predicted, interest in ECM solutions is growing in concert with the increasing complexity and demands of organizations to manage the contractual dimension of their operations. An Aberdeen Group survey of 220 companies revealed that 27% of enterprises will invest in commercially available contract management solutions within the next twenty-four months.* Organizations participating in three Aberdeen Group benchmark studies rated contract management among the top business application investments prioritized for the next twenty-four months.* It is, therefore, evident that most forward-looking organizations either already have or will soon initiate activities to achieve excellence in the area of contract management through adoption of more efficient and effective processes, acquisition and implementation of new and better technology solutions, or in most cases a combination of both.

## 2.6 IMPACT OF POOR CONTRACT MANAGEMENT

The short story about inefficient contract life cycle management is that (1) it costs money and (2) it increases risk. The three major consequences of poor contract management are in the areas of increased operational costs, reduced revenues, and complications associated with audits.

Researchers at the Aberdeen Group estimate that a $1 billion organization with annual purchases totaling $500 million, of which $400 million is under contract, loses $18 million every year due to lack of proper supplier contract management. A company with suboptimal contract processes will spend additional time, effort, and expense in manually managing its supplier contracts, costing another $12 million annually.**

Bottom line:

> **If you are not in control of your contracts, you are not in control of your business.**

Understandably, the problems associated with access to and maintenance of an organization's contracts can have a direct impact upon the quality of the contractual relationship—leading to execution of suboptimal contracts. Such contracts represent less than the best interests of the organization and arise not so much because of poor negotiating ability on the part of the organization's representatives but primarily because of inefficiencies in the contract manage-

---

* The Contract Management Solution Selection Report, Aberdeen Group, Boston, June 2005.
** Susan Avery, "Contract Management Is the Next Step in Smart Supply Strategy," *Purchasing Magazine,* vol. 133, no. 12, pp. 60–64, July 2004.

ment system and the underlying business processes. Suboptimal contracts can also arise due to:

- Inadvertent deferral to less favorable terms (due to inefficient monitoring of stop-loss provisions, provision dates, etc.)
- Inefficient monitoring of compliance (due in part to lack of adequate visibility)
- Failure to ensure adequate standards of performance and goal benchmarks

Examples of the negative consequences of inefficient contract management include the following (with ranges and data from recent industry studies):

- Maverick (unsupervised) spending by buyers, which some studies estimate occurs in 17 to 27% of purchases
- Overcharging by suppliers (deliberate or inadvertent), with studies indicating that 10% of transactions involve price discrepancies
- Unwanted/unnecessary automatic renewal of products and services, as evidenced by studies indicating that 10% of contracts renew automatically
- Inability to verify if payments and deliverables are accurate and timely
- Inability to analyze actual against planned or contracted spending
- Inability to track accounts payable, which includes inability to enforce discounts and dealing with time-consuming and complex rebate calculations
- Inability to monitor effectiveness of contract management in terms of cycle time and contract quality (e.g., deliverables against plan, profitability, competitiveness)
- Lack of insight into supplier performance vis-à-vis contractual obligations
- Inability to enforce supplier contract performance or to enforce consequences for policy and regulatory violations
- Significant losses in time and resources due to inefficient contract authoring, editing, negotiating, and monitoring

## 2.7  SUMMARY

During the evolution of contracts, it may have been easy, appropriate, and risk-free to view one-dimensional contracts as bottom-line (terms, cost, time) documents. Today's larger organizations operate in a different space, where multiple multidimensional contracts must inform and drive their daily business and, ultimately, have tremendous impact on *their* bottom line. Managing contracts from a life cycle point of view is a crucial part of maximizing their efficacy from birth through termination or renewal.

In this chapter, we examined the stages of the contract life cycle and the problems inherent in each stage. We also examined the impact that poor contract management can have on any organization. The next chapter will provide an introduction to the technology solutions—commonly referred to as contract life cycle management or ECM solutions—to manage all stages in the life cycle of an organization's worldwide contracts.

# 3

# ENTERPRISE CONTRACT MANAGEMENT SOLUTIONS: AN INTRODUCTION

## IN THIS CHAPTER:

- What Is an ECM Solution?
- How Does an ECM Solution Address the Challenges in the Contract Life Cycle?
- Is an ECM Solution Right for My Organization?
- Which ECM Solution Is Right for My Organization?
- What Are the Current Trends in the ECM Solution Market?
- Where Will This ECM Solution Fit in My Organization?
- What Benefits Can I Expect from This ECM Solution?

## 3.1 OVERVIEW

Enterprise Contract Management (ECM) solutions have recently emerged as a key tool enabling today's organizations to address challenges in the contract life cycle and to provide focus and direction in their journey to excellence in contracting processes. These solutions come in many shapes, sizes, and price ranges; however, all ECM solutions are designed to achieve certain core objectives:

- Automate and streamline the various stages of the contract life cycle
- Permit enforcement of consistent and efficient contracting processes
- Institute and formalize organizational controls
- Provide visibility into an organization's risks and opportunities
- Ensure compliance with regulatory and financial accountability requirements

That ECM solutions have emerged as a powerful management tool is evidenced by their impact on the bottom line. The Aberdeen Group reported that organizations using ECM solutions to automate contract life cycle management processes have been able to reduce material and services costs by 2 to 7%, cut process cycles in half, reduce contract administration costs, improve contract compliance 50 to 55%, diminish operational and regulatory risk, and increase revenues and profits.* Considering the current market pressures to reduce costs and risks, increase revenue, and address compliance requirements, it is not surprising to note that organizations today are placing a very high priority on implementation of ECM solutions.

This chapter, therefore, presents a brief primer on ECM solutions and answers some of the key questions that senior executives and managers considering an ECM solution would have, such as:

- What is an ECM solution?
- How does an ECM solution address the challenges in the contract life cycle?
- Is an ECM solution right for my organization?
- Which ECM solution is right for my organization?
- What are the current trends in the ECM solution market?
- Where will this ECM solution fit in my organization?
- What benefits can I expect from this ECM solution?

## 3.2  WHAT IS AN ECM SOLUTION?

Industry experts often use the terms contract life cycle management and ECM solutions interchangeably. For the purposes of this book, the term "ECM solutions" will be used and may be defined as follows:

---

* Contract Optimization: A Recession-Proof Strategy for Maximizing Performance and Minimizing Risks, Aberdeen Group, Boston, May 2003.

**ECM solutions** are those enterprise-wide information technology solutions that offer an organization the optimal combination of best practices and technology to effectively and efficiently manage its contractual agreements, both within the organization and with entities beyond its borders.

Most ECM solutions provide the following core capabilities to an organization:

- Content and document management capabilities, including control and access to workflow, change management, audit trail, document hierarchy, and document versions
- Contract authoring and configuration capabilities, including clause template library and wizard functionality to automatically create a contract framework based on a user's responses to a set of questions related to the contract
- Collaborative contract development capabilities that provide support for contract development processes and workflow and for reconciling terms and conditions with suppliers
- Resource planning capabilities, including the ability to plan, schedule, and control all tasks associated with a specific contract and the ability to track actual time and cost incurred in contract management
- Performance and compliance management capabilities, including the ability to monitor and report on the performance of the contracting partner against the contract and track compliance against terms negotiated as part of the contract
- Comprehensive integration and reporting capabilities, including integration with transactional systems such as enterprise resource planning (ERP), supplier relationship management (SRM), customer relationship management (CRM), business warehouse, document management, and reporting on an enterprise-wide basis

## 3.3 HOW DOES AN ECM SOLUTION ADDRESS THE CHALLENGES IN THE CONTRACT LIFE CYCLE?

Based on the high-level description presented of key capabilities offered by ECM solutions, they are a powerful adjunct in top management's arsenal, offering access, control, and reporting capabilities previously not possible. But in order to produce true value for an organization, an ECM solution must solve real problems in the day-to-day operating environment. It is therefore worthwhile to take a closer look (see Table 3.1) at how an ECM solution helps address the specific challenges faced by an organization in the contract life cycle in a tangible value-added way.

**TABLE 3.1.  How ECM Solutions Address Challenges in the Contract Life Cycle**

| Improvement Area | How ECM Solutions Address Challenges in the Contract Life Cycle |
|---|---|
| Contract request | ■ Enable employees to initiate requests for new goods/ services |
| Integration with RFx processing system(s) | ■ Information from contract requests forms the RFx (RFP, RFQ, RFI, etc.) and data generated from the RFx then form the basis of the contract, which eliminates duplication of effort and ensures process integrity |
| Contract authoring | ■ Enable contract authors to use standard clauses and contract templates to create new contracts<br>■ Allow changes to standard templates based on unique requirements per contract |
| Internal collaboration | ■ Determine appropriate contract approval workflow based on terms and conditions chosen, value of contract, deviations from standard template, and other similar parameters |
| External collaboration | ■ Provide a way to present contracts to suppliers and customers online, by e-mail, or offline<br>■ Capture the full audit trail (including comments, changes to terms and conditions, file attachments, etc.) |
| Contract execution | ■ Capture key execution parameters such as legal entity names, internal and external signatures, effective start and end dates, next review dates, scanned copies of contract, etc. |
| Invoicing | ■ Ensure compliance with contract terms<br>■ Enable four-way match between contract, purchase order, goods/service receipt, and invoice |
| Strategic sourcing | ■ Enable analysis and reporting on suppliers within spend categories, indicating those that outperform and are cost effective |

**TABLE 3.1.  How ECM Solutions Address Challenges in the Contract Life Cycle (continued)**

| Improvement Area | How ECM Solutions Address Challenges in the Contract Life Cycle |
| --- | --- |
| Supplements/amendments/change orders | ■ Automate and track contract amendments and supplements, thereby reducing net effort required in new revisions of a contract |
| Contract repository | ■ Provide a single data repository where all versions/revisions of contracts are visible to all users based on security levels defined in contracts<br>■ Allow quick searching/sorting capabilities<br>■ Allow creation of parent-child links between agreements created with key suppliers |
| Renewals | ■ Notify appropriate personnel about upcoming contract expiration/renewal events to ensure effective planning of resources |
| Compliance | ■ Enable monitoring operational compliance, contractual compliance, and regulatory compliance factors |
| Contract monitoring | ■ Validate required compliance measures in contracts and report infractions<br>■ Enable tracking performance of suppliers and flag those that are below acceptable levels |
| Reporting and business intelligence | ■ Provide standard reports and empower non-IT resources to generate custom/ad hoc reports<br>■ Provide dashboard functionality for leadership |

# 3.4  IS AN ECM SOLUTION RIGHT FOR MY ORGANIZATION?

Oftentimes, an organization's management grasps the role and value of an ECM solution, but remains unsure if there is a need for it at the present time. Following is a good general guideline and indicator of your organization's potential need for ECM. If you answer "no" to any of the following questions, there is a high probability that an ECM solution should be on your short list:

■ Are your organization's contracts routinely coordinated across divisions?

- Can you efficiently locate any contract or term within a given contract?
- Do you know what percentage of your total contract portfolio is maintained online?
- Do you know the expiration dates and renewal dates of your contracts?
- Do you have a foolproof system in place to alert appropriate levels of management to key contract dates?
- Are you capturing all rebates or discounts in your supply contracts?
- Do all of your contracts go through a formal approval process before being executed?
- Are you able to ensure regulatory compliance with your corporate contracts?
- Do all your contracts comply with requisite terms, approvals, and corporate policies?
- Do you know immediately when a contract term has been achieved or violated?
- Are your financial systems updated when a contractual risk event occurs?
- Are you certain that you are not losing money due to cost leakages in your procurement contracts?
- Do you know how many contracts have cost penalties or potential legal liability and exposure to your organization?
- Can you routinely and efficiently compare and analyze the performance and terms of various contracts?
- Can you analyze and report on your contracts by vendor and by product?

Also, if you answer "yes" to any of the following questions, there is a high probability that your organization will benefit from an ECM solution:

- Do you have evergreen contracts that renew before you have a chance to renegotiate or cancel (e.g., lease agreements)?
- Are you paying unwarranted annual software maintenance fees?
- Do you suspect that your suppliers are overcharging you?
- Are you paying fees due to missed or late payments to suppliers?
- Are you missing the opportunity to take advantage of negotiated volume price breaks from suppliers? How do you use your contracts as part of your strategic sourcing analyses?
- Have you neglected doing an audit to assess your contracts and accounts payable functions for both cost and risk performance?

■ Is your contract development process antiquated? Is it a critical path item for sourcing?

Following is a useful diagnostic checklist regarding your organization's potential need for ECM solutions—a list of possible symptoms, if you will, of an organization whose contract management processes are not functioning as well as they might:

1. **Contract procedures and processes are labor intensive and fragmented**
   ■ Manual processes are used to create new contracts, typically employing word-processing applications
   ■ Different business units within the organization use different processes, procedures, and systems for managing contracts
   ■ Local business units do not leverage contracts already executed at a national or global level
   ■ Excessive contract processing times persist
   ■ Audits are resource and time intensive
   ■ Low or poor visibility into contract workflow and life cycle
   ■ Lack of proven templates or guidelines defining which specific terms and clauses are required for different types and different dollar values of contracts
   ■ Inadequate or insufficient reporting for senior management
   ■ High-cost staff performs administrative/review tasks
2. **Excessive costs are associated with contract management**
   ■ Low contract renewal rates due to lack of awareness of approaching contract expiration dates
   ■ Inefficient monitoring of performance and terms, resulting in overpayments, late fees, penalties, or failure to collect rebates or discounts
3. **Contracts involve high risk due to lack of compliance**
   ■ Lack of published policies and/or inability to prove consistent adherence to published contract-related policies
   ■ Unable to determine supplier compliance with terms and conditions negotiated in the contract
   ■ Absence of controls ensuring that contract authors have approval from legal, risk management, or other appropriate authorities prior to modifying contract terms or language
   ■ Lack of necessary integration and automatic reconciliation with financial systems

- Inability to routinely and rapidly identify all high-risk clauses
- The organization lacks contract performance monitoring and reporting tools

## 3.5  WHICH ECM SOLUTION IS RIGHT FOR MY ORGANIZATION?

Like automobiles or personal computers, ECM solutions come in a wide range of shapes and sizes. How does a chief procurement officer know which solution will really solve his or her organization's contract management problems? Fortunately, there is a straightforward process for determining which ECM solution is right for your organization. An ECM solution is right for your organization if it passes seven categories of evaluation listed below. An ECM solution deserves serious consideration as being appropriate for your organization's needs if the following questions about it can be answered "yes."

### 3.5.1  Content and Document Management Capabilities

- Does the system provide for storing, searching, sorting, managing, and reporting contracts and related documents?
- Does the system provide functionality to search based on key fields, such as vendor number, effective start and end dates, and contract owner's name?
- Does the system allow an expanded search based on any other contract attributes?
- Does the system provide capability to add as many user-defined fields as required?
- Does the system provide functionality to link documents together or create a parent-child hierarchy between documents (for example, master services agreement linked to compensation agreement or a scope of work agreement)?
- Does the system provide rich analytics and audit tools?
- Does the system have its own reporting engine and reporting server?
- Does the system have the capability to integrate with the organization's existing reporting engine?
- What standard reports does the system ship with?
- Does the system provide capability to generate ad hoc reports?

- Does the system provide functionality to define a security model for executing and viewing reports (i.e., the ability to define who can execute a report versus who can only view reports)?
- Does the system provide role-based reporting and/or dashboards?
- Is the system scalable to several thousand documents and users?
- Is there a restriction on the size of contract documents that can be stored in the system (i.e., maximum number of clauses per contract template, maximum number of pages in a contract, maximum size of attachments to a contract)?
- Does the system include functionality to perform mass changes to master data or contracts (e.g., updating the internal contact on all records that meet particular criteria)?

## 3.5.2  Contract Authoring and Configuration Capabilities

So much for the "engine" of an ECM solution being well suited for your organization. What about "the driver's seat"? How well does a prospective ECM solution fit those who will use it? Again, an ECM solution is right for your organization if the following questions can be answered with an unequivocal "yes":

- Does the system support full contract life cycle?
- Does the system support self-service contract requests and creation?
- Does the system provide capabilities for precontracting activities, such as eRFx?
- Does the system allow the contract author to use the results of precontracting activities to create a new contract?
- Does the system provide the functionality to develop a template library (clause templates, contract templates, and e-mail notification templates)?
- Does the system allow a contract author to use alternate clauses (i.e., preapproved clauses that can be used in place of the standard clauses in the contract templates)?
- Does the system provide assisted contract authoring functionality (i.e., a wizard that helps a user select and build the right contract based on answers supplied to a series of questions)?
- Does the system provide functionality to create amendments and link them to the original contracts?

- Does the system support integration to word-processing applications such as Microsoft Word?
- Does the system have the scope to be expanded to all types of contracts (for example, sales agreements, lease agreements, maintenance or service agreements, and intellectual property agreements) even if you are planning on automating only procurement contracts initially?
- Does the system support management of other parties' paper contracts?
- Does the system support creation and management of multiparty contracts?
- Is the system flexible enough to allow configuring approval rules and workflow to support your specific organizational and process structure?
- Can the system enforce approval workflows at the clause level and contract level to ensure compliance with appropriate industry-specific or local, national, or international regulations?
- Does the system provide sufficient redlining, audit trail, version tracking, and document check-in and check-out capabilities to meet the organization's auditing and reporting requirements?
- Does the system support secure electronic signatures?
- Is the system flexible enough to allow configuring users, user groups, security roles, and permissions to support your specific access-control-related business requirements?

## 3.5.3 Collaborative Contract Development Capabilities

A third area of inquiry about the right ECM solution for your organization concerns its capabilities to interact efficiently within—and beyond—the limits of your organization:

- Does the system enable alerts and/or workflow triggers based on specific contract milestones, such as effective end date, next review date, volume thresholds, and payment schedules?
- Does the system support multiparty participation in contract review and refinement via e-mail, fax, or online?

## 3.5.4 Resource Planning Capabilities

Coordinating and tracking historical events in the contract life cycle, while essential, are only part of a full ECM solution. The right ECM solution for your organization should be well equipped to support your forward-looking needs as well:

- Does the system provide functionality to track contracts related to capital projects by project phase or milestones?
- Does the system enable the planning, scheduling, and resource management required during different phases of the contract development process?
- Does the system provide functionality to track actual versus planned time and costs for different phases of the contract development process?
- Does the system provide an easy mechanism to integrate data with project planning and scheduling software, such as Microsoft Project or Primavera?

### 3.5.5 Performance and Compliance Management Capabilities

Self-assessment and compliance are the two primary control functions of a well-designed ECM solution that is right for your organization:

- Does the system support analysis of contracts based on negotiated terms?
- Does the system provide standard reports to monitor and ensure effective use of clause templates and contract templates in the contract authoring process?
- Does the system provide a comprehensive audit trail for changes made to system configuration (e.g., who made changes to a clause or contract template, when the change was entered, what the change was, and who approved it)?
- Does the system support automated generation of reports required for Sarbanes-Oxley and other reporting requirements?
- Does the system provide functionality to set up e-mail alerts, escalations, and process triggers based on predefined milestones and thresholds?
- Does the system support creation of ad hoc reports in a fairly intuitive manner?

### 3.5.6 Integration and Services Capabilities

No information management system operates in a vacuum, and none are trouble-free. Adequate integration and service capabilities are key elements in the right ECM solution for your organization:

- Does the system come with prebuilt adaptors and graphical user interface (GUI) integration tools for linking to existing enterprise systems?
- Does the system support real-time integration with other procurement-specific systems, such as SRM, supplier portal, enterprise spend management, e-procurement, e-sourcing, or ERP?
- Does the system support integration with applications that manage associated financial processes, such as invoice verification and payment and commitment management?
- Does the vendor provide systems integration services?
- Does the vendor have strategic partnerships with third-party technology and service integration firms?
- Does the system provide utility programs for loading master data such as product data, vendor data, vendor contact information, and user data?
- Does the system provide functionality to load legacy contracts automatically?

## 3.5.7  Other Criteria

The final questions to be asked about a prospective ECM solution for your organization are:

- Is the system easy to use and intuitive?
- Does the system provide localization capabilities (i.e., multiple languages, multiple currencies, different date and currency formats)?
- Is the software built on standard-based architecture such as Microsoft .NET or J2EE?
- How does the solution provider's track record of success, customer references, and financial viability compare against competitors?
- What are the implementation costs as compared to the software license costs?
- What are the customization and future upgrade costs?

Not all the criteria listed above will be of equal importance to every organization; they will vary in priority depending on the current state of each organization's contracting processes, its current technology, and the skill sets of the contracting professionals. In order to efficiently rank ECM solutions according to the functionality they provide, each organization should develop a balanced scorecard prioritizing all relevant evaluation criteria. An overall rating can then be attained for each prospective ECM solution under consideration.

## 3.6 WHAT ARE THE CURRENT TRENDS IN THE ECM SOLUTION MARKET?

Until very recently, ECM was little more than a document management process to automate the workflow associated with contract creation, collaboration, execution, administration, and analysis. However, recent issues of corporate scrutiny, accountability, and governance, driven by local, national, and global regulations and general shareholder concerns, have forced organizations to improve their skills and techniques in ECM. The document-centric approach to contract management has evolved to include the analysis of risk and the performance of contract execution.

ECM is emerging as an organizational discipline and is enabled by a new generation of systems designed to meet such ends from vendors such as Accruent, Action, Ariba, A.T. Kearney, B2eMarkets, Blueridge, Comergent, Contiki, Covigna, Determine, Diligent, Documentum, Ecteon, Emptoris, Frictionless, Global eProcure, Hummingbird, I-many, Interwoven, Ketera, Memba, Nextance, Oracle, Procuri, SAP, Upside Software, and WorkplaceIQ, among others.

The key trends in ECM solutions are:

- **Demand for ECM solutions**: Corporate interest and demand for ECM solutions are on the rise and will continue to be for the next few years. In a recent survey of 220 industry executives and managers, the Aberdeen Group found that 60% of the survey participants plan to utilize an ECM solution to create and manage procurement contracts;* 27% of the companies represented in the survey planned to make investments in an ECM solution within the next 24 months.

- **Shift in ECM implementations by contract type**: Most ECM implementations in the past were focused on streamlining the contracting process on the buy side. The success of these projects has generated interest in application of these solutions to streamline the life cycle of other contract types such as sales contracts, intellectual property

---

* The Contract Management Benchmark Report: Procurement Contracts: Maximizing Compliance and Supply Performance, Aberdeen Group, Boston, March 2006.

rights, etc. Therefore, more nonprocurement-driven ECM implementations are being initiated.

■ **Shift in ECM implementations by delivery method**: In the past, most organizations chose to install ECM solutions on-site. However, as more organizations realize the benefits of hosted delivery models (i.e., faster implementation, lower license fees, lower maintenance costs, flexible pricing models, higher security, and improved system performance), a greater percentage of future ECM implementations will be hosted solutions.

■ **ECM vendors versus ERP, supply chain management (SCM), SRM, CRM, and content management vendors**:

☐ ECM vendors, such as Emptoris, Nextance, I-many, and Upside Software, primarily focus on ECM. As they continue to demonstrate success and profitability due to increased corporate interest and demand, they are attracting other software vendors (such as ERP, SCM, SRM/CRM, and content management vendors) to the ECM space. The ERP vendors (such as SAP and Oracle) and SCM vendors (such as i2) have traditionally lagged well behind in contract authoring and collaboration-related functions, but they are in a good position to provide better functionality for compliance management as they usually own an organization's transactional data. These vendors are trying to play catch-up with ECM vendors in terms of contract authoring and collaboration functionality. The SRM/CRM vendors (such as FreeMarkets, Emptoris, Procuri, and B2eMarkets) are attempting to extend their eRFx authoring capabilities into contract management. Finally, content management vendors (such as EMC Documentum, FileNet, Interwoven, and Vignette) are beginning to build their current content management and workflow capabilities into contract management.

☐ ECM vendors are broadening their offerings to support more types of contracts and design industry-specific solutions. In the past, most of the ECM vendors specialized in managing a particular type of contract. For example, I-many specialized in sell-side contracts, Determine in buy-side contracts, Accruent in real estate contracts, etc. However, as these ECM vendors feel the pressure from other software vendors, they are being forced to broaden their offerings to manage all types of contracts on an enterprise level.

- **Vendor consolidation and price discounting will occur**: While the ECM market stays hot, it will continue to attract many new vendors and new solutions. Consolidation will occur in the ECM vendor space due to stiff market competition. This is already occurring; for example, Emptoris and Procuri (strategic sourcing vendors) acquired diCarta and CMSI (ECM vendors), respectively. SAP, an ERP vendor with the largest market share, acquired Frictionless Commerce in 2006. New market entrants and new hosted and "on-demand" delivery models will force price depreciation and further consolidation in the ECM market.*

## 3.7 WHERE WILL THIS ECM SOLUTION FIT IN MY ORGANIZATION?

ECM solutions offer greatest value to organizations with relatively large and interrelated contractual profiles (e.g., companies with hundreds or thousands of ongoing contractual relationships, spanning different divisions, locations, and profit centers). It is against this backdrop of dynamic complexity, with all of its financial, legal, compliance, and strategic implications, that ECM solutions offer the greatest potential for significant improvement and streamlining of an organization's "contract universe."

By definition, an ECM solution influences many groups, divisions, and organizational strata within an organization. Virtually anywhere the contracts in question have potential impact is fair game for an ECM solution to exert its effects. In order to maximize the opportunities for beneficial outcomes from an ECM solution implementation, it is useful to have a good general understanding of how the organization and its constituent parts may be affected by an ECM solution.

By way of brief examples, an ECM solution forms a critical link between SRM functions and traditional procurement functions (see Figure 3.1). Such a solution, when used on the sales side, forms the vital link between CRM and traditional sales and distribution. On the financial side, an ECM solution provides a link in reconciling accounts receivable and accounts payable data to corresponding terms and provisions in sales and procurement contracts. In this

---

* The Contract Management Solution Selection Report, Aberdeen Group, Boston, June 2005.

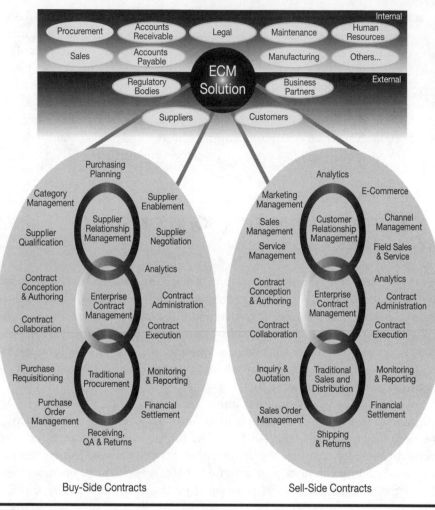

**FIGURE 3.1.  Where Does an ECM Solution Fit in My Organization?**

capacity, the ECM solution bridges a gap between the procurement or sales and finance and accounting functions within an organization. Similarly, ECM solutions link procurement functions to the divisions responsible for budgeting, planning, and forecasting.

Since contracts are constructed with legal terminology, provisions, and language, the linkages between all operating divisions of an organization and the legal, regulatory, and compliance functions are implicit.

In summary, an ECM solution should be viewed in terms of its comprehensiveness to link, weave together, and efficiently streamline communications and coordination for all of the essential operating, strategic, and financial divisions and levels within an organization. Unlike IT applications with a narrowly targeted end-user group, ECM solutions—by definition—are pervasive in their potential impact upon an organization's contractual activities and as such may have very substantial potential for positive change within an organization.

## 3.8  WHAT BENEFITS CAN I EXPECT FROM THIS ECM SOLUTION?

An ECM solution, when implemented as part of a larger continuous improvement initiative in ECM and when based on the ECM Maturity Model (presented in Chapter 6 of this book), can have a far-reaching impact upon the overall effectiveness and competitiveness of an organization. If configured and deployed correctly, such solutions offer both near-term and longer range benefits in five key areas to an organization:

- **Enhanced visibility**: An organization's need for contract visibility presents a perpetual and serious challenge—an organization's contracts must be simultaneously secure and accessible. ECM allows for improved visibility without compromising security, permitting improved communications among stakeholders from internal staff and management to customers and suppliers. Enhanced visibility into an organization's contracts leads to contract convergence and leveraging, thereby permitting the organization to consolidate spend and to drive better prices with suppliers and other business partners. It also enables contract administrators to view deviations from negotiated terms and conditions proactively and therefore undertake preventive and early-stage remedial actions before minor issues turn into showstoppers.
- **Increase revenue**: The strong contract authoring and collaboration capabilities of ECM solutions allow contracting professionals to focus their time and effort on negotiating better contracts for an organization and identifying increased up-selling and cross-selling opportunities. Automated reminders, notifications, and alerts enable accounts receivable personnel within an organization to invoice for all services rendered and collect penalties and charges where applicable.

- **Reduce costs**: An effective ECM solution can reduce costs for an organization in a variety of ways. As organizations begin consolidating their procurement contracts into a single repository within an ECM solution, they invariably find opportunities to consolidate or converge contracts and leverage global pricing and discounts. This leads to direct cost savings as better prices are negotiated with suppliers. The capabilities of an ECM solution to preflag automated renewals and automatically notify appropriate personnel in case of deviations from agreed-to terms and conditions help an organization in avoiding overpayment to vendors and in reducing hidden costs and penalties. By providing an audit trail of critical business transactions and strong reporting capabilities, ECM solutions assist in reducing the overall cost of external audits as well as the risk of regulatory penalties for noncompliance.

- **Contractual, regulatory, and procedural compliance**: An effective and efficient ECM solution implements an organization-wide contract creation, approval, execution, monitoring, and analysis system, with appropriate templates for clauses, contracts, and notifications/alerts. These templates allow organizations to remain within their stated procedures and reduce the time needed for contract creation and review. ECM solutions also facilitate contract management in such a way that other considerations such as budgetary constraints and corporate vision can be incorporated into the process of creating, executing, and monitoring contracts. Moreover, ECM ensures that designated staff is alerted when such considerations are negotiated or compromised. Since all contractual agreements involve risk, an essential benefit of ECM solutions is to provide assurance of the organization's contractual compliance, limiting exposure to undue litigation or expense. Moreover, an organization can be assured that its compliance with governmental regulations and those of other oversight agencies is being managed with the highest possible level of care.

- **Streamline processes and improve efficiency**: The net effect of a well-designed and appropriately implemented ECM solution is to simplify and streamline the communications process between all parties—within and beyond the organization. This leads to more accurate and timely exchange between employees and business partners, improved coordination of activities and resource allocations, and reduction of waste and duplication of effort. For example, an

ECM solution leads to more efficient and effective use of an organization's legal resources, focusing on review of contracts with exceptional circumstances versus reviewing all contracts regardless of need or priority. Effective ECM solutions also eliminate duplication of contracts and the need for shadow systems and tracking mechanisms.

According to AMR Research, "Automating purchasing contracts delivers significant ROI...Companies are implementing targeted projects in two to three months that deliver a 150% to 200% payback within a year."* Also, the Aberdeen Group has recently reported that "the ROI for an organization with $750 million in annual revenue and $200 million in annual spend from an ECM implementation is more than 3X in the first year!"** In addition, the Aberdeen Group also reported that organizations that implement an ECM solution typically experience about 55% improvement in compliance, 25 to 30% improvement in rebate/discount management, 25% improvement in contract renewal rates, 1 to 2% improvement in revenues, 2 to 7% reduction in material/service costs, and 25 to 30% reduction in administrative costs.** While the estimates vary by organization and by industry, it is evident that research groups and organizations agree that implementation of an ECM solution, if done correctly, can help reduce costs, maximize revenues, minimize risks, and in general improve business insight for any organization.

## 3.9  SUMMARY

Contracts are the lifeblood of any organization and in particular of the modern organization. They define and underpin all commercial relationships, thereby providing a platform for profitable growth of an organization. Despite their importance, most organizations lack the necessary controls, processes, and infrastructure needed to manage contracts at every stage of their life cycle. As a result, organizations lose billions of dollars every year due to contract leakage, suboptimal contract terms, unredeemed rebates, slow contract cycle times, renegade contracting processes, and missed savings opportunities. As presented in this chapter, these challenges can be overcome by implementing and adopting

---

* The Compelling ROI of Contract Management, AMR Research, Boston, February 2003.
** The Contract Management Solution Selection Report, Aberdeen Group, Boston, June 2005.

ECM solutions that provide a central repository for contracts, automate all stages of the contract life cycle, and provide tools to effectively monitor and analyze contract compliance and performance. In the next chapter, we will examine in detail how ECM solutions prepare and enable organizations to achieve sustained compliance.

# ENTERPRISE CONTRACT MANAGEMENT: THE VANGUARD OF SUSTAINED COMPLIANCE

## IN THIS CHAPTER:

- Compliance: Past, Present, and Future
- Sustaining Compliance
- Role of Technology in Achieving Sustained Compliance
- ECM and Compliance Management

## 4.1  OVERVIEW

To the casual student of business history, the recent evolution of modern enterprises may seem to be traveling a logical and gradual path, much as it has over prior centuries. Day-to-day market forces and the basic laws and paradigms of modern business may appear to be operating as they should, and except for the dramatic impact of information technologies and globalization and the ripple effects of crises such as 9/11 and Katrina, it might appear that the past decade has been one of evolution rather than revolution.

The casual student of business history would be wrong. While external appearances may not offer ready evidence of the underlying reality, modern business enterprises, especially those based in the United States, have undergone a quantum shift in priorities and practices—the corporate equivalent of a tectonic shift in the very center of gravity of modern business. Its name: *compliance*.

Compliance was thrust upon the business scene with the full force of every conceivable governmental agency, investor, and customer, driven by forces which had long been shifting under the surface. And in the aftermath of the era of Enron, modern business is faced with a new landscape, one defined by the strictest standards and codes of conduct ever imposed upon the free market system.

One of the great legacies of the revelations of corporate noncompliance during recent years is not the elucidation of the misdeeds themselves, but the exposure of the underlying weaknesses and vulnerabilities at the core of modern corporate culture. Historically, compliance has been viewed by businesses largely as a problem that had to be either circumvented or dealt with, a necessary cost of doing business, something to be tolerated. Even those companies not found guilty of deliberate violations of compliance requirements frequently sought the shortest possible path to meet minimum requirements in order to get on with business as usual.

Prior to the Enron era, compliance was not embraced as a potentially proactive force in the long-term growth and success of an enterprise. Compliance departments were not viewed as autonomous agents of quality and change, put in place to ensure a corporate culture of sustained quality and risk minimization. Utilizing a health metaphor, compliance has historically been regarded as a Band-aid, when in fact the patient was in need of a heart transplant.

Since compliance concerns virtually every aspect of an organization's activities, it is fundamentally linked to that organization's information technology architecture. Historically, compliance managers had little if any say over the design or role that IT played in the execution of their responsibilities. Compliance managers were expected to adapt to existing IT systems, instead of requiring that such systems be tailored to serve the purpose of compliance. When IT did not fit compliance, historically it was compliance that had to change.

But the compliance "earthquake" has permanently altered the modern business landscape. With compliance initiatives clearly at center stage for virtually all organizations, the relationship between proactive compliance and state-of-the-art IT solutions is at the vanguard of an organization's survival. Moreover—and as a final chapter on the Enron era—compliance is now emerging as a force for vision in defining the core culture of modern enterprises, ushering in what some have recently referred to as the era of compliance, where corporate governance is not a subject that deals with the avoidance of pain, but rather a standard to be sought and achieved through a systematic implementation of compliance initiatives by which compliance monitoring occurs in the normal course of business activities. Out of the debacles and shattered financial landscapes of the 1990s, a new attitude about compliance in modern business has emerged. In short, the rebuilding of corporate culture has begun, and forward-looking enterprises are now seeking their own road maps to ensure the future is built on bedrock.

One of the most profound consequences of this shift in corporate priorities and cultures has been the assignment of accountability up the corporate ladder to executives, directors, and senior managers. Shareholders, government agencies, watchdog groups, and the general public have all raised the bar for senior management in terms of assigning direct responsibility and consequent liability for noncompliance. No longer does turning a blind eye result in a slap on the wrist—real prison time and real financial loss await modern executives who do not place compliance at the forefront of their corporate agendas and mission statements. This shift in consequence and responsibility has led to an unprecedented top-down penetration of compliance as a priority at every level of an organization—a new ripple effect felt both deeply and broadly through an organization's operations, staff, accounting, and record keeping.

A second factor shaping the landscape of the new era of compliance is the increasing level, complexity, and scope of challenges and demands placed upon large organizations, including:

- Increased regulatory, fiduciary, and legal demands
- Increasing competitiveness for public confidence and financial performance
- Increasing digitization of business relationships, including contracts
- Need for flexible systems that can respond to new compliance demands

Given the scale and complexity of large modern organizations, and the unprecedented compliance challenges they face, a logical question is:

**What role can technology play in modern compliance management?**

Clearly, information management is at the heart of compliance management; information is, after all, the very currency of compliance—from the manufacturing floor to the marketplace, from the boardroom to the courtroom.

Companies that manage and control their information in a compliance-oriented framework are best positioned to avoid problems and remain competitive.

The subtitle of this chapter on the subject of Enterprise Contract Management (ECM) is "The Vanguard of Sustained Compliance." A fundamental premise of this chapter is that compliance involves an organization's behavior in its relationships—with its employees, its shareholders, its customers, its suppliers, and with the public. Since the terms of such relationships are documented in a spectrum of contracts (including legislation, agreements, and resolutions), ECM is an essential compliance function. Moreover, ECM solutions best serve an organization's efforts to achieve sustained compliance when they are designed, implemented, and monitored to integrate seamlessly into an enterprise's IT architecture and fully embrace that organization's contract universe.

In this chapter, the following aspects of ECM and compliance management are covered:

- An overview of compliance in both its historical and contemporary contexts
- An approach to achieving sustained compliance
- The role of technology in achieving sustained compliance
- The role of ECM in achieving sustained compliance

## 4.2  COMPLIANCE: PAST, PRESENT, AND FUTURE

### 4.2.1  Definition of Compliance

The first reaction of most people when they hear the word compliance is to think about regulations and legislation. However, in today's business environment, compliance stands for much more. It involves ensuring not only that an organization meets the requirements of regulations, legislation, and standards defined by agencies that are external to the organization, but that it also enforces and ensures adherence to its own policies, procedures, standards, best practices, and plans.

Given this definition of compliance, there are three major domains of compliance within an enterprise:

- Regulatory (governmental and legal)
- Procedural/operational (within an organization's business functions)
- Contractual (between an organization and other entities)

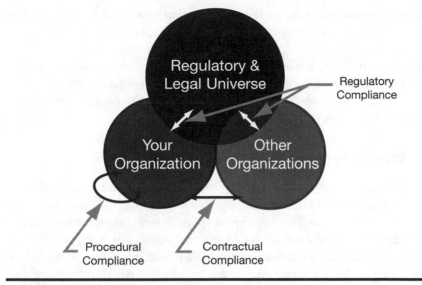

**FIGURE 4.1.  Compliance Domains**

These domains are depicted graphically in Figure 4.1. The impact of each of these compliance domains upon an organization is evident when one considers the intimate linkages between the individual domains.

## 4.2.2  Evolution of Compliance in Modern Business

It is useful to reflect upon how compliance achieved its current status among corporate priorities. As stated earlier, the subject was once one of the least discussed among many organizations, and only in the past few years has it recently emerged as the buzzword in corporate mission statements.

Historically, many companies regarded compliance as a necessary cost center to mitigate the risk of lawsuits and to appease regulatory agencies. The saying "do enough to get by" might have been coined to characterize the culture of many organizations regarding compliance. "Tolerated but not embraced" and "pulled to the forefront only when needed"—these phrases do not inaccurately portray the general attitude of many corporate executives toward compliance before the decade of Enron and WorldCom.

It is not the intent of this chapter to suggest that all enterprises in the pre-Enron world deliberately attempted to circumvent the purpose of compliance. In fact, it is evident that most of the compliance failures of the past were not deliberate, but rather were the inadvertent consequences of misplaced priorities. There was, however, plenty of blame to go around in the wake of Enron and WorldCom, the dot-com bust, and the stream of accounting scandals, fraud and corporate bankruptcies, insider trading, and executive compensation schemes. These events brought to light a reality that had long gone unobserved by the general public: in some corporate spheres, consistent disregard for compliance had become the norm.

## 4.2.3  The Current State of Compliance

In the aftermath of this era of corporate compliance debacles arose a network of rules, regulations, codes, standards, policies, procedures, and expectations that have permeated virtually every level of modern business—in many respects for the better. These regulations affect different industry sectors (such as healthcare organizations, financial institutions, insurance agencies, brokerage firms, federal agencies, publicly traded companies, etc.) in different ways and require that differing initiatives be put in place to meet a myriad of requirements. A high-level overview of some of the key regulations impacting businesses across industries today is presented below. An even more detailed list of such regulations is presented in the appendix of this book.

- **Sarbanes-Oxley Act (SOX)**: Of all the recent regulations, the one that has received the maximum attention from organizations across all industries is the Public Company Accounting Reform and Investor Protection Act, also commonly known as SOX. This act has brought about the most extensive reform that U.S. financial markets have seen since the enactment of the Securities Act of 1933 and the Securities Exchange Act of 1934. While the complete SOX has eleven titles, Sections 302 and 404 have had the greatest impact in terms of ongoing compliance obligations. Section 302, which pertains to corporate responsibility for financial reports, requires the certification of disclosure in quarterly and annual reports by the chief financial officer. Section 404 requires that annual reports contain a discussion of the effectiveness of internal controls. These two sections place significant responsibility on the chief financial officer and an organization's external auditors, who for the first time must provide an opinion on the reliability and effectiveness of the internal control representation made by an organization's CEO and CFO. Finally, SOX Section 409 mandates significantly expanded disclosure requirements, with disclosures made as quickly and completely as possible after pertinent events affect an organization's performance.

- **Gramm-Leach-Bliley Act (GLBA)**: GLBA impacts banks and other financial institutions such as securities firms, insurance agencies, lending firms, brokerages, and credit counseling firms. It requires financial services companies to implement safeguards for customers' current and legacy information. The act makes it illegal for a financial institution to share customers' nonpublic personal information with third parties unless the organization first discloses its privacy policy to consumers and allows them to opt out of that disclosure.

- **Health Insurance Portability and Accountability Act (HIPAA)**: HIPAA was originally passed in 1996 to help expand insurance coverage to the unemployed, but over the past several years it has been expanded to include privacy clauses and security requirements. HIPAA regulations require healthcare and insurance organizations to have procedures in place to prevent, detect, contain, and correct security violations. They must also have procedures and processes to regularly review records of information system activity.

- **Basel II**: Already a part of international banking law, the Basel II Accord is essentially a risk management mandate that requires proven IT security and administration. Capital reserves, supervision, and market discipline are Basel II's three risk management pillars. Basel II requires banking institutions to reserve capital that can be used to cover operational risks, including those that arise from inadequate internal processes or external events.

- **FDA 21 CFR Part 11**: This legislation became effective in August 1997 and affects companies in all industries regulated by the U.S. Food and Drug Administration (FDA), including but not limited to biopharmaceutical (human and veterinary), personal care products, medical devices, and food and beverage. It establishes the criteria for the use of electronic records and signatures. For companies that meet Part 11 compliance, electronic records and signatures can replace traditional paper records and signatures, thereby enabling pharmaceutical and other FDA-regulated industries to streamline processes and reduce costs by moving to digital records.

- **Federal Information Security Management Act (FISMA)**: Expansive in scope, FISMA was enacted by the Bush administration in 2002 in response to concerns about cyber-security. The act requires all federal agencies to develop, document, and implement agency-wide programs to secure data and information systems that support agency operations and assets, including those managed by other agencies or contractors. Agencies will be subject to annual tests, including evaluations of their IT security systems. With some 3.4 million cybersecurity incidents documented by the U.S. government in 2005, many analysts believe the government will put additional pressure on federal agencies to secure their IT infrastructure quickly.

- **European Union Data Protection Directive (EUDPD):** The EUDPD is applicable to all local and international organizations doing any business with an organization in the member states of the European Union regardless of industry, shape, or size. It specifies that user data must be collected for a specific purpose, must be processed lawfully, and cannot be retained any longer than required. The intent behind the directive, therefore, is to protect the fundamental rights and freedoms of individuals and in particular their right to privacy with respect to the processing of personal data.

- **Personal Information Protection and Electronic Documents Act (PIPEDA):** PIPEDA is a Canadian federal act that governs the collection, use, and disclosure of personally identifiable information in the course of commercial transactions. The act was created in response to EUDPD, which limits trade with nations that do not provide privacy protection equivalent to the European Union directives. The law requires organizations to obtain consent when they collect, use, or disclose personal information; provide an individual with a product or a service even if the individual refuses consent for the collection, use, or disclosure of his or her personal information unless that information is essential to providing the product or service requested; collect information by fair and lawful means; and have personal information policies that are clear, understandable, and readily available.

- **Department of Defense 5015.2**: This regulation provides implementation and procedural guidance on the management of records in the Department of Defense. This standard sets forth mandatory baseline functional requirements for records management application software used by Department of Defense components in the implementation of their records management programs. In addition, this standard also defines required system interfaces and search criteria to be supported by the records management applications and describes the minimum records management requirements that must be met, based on current National Archives and Records Administration regulations.

■ **Securities and Exchange Commission 17a-4**: This rule requires the retention of all customer records, financial transactions, bank records, and buy/sell orders. All correspondence is to be retained for six years. This includes e-mail and instant messages if an organization uses these for transactions. Organizations are required to keep a secure copy of every transaction, and records must be maintained on nonalterable, nonerasable media.

It is evident that compliance covers a much broader arena than just corporate accounting for most companies. These regulations have emerged for reasons ranging from data privacy to IT security, from workplace to employee safety, and from tighter controls around financial management to environmental concerns. There are regulations that apply to specific vertical sectors, such as the Federal Energy Regulatory Commission to energy, OSHA and ISO to manufacturing, HIPAA to healthcare and insurance, and Department of Defense 5015.2 to defense. In addition, companies with a global presence are required to comply with regulations not just in the United States but also in regions worldwide where they conduct business.

## 4.2.4 The Future of Compliance

As organizations across industries and geographies have rushed to meet the requirements of legislation, regulations, and standards, some key trends—and lessons learned—have emerged which will shape the future of compliance:

■ **Execution approach**: Achieving compliance with regulations was often treated by many organizations as a distinct project with a definite beginning and end. Resources were reallocated from multiple departments, the focus of internal audit departments was redirected, consultants were hired to assist in achieving compliance, and the compliance initiative was assigned a higher priority over other business initiatives. However, achieving compliance is no longer a one-time requirement; the project implementation approach, which worked well for initiatives with a definite beginning and an end, no longer applies to current compliance initiatives. In the compliance environment of today and tomorrow, organizations need to institutionalize good corporate governance and effective internal controls as part of day-to-day operations in order to achieve sustained compliance.

- **Business processes**: Much of the initial effort around achieving compliance was heretofore focused on implementing manual processes or custom applications to address specific compliance issues. While such efforts helped organizations achieve compliance in the short run, they did little to address the root cause of the problem—inefficient business processes. Leading organizations, therefore, must understand that sustained compliance requires a retooling of their underlying business infrastructure, architecture, and procedures. These elements need to be carefully designed, implemented, and monitored to ensure that good corporate governance and solid internal controls are embedded within the organization for sustained compliance.

- **Technology**: When many compliance efforts were initiated by organizations a few years ago, those responsible for implementation did not fully comprehend the role that technology could play in achieving compliance. At the same time, IT departments did not know how they would be impacted by these compliance efforts. However, as businesses began to dig deeper and came up with solutions to address compliance issues, it became clear that technology could, and eventually would, play a significant and perpetual role in an organization's effort to sustain compliance.

  The software industry responded immediately to this need. A large number of technology solutions have emerged in recent years, each attempting to address the new and more stringent needs of organizations in managing newly required documentation, evaluation, testing, monitoring, and reporting activities. Most of these solutions are still in their infancy, and the compliance software market will undoubtedly go through a maturing period characterized by consolidation over the next three to five years. Organizations will need to continue to invest in technology solutions to support compliance efforts in some key areas such as document management, records management, workflow, and reporting.

- **Corporate communications**: Not surprisingly, considerable confusion has resulted from interpreting the numerous compliance regulations that have appeared on the corporate horizon during recent years. The need to resolve such confusion has given rise to an emerging interest in improving corporate communications and information systems as they relate to compliance issues, policies, procedures, and training. Organizations have begun to understand the importance of defining roles and responsibilities of employees explicitly and ensuring that employees understand their changing roles in achieving compliance in the new regulatory environment. Business-to-employee communication and employee education are of critical significance in the effort to sustain compliance over an extended period of time.

■ **Governance and risk management**: Given the present and future compliance environment which demands the embedding of good governance within an organization, it makes sense to view compliance initiatives within a larger corporate governance and risk management framework. In the past, the absence of a formal governance and risk-management-based approach left organizations with no way to prioritize their activities. Some initiatives focused on the wrong areas, resulting in a disproportionate amount of resources being spent on documenting and testing controls that did not truly mitigate risk.* To achieve compliance on an ongoing basis, organizations need to implement a comprehensive and structured governance, risk, and compliance management (GRC) model that is consistent with their strategy and risk management objectives and properly aligns people, process, and technology capabilities to meet these objectives.

Armed with knowledge of trends and lessons learned from the past, most forward-thinking organizations have realized the importance of aiming to achieve sustained compliance instead of focusing solely on the near-term low-hanging fruit (i.e., achieving compliance in the short run by putting manual processes or workarounds in place). Forward-looking organizations view compliance:

■ Not as a burden, but as an opportunity to make positive changes throughout the organization
■ Not as a one-time or just-in-time project, but as an ongoing process of continuous improvement
■ Not from a silo approach, but with a holistic view across the enterprise within an integrated GRC framework

---

* Under Control: Sustaining Compliance with Sarbanes-Oxley in Year Two and Beyond, Deloitte Consulting, New York, 2005.

- Not as a necessary and burdensome cost, but as an investment and a way to improve the overall efficiency and effectiveness of internal business processes and ultimately to reduce costs

The next section in this chapter, therefore, describes a new vision of compliance and what organizations across various industry sectors can do to sustain compliance.

## 4.3  SUSTAINING COMPLIANCE

### 4.3.1  A New Vision of Compliance

As is evident from our discussion in the previous section, compliance efforts in most organizations have historically been treated as ad hoc, silo-ed, and disconnected one-time projects, growing layer upon layer, adding to the cost and resources, not fully realizing the advantages of sustained compliance. Instead of this reactive and often unproductive approach to compliance (which reduces the overall agility of an organization and thereby increases its risk), organizations would be better served with a new vision of compliance—one that embeds a culture of compliance into the underlying business fabric, supporting organizational efficiency with repeatable and sustainable processes.

This new vision of sustained compliance puts stakeholders first by embracing internal governance, ethics, and risk management guidelines. It also addresses external regulations and supports compliance with both the letter and the spirit of the relevant laws and regulations. Such a vision approaches compliance with financial and operational policies and procedures, as well as commitments to stakeholders, as seriously as it approaches legal and regulatory mandates.* It views stakeholders as any group that can impact the value of the organization, including customers, investors, employees, regulators, and society as a whole.

This new vision of compliance (see Figure 4.2) aligns compliance efforts within an organization through ongoing implementation of its goals and objectives. Moreover, this vision functions within an integrated enterprise-wide GRC strategy as opposed to treating compliance as a discrete function within the organization (see Figure 4.3). Treating compliance as a discrete function leads

---

* Integrity-Driven Performance: A New Strategy for Success through Integrated Governance, Risk and Compliance Management, PricewaterhouseCoopers, New York, 2004.

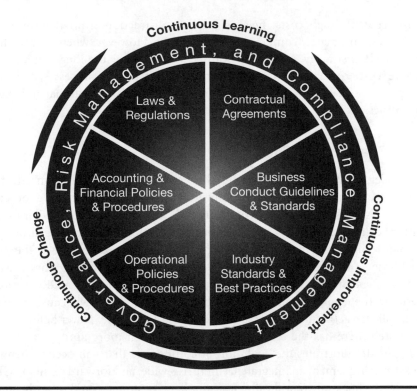

**FIGURE 4.2. A New Vision of Compliance**

**FIGURE 4.3. Governance, Risk, and Compliance Management Strategy**

to unacceptably high costs, heightened risk, distraction from the corporate mission, and ultimately competitive disadvantage. However, when dealt with as part of a GRC strategy, compliance can be sustained for the long run and can become self-perpetuating because corporate culture, people, processes, and technology work collaboratively to ensure compliance with both internal and external policies.

## 4.3.2  The "Ripple Effect"

It is evident that a forward-thinking GRC strategy is founded upon effective compliance management. Such a strategy requires that the tenets of good governance, risk assessment, and compliance be completely integrated into the mission, culture, and daily activities of an organization, from the boardroom to the mail room. Only then will a strategy lead the organization down the path of achieving sustained compliance. When different organizations work toward individually achieving sustained compliance by deploying such a GRC strategy internally, the ripple effect and synergy between their efforts will cause the level of compliance across the corporate world to rise as a whole. Never before in the corporate sphere has the term "raising the bar" been more apropos.

Figure 4.4 illustrates the evolution of compliance that will occur when organizations implement an integrated, enterprise-wide, and forward-thinking GRC strategy. Such a strategy will influence suppliers, customers, and other business partners to follow suit. The "current state of compliance" depicted in Figure 4.4 indicates that the legal and regulatory universe is changing and expanding dynamically. In this current universe, with mandated deadlines looming, legal departments and compliance officers (the traditional risk managers within organizations) make their best guesses as to how to interpret and enact compliance requirements. Top management views such compliance efforts as a "one-time deal," redeploying employees and pulling resources away from other efforts in order to meet compliance deadlines. In other words, the focus in the "current compliance universe" is almost exclusively internal and discrete. Those in senior management lack the visibility to see how compliance mandates affect their counterparts (i.e., their customers, suppliers, and other business partners). Moreover, senior management is not aware that the compliance engine is not running on all cylinders available to it.

Fortunately, the model of compliance evolution does not stop here. By the time the corporate world reaches the "intermediate state of compliance," top management and legal officers will have been successful in complying with the letter of the law but, mindful of the disruption and costs such initiatives can

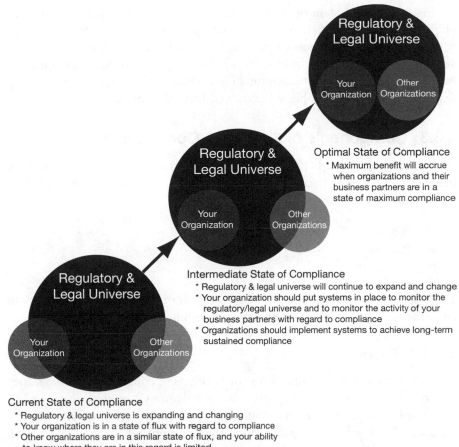

Optimal State of Compliance
  * Maximum benefit will accrue
    when organizations and their
    business partners are in a
    state of maximum compliance

Intermediate State of Compliance
  * Regulatory & legal universe will continue to expand and change
  * Your organization should put systems in place to monitor the
    regulatory/legal universe and to monitor the activity of your
    business partners with regard to compliance
  * Organizations should implement systems to achieve long-term
    sustained compliance

Current State of Compliance
  * Regulatory & legal universe is expanding and changing
  * Your organization is in a state of flux with regard to compliance
  * Other organizations are in a similar state of flux, and your ability
    to know where they are in this regard is limited

**FIGURE 4.4.  Progression of Compliance States**

entail, will not want to repeat the monumental effort required to achieve compliance beyond its present state. In our model, such managers will realize that a superior way to address the demands of today's regulatory environment is to deploy compliance efforts as part of an integrated and enterprise-wide GRC strategy, thereby transforming the perception of compliance within the organization from a burden to a catalyst for better business performance. At the same time, organizations will realize that, in order to achieve sustained compliance, they will also need to influence their business partners, customers, and suppliers to move toward a culture of compliance.

In the "optimal state of compliance," all organizations make a conscious effort to function in a state of sustained compliance. Organizations encourage, if not require, their business partners to be compliant as well. Such peer pressure, coupled with a growing awareness of the long-term benefits and financial rewards of compliance, would ultimately transform the corporate world as a whole to function at this higher, sustained level of compliance.

## 4.3.3 Components of Sustained Compliance

As illustrated in Figure 4.5, to the extent that sustained compliance is a machine being assembled by an organization, there are three component parts that must be put together to work as a unit:

- People
- Process
- Technology

The following sections discuss the role that each of these components plays in ensuring that compliance can be sustained within an organization.

### 4.3.3.1 People

People are the agents responsible for the very acts of compliance. As such, they play the central role in ensuring sustained compliance via implementation of an integrated, enterprise-wide GRC strategy. Organizational executives, such as the CEO and CFO, are explicitly and often solely responsible for internal control. As they survey the corporate culture, they must reasonably map out how com-

**FIGURE 4.5. Components of Sustained Compliance**

pliance will be achieved and by whom. If a new GRC strategy calls for new tasks, executives have the responsibility of creating new positions or restructuring existing ones so that compliance demands can be met. As part of this exercise, organizations should identify the skills and competencies needed in these new or changed positions and ensure that a staff development or augmentation strategy will enable the transition from the current state to the desired state.

Most importantly, executives should remember that their vision is a guidepost for their employees. They need to set high standards and hold employees accountable to meet them. They also need to institute incentives to promote a culture of compliance and establish training programs to arm employees with all the tools and information needed to achieve and sustain compliance. Finally, they should continually communicate progress to employees and managers so that everyone is on board with establishing sustained compliance via a new GRC culture.

### 4.3.3.2 Process

Organizations are only as strong as the business processes in place that allow employees to carry out their responsibilities in an accurate, timely, and effective manner. Not only does compliance impact existing business processes, but it may also require that new processes be put in place to directly manage compliance-related issues. Therefore, organizations must survey both the processes required and how they will allocate/designate resources to carry out compliance-related tasks. Typical questions that arise during this phase of the consideration are:

- What processes and activities must be accomplished routinely to ensure the effectiveness of an enterprise-wide GRC program?
- What processes expedite compliance rather than add complexity?
- What processes need to be standardized or formalized?
- What processes are in place for training and for ensuring accountability?

A fundamental process to be considered is risk management, a primary function of which is to identify shortcomings in organizational infrastructure, policies, and related systems. In addition to preparing for proactive compliance, process developers must consider risk management and remember to incorporate elements into their strategies that proactively address the systematic identification of failures, errors, and other forms of inadvertent and deliberate risks to the organization. Similarly, mandates such as SOX require protection for whistle-blowers. Processes for addressing these issues should not be secondary to other processes designed to improve the GRC structure, but rather should be logically and systematically included as part of the overall compliance initiative.

The key to optimizing the process dimension of compliance is balance. In addition to preparing for the proactive aspects of new compliance implementation, process developers should also focus on incorporating and refining systems to address failures and errors in information flow and its operational consequences.

Because some employee turnover is inevitable, executives and employees should create process documentation regarding the fulfillment of all of their relevant duties. This is critical not only for new employees to understand an organization's business processes, but also for auditors and regulators who inspect corporate records to ensure that document retention and disposition policies are enforced and followed consistently throughout the organization.

### 4.3.3.3 Technology

It goes without saying that achieving the state of sustained compliance via an integrated, enterprise-wide GRC strategy would be a more daunting task without the aid of technology. Technology provides the necessary basis for a seamless GRC and fluid work environment in any organization. Businesses across geographies and industry sectors have already experienced firsthand that inefficiencies related to suboptimal automation of business processes can have a significant negative impact on an organization's profitability and competitiveness. Further, a piecemeal approach to addressing specific regulatory requirements using technology solutions adds IT applications layer by layer, thereby increasing the initial as well as ongoing costs and resources for an organization.

Leading organizations are utilizing an array of new and existing technologies to achieve sustained compliance. Although organizations may be able to use the tools currently in place, many are finding that more versatile technology solutions are necessary to meet GRC requirements. Such new technology solutions also aid in enterprise-wide congruency and process augmentation. Technology vendors have already developed a wide range of such solutions (see Section 4.4.3). These solutions, if implemented correctly, can provide the margin of difference between compliance success and failure, especially in large and complex organizations. Also, the process efficiencies and other related benefits obtained from implementing such solutions can rapidly offset their implementation costs. However, it is crucial that the developers and implementers of a GRC framework keep their eyes open to redundancies and complexities in processes and technology solutions—unnecessary elements that can actually negate otherwise constructive compliance efforts.

As organizations begin to implement GRC into their business cultures, no decisions should be made without taking into account all three of the interlocking components of compliance—people, process, and technology. The subsequent sections of this chapter focus on the role of technology and specifically one particular emerging technology solution—the ECM solution—in guiding an organization down the path of sustained compliance.

## 4.4 ROLE OF TECHNOLOGY IN ACHIEVING SUSTAINED COMPLIANCE

In today's corporate environment, technology plays an essential role in addressing compliance issues. This section focuses on the critical and growing importance of information and related technologies in both addressing current compliance issues and as a powerful tool for forward-thinking managers seeking sustainable solutions for their organizations' future compliance demands.

### 4.4.1 The Relationship between Technology and Compliance

A fundamental mandate in this new era of compliance is for organizations to reexamine and reengineer their underlying business processes. Once viewed as optional (and consequently piecemeal), rethinking and retooling are now comprehensive, embracing virtually every level of an organization: user access, inbound and outbound e-mails, reports, public relations, employee data, and every other source of information generation, transmission, flow, and storage.

Understandably, such changes in business processes often require changes in the IT systems that support and enable them. Thus, compliance has generated a new and never-ending workload for IT departments. To complicate this process, compliance departments have traditionally operated under considerable IT constraints and have had little influence over IT strategy to achieve either their own objectives or those of the organization. Their involvement has usually been after the fact, only to ensure that whatever has been done was in compliance with regulatory requirements.

Due to this reactive defensive, rather than proactive offensive, approach of compliance departments, specialized technology solutions were not traditionally procured and implemented with the goal of enhancing the compliance function within an organization, with the notable exceptions of when such changes were required to meet a specific regulatory requirement or in response to a breach of a regulatory requirement. Not surprisingly, the resulting evolution of compliance-related IT has proven suboptimal in relation to the challenge, further exacerbating the process and costs associated with achieving tangible results.

The solution to this dilemma is emerging as the relationship between technology and compliance becomes increasingly evident. Today's leaders in corporate compliance function proactively at an early stage in the development of enterprise-wide applications so that compliance requirements can be embedded in the business processes of the organization, leading to sustainable compliance.* Compliance managers are reinventing themselves in response to the urgent need to fulfill a more visionary, active, and influential role in the organization, thereby strengthening the relationship between compliance and IT at a strategic, as well as operational, level.

While it is critical for compliance managers to be actively involved in IT initiatives from an early stage, it is equally important to engage the IT department in proactively identifying opportunities based on clearly defined compliance processes. By so doing, such initiatives can leverage technology, both to improve controls and to enable compliance managers to spearhead truly effective compliance programs. Because the compliance function touches virtually every business process, and because many of the IT systems within an organization are disparate and poorly integrated, the challenge for IT professionals is often to leverage the organization's existing IT infrastructure to the extent possible. Amidst such challenging conditions, the goal is to create a compliance management information system that secures, monitors, and preserves information from multiple systems (e.g., enterprise resource planning, supplier relationship management, customer relationship management, finance and accounting management, and human resources management) and to do so in a manner that minimizes compliance breaches and related shortcomings. Moreover, the compliance manager's task does not end at the corporate front door; in the event of an audit, IT must serve to expose and present the organization's information in the most accurate yet least incriminating way, which requires timely and sophisticated linkages of IT across the enterprise.

---

* The Future for Compliance—Using Technology to Deliver Value, PricewaterhouseCoopers, New York, 2003.

The preceding discussion highlights the fact that in this new era of compliance, IT professionals are faced with new, significant, and ever-changing challenges. However, current technology often does not offer IT managers the capability to adequately address compliance challenges presented to them, nor to efficiently perform compliance-related tasks. In the absence of technology designed to meet today's compliance challenges, the goal of achieving a seamless enterprise-wide compliance interface often eludes even the most capable of today's IT professionals. Oftentimes, IT professionals must interlace applications in an attempt to create compliance continuity across different departments. Additionally, while such programs are under way, IT is expected to maintain data integrity and security to protect against the misuses of such data, even including potential actions by disgruntled employees or administrators. Thus, while IT may not address all of an organization's compliance needs, it is— and will remain—an integral part of an overall long-term compliance implementation program. This fact places technology squarely in the center of an organization's compliance future.

## 4.4.2  How Does Technology Address Compliance Requirements?

The previous section illustrated how technology is an integral part of an organization's overall long-term compliance implementation program. Without adequate and appropriate technology, companies would incur significant risks at all levels and expend inordinately high overhead costs attempting to staff a department solely for the tracking and management of organizational information. In this section, we will see how technology addresses compliance in a way that both systematically organizes data flow and cuts costs.

Technology helps an organization meet compliance requirements in the following ways:

1. **Efficient and effective business processes:** Technology instills confidence that in addition to reducing and automating business processes and cycle times, an organization's policies, procedures, guidelines, and best practices are followed consistently across the board. While it is important to ensure consistency in business transactions, it is equally important to ensure that the meeting of compliance requirements does not reduce an organization's efficiency or dramatically increase costs related to core operational functions. Technology helps translate this burden of compliance into a benefit for an

organization by embedding and systematizing compliance into the fabric of the organization's culture, thereby leveraging the results of compliance implementation to provide greater visibility and transparency to senior management for key decision making.

2. **Single version of the truth**: Technology enables an organization to organize, monitor, and archive documents and information in a common repository or other integrated IT systems. This ensures that a single active version of each document (such as organizational policies, procedures, and contracts) exists and that prior versions have been correctly archived for future reference or audits. While the initial focus of most organizations has been on implementing some form of an ECM solution to achieve this single version of the truth, recent compliance requirements have caused a shift in focus. The focus has moved from content management to rigorous records management protocols, a more stringent approach to the management, retention, and disposal of critical business records. Technology solutions that provide such records management capabilities enable organizations to archive documents for efficient retrieval and viewing without placing them at risk of alteration. Such systems greatly foster automation of an organization's policies and procedures regarding document retention and disposal. Furthermore, as new regulations have emerged on the corporate horizon, and as new requirements are added, IT solutions must continue to provide records management capabilities tailored to existing and newer forms of document retention and disposal (e.g., data generated and stored in electronic documents such as e-mails and instant messages).

3. **Collaboration and workflow**: Technology provides organizations with a digital work space that facilitates content collaboration between co-workers and business partners on documents, records, Web content, and other digital assets. This allows organizations to apply user-controlled document-level security limitations regarding access to generate, read, edit, or delete documents and information. It further provides the capability to track revisions of content including associated comments, e-mails, and discussions. In addition to facilitating collaboration, such technology also facilitates workflow management though the automation of structured business processes, transactions, and events. This includes routing of tasks, documents, and information from one user to another in a way that ensures compliance with an organization's policies, procedures, and guidelines. Workflow

management results in streamlining and simplifying business process and in improving organizational efficiency, flexibility, process control, and procedural compliance.

4. **Secure and role-based access:** The advent of Internet-enabled IT solutions, intranets, and extranets has helped organizations make the transition from closed business models to more open and adaptive forms. While this has helped improve efficiency and productivity across organizations and geographies, it has also led to an exponential increase in the complexity involved with managing users and user access to systems and documents. To address this rapidly changing and complex issue, current technology provides role-based access to facts, figures, and business transactions, enabling the establishment, enforcement, and segregation of duties and access levels. Such technology increases the probability that users execute business events and transactions in accordance with their roles and responsibilities as they are documented and approved by upper management. Moreover, in such a system, no one person has total administrative control, but rather authority is distributed so that data integrity and confidentiality remain intact and locally monitored. No single person has the freedom to change information without appropriate authorization, knowledge, and understanding of the system as a whole. In addition to providing secure and role-based access to users within an organization, technology also enables maintaining an audit trail of all business transactions (i.e., tracking and recording critical information such as who made what changes, when, and where).

5. **Real-time monitoring and alerts:** Technology enables proactive and real-time monitoring of business transactions and data activity across multiple systems and locations, providing the capability to automatically alert administrators or authorized personnel to any abnormalities, exceptions, threats, or security breaches. This dramatically improves the capabilities of senior management to understand and respond to problems before they become showstoppers or outright compliance breaches. The net effect of such real-time monitoring capability is to significantly reduce the overall risk and the cost and time an organization spends in reparative versus preventive measures associated with data integrity and security.

6. **Real-time, reliable reporting:** The new era of compliance demands that organizations respond rapidly to evolving markets and changing supplier/customer dynamics. Analyzing such information requires

substantial analytical horsepower operating in real time, without which routine conduct of such analysis would be considered impossible given the complex IT infrastructure of most organizations. Such infrastructure is often an amalgam of application silos, each dedicated to separate divisional data populations, such as supplier relationship management (SRM), customer relationship management (CRM), supply chain management (SCM), finance and accounting management, and human resources management. Today's IT enables rapid and seamless integration between such individually useful but often disparate and constantly changing data structures. When integrated correctly, such information silos turn into a comprehensive gold mine of information from which data can be rapidly extracted using today's advanced analytics tools. These analytical tools facilitate development of business forecasts, optimization of resources on the fly, and recommendation of appropriate actions with unprecedented speed, agility, and accuracy based on near real-time reports, synthesis of previously submerged information via data mining, and other advanced techniques. Some of the newer IT tools also provide interactive analysis capabilities through which users can slice and dice extracted data and execute a wide variety of what-if scenarios and other higher level logical analyses, correlations, and forecasts. Thus, businesses are no longer restricted to using the rearview mirror technique for making critical decisions to respond to changing market conditions. They can now operate with greater agility, adaptability, and compliance by making informed decisions based on reliable real-time reports and supporting tools.

No single technology solution provides all the benefits mentioned above. Instead, organizations need to combine the functionality of several different technology platforms, some of which may already be in place and some that will need to be acquired. The goal of the next section is to shed some light on a variety of emerging IT solutions designed to assist organizations in addressing today's compliance requirements and those that will undoubtedly arise in the future.

## 4.4.3 Technology Solutions That Are Being Used to Address Compliance Issues

Compliance management is a term that describes a rapidly maturing software category that combines applications and provides capabilities in integration, collaboration, reporting, and monitoring. Software vendors in this space can be classified into the following segments:

1. **Compliance management specialists**: This category includes the best-of-breed software applications that were designed specifically to address compliance management within an organization. These applications automate the design, documentation, review, approval, and testing of an organization's internal controls framework, thereby reducing the time to compliance and expediting audits. Some of the key vendors in this space are Certus, HandySoft, OpenPages, Paisley Consulting, and Stellent. Such vendors are expanding the functionality of their products to support broader enterprise risk management strategies. Since these products are relatively new to the market and have not completely achieved maturity, user-friendly functionality and integration with other enterprise-wide applications are still in development.

2. **Enterprise risk management (ERM)**: ERM solutions enable senior management to effectively prepare for both uncertainties and their associated risks as well as for opportunities for the organization to grow and remain competitive. Such solutions help identify, analyze, and manage the risk of loss resulting from inadequate or failed internal processes, people, and systems or from external events. Since regulatory risks fall under the greater umbrella of enterprise risks, ERM solutions can be very effective and efficient in identifying and addressing compliance-related issues. Some of the key vendors in this compliance software space are Capterra, CSC, Methodware, Noweco, OpenPages, Paisley Consulting, Risk Track, and Vericept.

3. **Enterprise resource planning (ERP)**: ERP applications are multimodule software applications that enable organizations to manage a variety of business processes such as finance, controlling, SCM, product life cycle management, asset management, etc. This category includes vendors such as SAP and Oracle. SAP released its Management of Internal Controls solution in September 2004, while Oracle had released its Internal Controls Manager product in August 2003. The strength of these applications lies in their ability to integrate seamlessly with the other products in the suite of applications provided by the individual vendors. This seamless integration allows organizations to leverage their current configurations and master data, including security and access controls, from their ERP

applications. However, ERP systems have traditionally demonstrated poor integration with existing document management and records management systems.

4. **Enterprise content management (CM)**: CM applications support the evolutionary life cycle of all digital information resources, such as images, documents, and text, from creation, review, storage, and dissemination to destruction. CM systems provide an infrastructure for the compliance framework, providing functionality such as enterprise search, electronic forms processing, scanning and imaging support, e-mail archiving, records retention, security and access control, versioning, audit trail, electronic signatures, spreadsheet remediation, check-in/check-out, and interfaces to archive content to permanent media. However, CM systems usually lack the functionality to assist in authoring standard business documents such as purchasing contracts, sales contracts, and service agreements, which should be developed using standard—and approved—clause language and contract templates. Some of the key vendors in this category are Documentum (recently acquired by EMC), FileNet, Interwoven, OmniRIM, Stellent, Vignette, and Xerox DocuShare.

5. **Financial control management (FCM)**: FCM applications automate much of the day-to-day work performed in finance organizations to ensure that users complete all critical work in a timely and consistent manner and in compliance with regulations and organizational policies. This creates greater confidence in the production of financial statements. These applications record and produce evidence about control activities and financial control procedures, and detect and manage exceptions to resolution through review to disclosure, if applicable. Some of the key vendors in this category are Movaris and Cartesis.

6. **Business intelligence (BI) or business analytics (BA)**: This is a broad category of applications for gathering, storing, analyzing, and providing access to data to help end users make better business decisions. By providing full, role-based access to financial information, these applications assist in establishing and enforcing standards for data retrieval, usage, and review across an organization. This secure and controlled access provides a basis for automating the financial review process, minimizing error-prone manual processes and solidifying the effectiveness of internal controls required to achieve compliance with numerous regulations. Some of the key vendors in

this space are Actuate, Business Objects, Cognos, Hummingbird, Hyperion, Informatica, SAS, and Siebel Analytics.

7. **Business performance management (BPM)**: BPM applications are often touted as the next generation of BI applications. The concept behind BPM applications is that all aspects of business planning, operational and financial management, and performance management should be treated as an integrated platform. This is in contrast to the common approach of providing scorecards, analysis, and reporting as a set of disconnected applications. These applications emphasize the use of metrics beyond financial ones to guide business process management strategies. Some of the key vendors in this software category are Chordiant, Exigen, FileNet, Fuego, HandySoft, Hyperion, Insession, Plexus, Proforma, Savvion, and Ultimus.

8. **Business activity monitoring (BAM)**: BAM applications specialize in monitoring transactions, applying controls in gaps between separate IT systems, and gaining access to data combined in stand-alone systems or blocked by proprietary software platforms that do not communicate well with other software applications. BAM applications can detect potential fraud and anomalies in financial process execution, which can provide additional assurance that internal controls are in place and can substantiate assertions for the SOX Section 404 controls evaluation. Some of the key vendors in this space are ACL Services, Active Reasoning, Akonix, Approva, Oversight Systems, and Tripwire.

9. **Business-to-employee (B2E) portals**: B2E portals are also known as employee relationship management systems. These portals are a customized, personalized mix of news, resources, and applications that simplify access to corporate information, personal data, transactions, and services. They enable employees of an organization to stay up-to-date with what is going on within the organization, from daily news and information to communications across all business functions around the world. Many organizations are increasingly using B2E portals today as a means to collaborate and communicate on compliance-related policies, standards, guidelines, and training. The portals enable the direction of compliance-related material, in text and video format, to targeted audiences and help improve awareness of the organizational and individual obligations to achieve compliance. Some of the key vendors in this software category are HP, Kronos, Microsoft, Oracle, SAP, Soffront, and Vignette.

10. **Complaint handling systems**: Although the function of complaint handling is closer to CRM, it is mentioned here because it can provide critical information associated with an organization's compliance-related actions. For example, a complaint handling system can highlight the concentration of complaints by product or by region, along with applicable market indicators. Such information would be important in order to understand what type of regulation risks an organization might have to address so that remedial actions could be taken immediately. Several functionality-rich complaint handling systems are available in the market today from vendors such as Remetrex or Lynk Software. These systems provide strong workflow management, monitoring, and reporting capabilities. This functionality is also embedded in most advanced CRM tools such as the ones provided by Oracle, Right Now, Sales Logix, SAP, SAS, and Siebel.

11. **Issue management systems**: Issue management systems have been used for several years to record, track, and report issues with an organization's enterprise-wide applications such as ERP, SCM, CRM, and SRM. However, their use within the compliance space has been restricted so far primarily because of the risk that such information may be used during litigation. Forward-thinking organizations that wish to become more proactive understand that they can deploy such systems to gather information in order to address and mitigate risks before they become major issues. Some of the key vendors in this software category are AutoTask, ExtraView, LinkEdge, Serena, and TrackStudio.

12. **Enterprise Contract Management (ECM)**: ECM solutions support the life cycle of all contracts within an organization, from contract creation, collaboration, execution, and administration to analysis and reporting. The capabilities of an ECM system overlap with those of many other software categories described above. For example, a major component of an ECM solution is document management, including records management and workflow management, which is the focus of CM solutions. ECM solutions minimize error-prone manual contracting processes, provide secure and controlled role-based access to contracts, and provide extensive reporting capabilities. In this respect, they share the capabilities of BI, BA, BPM, and BAM applications. These applications also integrate to a wide variety of existing enterprise-wide applications, such as ERP, ERM, SRM,

CRM, portals, etc. Some of the key vendors in this space are Accruent, Ariba, Contiki, Ecteon, Emptoris, I-many, Ketera, Nextance, Procuri, SAP, and Upside Software.

The remaining sections of this chapter describe the capabilities of ECM solutions and how such applications address the demands placed on an organization by a multitude of regulations discussed in previous sections.

## 4.5 ECM AND COMPLIANCE MANAGEMENT

ECM has profound potential for sustained compliance, especially in three critical areas:

- Procedural compliance
- Contractual compliance
- Regulatory compliance

By establishing an integrated ECM/compliance system, an organization not only instills a culture of compliance for present operations, but it lays the foundation for future compliance challenges and opportunities. Figure 4.6 illustrates the critical role that ECM plays in compliance management within, and across, organizational boundaries.

### 4.5.1 Procedural Compliance

As an organization continues to work toward the new vision of sustained compliance by adhering to its own operational and financial policies and procedures along with business conduct guidelines and standards, the organization is participating in procedural compliance. This is an organization's attempt to self-govern and impose guidelines so that each transaction is in line with certain boundaries the organization has created to ensure success. Such procedures govern the type of sales an organization conducts, the type of vendors from which it procures goods and services, and the type of communication it makes available to both internal and external audiences.

Without ECM, companies face the tedious task of manually entering clauses that communicate the organization's boundaries in each contract; however, unless a template is developed and made available to the contract authors, chances are the language used in the clauses will not be standard across the

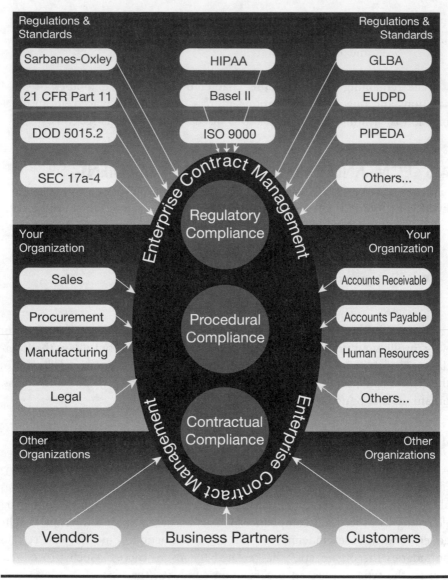

**FIGURE 4.6. Role of ECM in Compliance Management**

enterprise. Each contract, therefore, requires meticulous review by designated individuals who are charged with ensuring and enforcing procedural compliance. This greatly increases the risk to an organization that uses several contracts and has limited staff to ensure their integrity. Furthermore, without a standard contractual system, some employees may unethically take the liberty of executing their own contracts with unacceptable terms. This generates tremendous risk for an organization in many regards.

An effective and efficient ECM solution implements an organization-wide contract creation, approval, execution, monitoring, and analysis system, with appropriate templates for clauses, contracts, and notifications/alerts. These templates allow organizations to stay within their said procedures and reduce the time needed to both create and review the contracts. ECM solutions also manage contracts in such a way that other critical considerations such as budgetary constraints and corporate vision are included in the process of creating, executing, and monitoring contracts, and designated staff is alerted when these considerations are compromised.

## 4.5.2  Contractual Compliance

One of the biggest challenges facing CEOs, CFOs, and other senior managers is that of contract life cycle management. Contracts have life terms and stipulations that must be heeded to make them effective. This includes proper payment, reporting, and renewal. As contracts continue to determine things such as employment, sales, vendors, federal grants and loans, supplies, and more, they must be monitored so that both the organization and the party to which it is bound fulfill their responsibilities for mutual profitability. Furthermore, contracts must remain highly visible while remaining secure against unlawful access or changes.

ECM provides mechanisms for monitoring contractual stipulations as well as for securing the contracts themselves. Alerts can be issued when certain terms need attention, and methods for automatic payment and reporting take the managerial responsibility from staff. Systems may be set up to send contracts to certain staff automatically, and safeguards can be put in place so that only appropriate individuals can edit contracts and their terms.

ECM takes much of the burden of contractual maintenance from staff and automates it in an organized, efficient, and streamlined system that allows for much better contractual compliance and, overall, better profitability for the organization. As contracts are fulfilled by both the business and outside parties, companies face fewer audits and fewer instances of delinquent accounts.

## 4.5.3  Regulatory Compliance

Regulatory compliance is defined as compliance to mandates imposed by outside organizations or government. Contractual management must address regulatory compliance in great detail, as the consequences of not meeting such regulations are grave, resulting in costly penalties or even a cessation of business opportunity.

Organizations enter into various contracts regarding sales practices, property rights, employment stipulations, and other legal matters that outside regulators have determined. These types of contracts allow businesses to operate and thrive in their given industries. These contracts, in turn, require a certain level of awareness of their stipulations and clauses for either party to be successful. Noncompliance with regulations most often results in steep fines or restriction of service.

ECM addresses regulatory compliance in the most crucial of ways. In contrast to the high-maintenance properties of contracts, ECM allows organizations to incorporate several methods to ensure regulatory compliance, not only efficiently but in a proactive and consistent manner. As mentioned before, ECM allows any given organization to automate payments according to the demands of a contract without any other action required by staff. ECM may act as a calendar to address every segment of a contract's life cycle, including its execution, review, payment schedule, and renewal. In the case of evergreen renewals, simple notices can alert executives that such renewal is about to occur in case they care to review the contract or other party's performance. Given the far-reaching impact ECM solutions have in addressing regulatory requirements, it makes sense to dive deeper into this aspect of ECM.

## 4.5.4 ECM Solutions Address Sarbanes-Oxley Requirements

SOX, enacted in 2002, has arguably been one of the most stringent and far-reaching set of business regulations to ever be enacted on the corporate world. This regulation explicitly and directly affects all U.S. public organizations; however, its impact is being felt by smaller organizations as well, because the larger customers and suppliers of such smaller organizations have begun to assert control over their internal processes for all business activities. It makes sense to discuss the role of ECM solutions in addressing SOX requirements before jumping into the discussion of how ECM solutions address common requirements of most regulations. Table 4.1 describes how ECM solution capabilities enable an organization to address the requirements of different sections of SOX regulation.

**TABLE 4.1. How ECM Addresses Sarbanes-Oxley Act Requirements**

| Regulation | How ECM Addresses the Requirements |
|---|---|
| **Sarbanes-Oxley Act Section 302: Corporate Responsibility for Financial Audits**<br>■ The CEO and CFO of an organization need to attest that the financial statements and disclosures released are accurate.<br>■ The officers of an organization will be held personally responsible for willful violations of this section.<br>■ Signing officers are responsible for establishing and maintaining internal controls. | ■ Provides role-based access and information along with a rule-based engine to ensure that business processes set up by an organization (such as segregation of duties and approvals based on criteria such authority limits, material groups, divisions, etc.) are adhered to.<br>■ Ensures that executive-level staff of an organization has complete visibility to all new or amended contracts, controls, approvals, and transactions using automated e-mail notifications, alerts, and executive dashboards.<br>■ Delivers proactive and advanced alerts to appropriate personnel, highlighting exceptions that require specific filings or actions.<br>■ Provides audit trail and log to ensure accurate tracking.<br>■ Provides capabilities to ensure that revenue recognition rules are complied with systematically. |
| **Sarbanes-Oxley Act Section 401: Disclosures in Periodic Reports**<br>■ Adequate and comprehensive disclosures are required where there may be some conflict in relationships with customers or suppliers.<br>■ Compliance with this regulation also requires a reconciliation of all financial information of a firm with its operational information. | ■ Provides capability for storing, searching, sorting, managing, and reporting contracts and related documents.<br>■ Provides functionality to search based on key fields such as vendor number, effective start and end dates, contract owner's name, etc.<br>■ Provides functionality to add an unlimited number of custom fields which can be used by an organization to capture stakeholder information that may be deemed important.<br>■ Legacy data load utility programs allow an organization to pull its existing contracts with suppliers and customers into a central repository. This enables complete accounting of all the contractual relationships of an organization.<br>■ Integration of an ECM solution with ERP, SRM, CRM, and other enterprise-wide applications ensures that business transactions are conducted in accordance with negotiated terms and conditions listed in contracts. |

**TABLE 4.1. How ECM Addresses Sarbanes-Oxley Act Requirements (continued)**

| Regulation | How ECM Addresses the Requirements |
|---|---|
| **Sarbanes-Oxley Act Section 401: Disclosures in Periodic Reports (continued)** | ■ Provides reliable and real-time reporting with capabilities to report exceptions to approved business processes in a standard format.<br>■ Allows exporting contract information and other related data (such as total quantity of goods ordered versus received, total number of purchase orders generated against a contract, total value of items ordered against a contract, sum total of invoices paid to date against a contract) to third-party reporting applications to meet the requirements of timely and accurate reporting.<br>■ Delivers proactive, advanced, and varied alerts to appropriate personnel, highlighting exceptions that require specific filings or actions. |
| **Sarbanes-Oxley Act Section 404: Internal Controls Report**<br>■ Each annual report shall contain an "internal control" report which shall:<br>  □ State the responsibility of management for establishing and maintaining an adequate internal control structure and procedures for financial reporting.<br>  □ Demonstrate an assessment of the effectiveness of the internal control structure.<br>■ External auditors need to attest to and report on the organization's internal control report. | ■ Provides capability to configure contracting processes with the system along with flexibility to set up approval rules, workflow, notification triggers, alerts, and report schedules, which help establish, facilitate, and institutionalize internal controls across an organization.<br>■ Customized workflow allows organizations to tailor the system in accordance with their contracting processes. This ensures and enforces consistent handling and routing of contracts and enables adherence to prescribed business rules and best practices.<br>■ The document repository provided within an ECM solution ensures that all contractual documents are secured, stored, and archived in accordance with a document retention and disposition policy.<br>■ User roles that define who can do what in the system, along with approval rules based on delegation of authority, ensure appropriate segregation of duties.<br>■ Maintains an audit trail for each business transaction that includes details such as who, what, when, and how. This enables attestation that internal controls are being complied with. |

**TABLE 4.1.  How ECM Addresses Sarbanes-Oxley Act Requirements (continued)**

| Regulation | How ECM Addresses the Requirements |
|---|---|
| **Sarbanes-Oxley Act Section 404: Internal Controls Report (continued)** | ■ Provides standard (or out-of-the-box) reports to assist with SOX reporting. Also enables creation of custom and ad hoc reports that assist in managing, monitoring, and tracking supplier/customer performance against negotiated terms and conditions. |
| **Sarbanes-Oxley Act Section 409: Real-Time Disclosures**<br>■ Issuers shall disclose to the public on a rapid and current basis additional information concerning material changes in the financial condition or operations of the issuer, which may include trend and qualitative information and graphic presentations, and may be deemed as useful or necessary to protect the investors or in the public interest. | ■ Provides rich reporting and analytics tools.<br>■ Capable of integrating with an organization's existing reporting engine.<br>■ Provides several standard reports and capability to generate ad hoc reports.<br>■ Provides role-based reporting and/or dashboards.<br>■ Provides standard reports to monitor and ensure effective use of clause templates and contract templates in the contract authoring process.<br>■ Supports analysis of contracts based on negotiated terms.<br>■ Supports automated generation of reports required for SOX and other reporting requirements.<br>■ Sends notification (exception reporting) to appropriate person to highlight any unusual or suspicious accesses based on predefined triggers. |
| **Sarbanes-Oxley Act Section 802: Records Retention and Records Management**<br>■ Requires retention and protection of audit and financial documents, including electronic records (such as e-mails, instant messages, and even chat sessions).<br>■ Destruction, alteration, or falsification of corporate records can have serious consequences. | ■ Provides capability for storing, searching, sorting, managing, and reporting contracts and related documents.<br>■ Provides mechanism to execute document retention and disposition policy.<br>■ Maintains an audit trail for each business transaction that includes details such as who, what, when, and how.<br>■ Provides elaborate redlining, audit trail, version tracking, and document check-in and check-out capabilities to meet an organization's auditing and reporting requirements.<br>■ Supports secure electronic signatures. |

**TABLE 4.1. How ECM Addresses Sarbanes-Oxley Act Requirements (continued)**

| Regulation | How ECM Addresses the Requirements |
|---|---|
| **Sarbanes-Oxley Act Section 906: Financial Reporting**<br>■ CEOs and CFOs need to personally guarantee that the periodic reports containing financial statements fully comply with the Securities Exchange Act of 1934 and that they present the financial condition and results of operations of the organization accurately. | ■ Provides a mechanism to verify compliance against contracted terms and conditions, regulations, and internal organizational policies, standards, and best practices. This helps ensure the accuracy of financial reports.<br>■ Provides a mechanism to integrate with ERP applications where the financial data are usually recorded and tracked.<br>■ Provides reports that help compare data from the application housing the financial data with the contractual data maintained in the ECM solution. This helps determine if material difference exists between negotiated terms and actual business transactions and forms critical input to generate real-time and accurate financial reports. |

## 4.5.5 ECM Solutions Address Common Requirements of Multiple Regulations

The previous section presented the role of ECM solutions in addressing requirements of SOX regulations. However, it is imperative to remember that ECM solutions (or for that matter any technology solution) should not be implemented to address specific requirements of a specific regulation. The regulatory environment is changing rapidly in terms of the number of regulations and their requirements and complexity. Therefore, instead of focusing on the letter of the law, the goal of every organization should be to achieve compliance with the spirit of the law. Only then will an organization stay ahead of the curve regardless of the new regulatory requirements or changes to existing regulations that may occur. With this in mind, Table 4.2 presents a discussion of how ECM solutions address the common requirements of multiple regulations or, in other words, how ECM solutions help organizations achieve compliance with the spirit of the law.

**TABLE 4.2. How ECM Solutions Address the Common Requirements of Multiple Regulations**

| Requirement | How ECM Addresses the Requirement |
| --- | --- |
| **Process focus** | ■ Supports contract life cycle end to end<br>■ Supports other parties' paper process<br>■ Supports creation of multiparty contracts<br>■ Supports integration with precontracting processes such as RFQ, RFP, RFI, etc.<br>■ Supports multiparty participation in contract review and refinement via e-mail, fax, or online<br>■ Configuration options allow setting up an organizational structure within the software that mimics the real-life organizational hierarchy<br>■ Ability to assign users in roles and departments and set up approval rules to enable desired workflow, approval flow, and e-mail notifications<br>■ Supports planning, scheduling, and controlling resources required during different phases of the contract development process<br>■ Enforces approval rules at clause level as well as contract level |
| **Content and document management** | ■ Provides real-time visibility across functions or geography based on security roles and permissions assigned to any user<br>■ Provides capability for storing, searching, sorting, managing, and reporting contracts and related documents<br>■ Provides mechanism to execute document retention and disposition policy<br>■ Provides functionality to search based on key fields such as vendor number, effective start and end dates, and contract owner's name<br>■ Allows expanded search based on any other contract attributes<br>■ Provides capability to add as many user-defined fields as required<br>■ Provides functionality to link documents together or create a parent-child hierarchy between documents (for example, master services agreement linked to compensation agreement or a scope of work agreement)<br>■ Provides functionality to perform mass changes to master data or contracts (for example, updating the internal contact on all records that meet particular criteria), and provides extensive audit trail functionality for any changes made to the data or documents in general |

**TABLE 4.2. How ECM Solutions Address the Common Requirements of Multiple Regulations (continued)**

| Requirement | How ECM Addresses the Requirement |
|---|---|
| **Mechanism to enforce and ensure use of standards, rules, and best practices** | ■ Allows the contract author to use the results of precontracting activities to create a new contract<br>■ Allows configuring users, user groups, security roles, and permissions to support specific access-control-related business requirements<br>■ Provides the functionality to develop a template library (clause templates, contract templates, and e-mail notification templates)<br>■ Allows a contract author to use alternate clauses (i.e., preapproved clauses that can be used in place of the standard clauses in the contract templates)<br>■ Provides assisted contract authoring functionality (i.e., a wizard that helps a user select and build the right contract based on answers supplied to a series of questions)<br>■ Provides functionality to create amendments and link them to the original contracts<br>■ Supports integration with word-processing applications such as Microsoft Word and to spreadsheet applications such as Microsoft Excel<br>■ Supports integration with project planning and scheduling software such as Microsoft Project or Primavera<br>■ Supports multiparty participation in contract review and refinement via e-mail, fax, or online<br>■ Capability to support and manage life cycle of all types of contracts (for example, sales agreements, lease agreements, maintenance or service agreements, intellectual property agreements)<br>■ Enforces approval workflows at clause level and contract level to ensure compliance with appropriate industry-specific or local, national, or global regulations<br>■ Enables alerts and/or workflow triggers based on specific contract milestones, such as effective end date, next review date, volume thresholds, payment schedules, etc.<br>■ Provides standard reports to monitor and ensure effective use of clause templates and contract templates in the contract authoring process<br>■ Provides prebuilt adaptors and graphical user interface (GUI) integration tools for linking to existing enterprise systems<br>■ Provides real-time integration with other procurement-specific systems, such as SRM, supplier portal, enterprise spend management, e-procurement, e-sourcing, and ERP |

**TABLE 4.2.  How ECM Solutions Address the Common Requirements of Multiple Regulations (continued)**

| Requirement | How ECM Addresses the Requirement |
| --- | --- |
| **Mechanism to enforce and ensure use of standards, rules, and best practices (continued)** | ■ Supports integration with applications that manage associated financial processes, such as invoice verification and payment and commitment management<br>■ Provides utility programs for loading master data such as product data, vendor data, vendor contact information, and user data<br>■ Provides functionality to load legacy contracts automatically<br>■ Provides localization capabilities (i.e., multiple languages, multiple currencies, different date and currency formats) |
| **Accountability** | ■ Allows configuring users, user groups, security roles, permissions, and approval rules to support workflow and approval process per business requirements<br>■ Provides capability to track cycle time of contract life cycle, along with the ability to identify bottlenecks in the process |
| **Audit trail** | ■ Provides sufficient redlining, audit trail, version tracking, and document check-in and check-out capabilities to meet an organization's auditing and reporting requirements<br>■ Captures the following:<br>  □ Who: Who accessed the data?<br>  □ What: What tables, columns, records, fields, and file attachments were accessed?<br>  □ When: When was it done?<br>  □ Where: From what location (IP address) within or outside the network?<br>  □ How: From which part of the application was the change made?<br>  □ Result: Was the change successful? Was the query/report successful?<br>  □ Exception reporting: Sends notification to appropriate person to highlight any unusual or suspicious accesses based on predefined triggers<br>■ Provides functionality to track contracts related to capital projects by project phase or milestones<br>■ Provides functionality to track actual versus planned time and costs for different phases of the contract development process<br>■ Provides standard reports to monitor and ensure effective use of clause templates and contract templates in the contract authoring process<br>■ Supports secure electronic signatures |

**TABLE 4.2. How ECM Solutions Address the Common Requirements of Multiple Regulations (continued)**

| Requirement | How ECM Addresses the Requirement |
|---|---|
| Reliable, real-time reporting | ■ Provides rich reporting and analytics tools<br>■ Capable of integrating with an organization's existing reporting engine<br>■ Provides several standard reports and capability to generate ad hoc reports<br>■ Provides role-based reporting and/or dashboards<br>■ Provides standard reports to monitor and ensure effective use of clause templates and contract templates in the contract authoring process<br>■ Supports analysis of contracts based on negotiated terms<br>■ Supports automated generation of reports required for SOX and other reporting requirements |

## 4.5.6 Lessons Learned from Initial ECM Solution Implementations

It is evident from our discussion in the previous section that ECM solutions are powerful tools that offer enhanced capabilities to manage all stages in the life cycle of contracts. If deployed correctly, use of such solutions can lead to superior visibility; procedural, contractual, and regulatory compliance; and an overall improvement in competitiveness both within and beyond the organization. It is therefore of great importance to discuss the lessons learned from past ECM implementations in the context of achieving sustained compliance to promote recurrence of successful outcomes and to preclude the recurrence of unsuccessful outcomes. Listed below are some of the key lessons learned from the first wave of ECM solution implementations:

■ **Silo-ed implementations**: Historically, many organizations have missed "the big picture" regarding ECM initiatives and their role in compliance management. Often, organizations fail to align their ECM initiatives with other enterprise-wide programs, treating ECM implementation in a "silo-ed" manner rather than making it an integral part of an overall enterprise-wide compliance initiative or an even bigger GRC framework. A related shortcoming of past approaches has been to treat ECM solutions separately from the contract life cycle management process improvement initiative. Managers must realize that, in and of itself, ECM is not a silver bullet. The true return on investment of an ECM initiative is best viewed and enacted within the broader context of the contracting process, with a view toward a fully integrated system.

■ **Project-focused implementations**: Several organizations have treated their ECM solution implementation as a one-time project. They approached the implementation with the idea of using technology to achieve compliance with one or more specific regulations, but did not take this opportunity to analyze, redesign, and optimize the underlying contracting processes. When technology is used to automate suboptimal business processes, it merely results in bringing what is wrong in the processes to the surface much more quickly than manual processes do. Thus, while the approach of implementing ECM as a one-time project may be successful in the short run, this success—and ultimately compliance—cannot be sustained in the long run unless compliance is embedded in the culture of the organization by using repeatable, sustainable, efficient, and effective contract life cycle management processes.

■ **Functional-group-focused implementations**: It is understandable that organizations need to learn how to walk before they can start running. Some of the early adopters of ECM implemented the solutions for the procurement function; others implemented it for sales or human resources or for managing real estate or intellectual property contracts. However, the ECM solution implementation was treated as a project with a definite start and a definite end; once the software application was installed and ready to use by the first functional group within the organization, members of the implementation team were sent back to their routine jobs of contract author or contract administrator. Instead, organizations should continue to roll out the chosen ECM solution to other organizational functional groups that were not included in the initial rollout. Only when ECM solutions are embedded deeply and across the entire organization can compliance be sustained.

■ **Stand-alone implementations**: Compliance with regulations requires the ECM solution to talk to multiple applications, such as ERP, SRM, CRM, etc. However, most early adopters of ECM solutions did not integrate them with other enterprise-wide applications. This led to swivel-chair integration, where the end users would log in to one application to retrieve some data about a transaction, then either toggle to the ECM solution on the same workstation or move to a different workstation and enter the same data in the ECM solution. This results in errors and discrepancy in data. Instead, organizations should integrate their ECM solution with ERP, SRM, CRM, and other enterprise-wide solutions to get the maximum benefit from their investments.

- **The paradox of compliance**: Another frequently misunderstood area is the "paradox" of compliance; going above and beyond in regulatory compliance usually results in lower overall costs compared to doing the bare minimum to comply. This is because there is a significant overlap between multiple regulations (e.g., Basel II and SOX Section 409 both require timely disclosure of material changes in operations and financial condition). ECM frequently has been deployed in the past with the objective of addressing a specific regulatory requirement rather than a host of similar, if not identical, requirements in one consolidated effort. This obviously has proven to be an expensive and inefficient approach.

- **Compliance with the "letter of the law"**: ECM applications are often underutilized when management waits for regulatory bodies to provide direction and a road map for implementing processes and systems to achieve compliance. This situation has left many organizations in the uncomfortable position of having to create their own interpretation of what a given regulation implies. Instead of focusing on complying with the letter of the law, organizations need to improve the underlying business processes to comply with the spirit of the law.

- **Lack of use of proven implementation methodologies**: Several organizations did not use proven project management, change management, and continuous improvement methodologies while implementing an ECM solution. This led to inefficient and ineffective implementation, long lead times, and not enough buy-in from key stakeholders. Once the ECM solution was implemented, many organizations did not use a continuous improvement approach (such as Six Sigma) to keep moving the organization and its contracting processes toward greater efficiency.

- **Lack of direction and support from senior management**: A final area of underutilization of ECM is related to fundamental management communications. Oftentimes, those responsible for ECM implementation lack the support, guidance, and clear direction from upper

management regarding the relevance of ECM solutions and processes to the broader organization. This often leads to suboptimal
implementation and failure to realize the full potential of a corporate
culture of continuous improvement in the contracting process, the
establishment of incentives aligned with the organization's goals, and
the ultimate attainment of sustainable compliance. The very lack of
communication that gave rise to this suboptimal result often gives
rise to problems in related areas such as instilling changes in the
organization's culture as it relates to compliance as a whole.

■ **Beyond document management**: Many early ECM adopters have
treated ECM implementations as a document repository implementation only. While this is one of the key components of an ECM
solution, such applications provide much more functionality, for
example capability to author contract documents using clause and
contract templates. Most current content management solutions do
not provide this capability which is at the core of ensuring and
enforcing compliance. The other capabilities offered by ECM solutions should be used to ensure that they institutionalize, industrialize, and embed compliance at all levels within organizations.

The prospect of implementing an ECM solution can be daunting, especially
for senior managers with limited familiarity in the world of contract management applications. It is understandable that a number of issues could arise in
the implementation of such an application that could have a far-reaching impact
on almost all functions within an organization. However, through a combination of sound planning, careful team building, good consultative support, and
periodic evaluation of value added, the process of ECM solution implementation can be achieved with minimal risk and disruption to operations and a near-
seamless conversion to superior control over this critical area of an organization's
information management systems.

## 4.6 SUMMARY

The intimate, complex, and potentially powerful relationship between ECM
applications and compliance management was described in this chapter. This
relationship is based on the fact that contracts are the very currency of compliance—they represent communications between individuals, organizations, and
agencies that, woven together, form the fabric of a company's relationships. To

the extent that ECM serves to promote and foster sustained compliance, the organization and its stakeholders benefit. Suboptimal or ineffective ECM, on the other hand, leaves a company ill-equipped to address the challenges of compliance and prevents it from taking full advantage of the many benefits offered by a proactive culture of compliance.

The three major domains of compliance for an organization—regulatory, procedural, and contractual—were outlined. Also discussed were the interrelationships between these domains and the demands these relationships place upon an organization—both internally and externally. These demands arise from the need to interact with the various agencies involved in establishing and monitoring compliance policy, the divisions within an organization that must work effectively to achieve sustained compliance, and the various vendors, customers, and business partners with which a company must interact in a compliance-friendly environment. The role of ECM in streamlining these relationships was emphasized, including the role of ECM as a tool in contract creation, approval, execution, monitoring, and analysis, utilizing appropriate templates, reporting mechanisms, and notifications of compliance activities as they relate to predetermined standards.

In point of fact, the extent to which ECM is utilized and implemented by an organization has a dramatic impact on every aspect of operations and financial performance. Underutilization or nonutilization of appropriate ECM applications leaves a company's compliance framework incomplete, elevating regulatory risks, reducing competitiveness, and leaving opportunities for growth unrealized. The benefits of proactive implementation and utilization of ECM applications as part of an overall compliance initiative are numerous. They include enhanced contract visibility without sacrificing security, increased revenue and reduced costs, and streamlining of a company's procedures, operations, and processes to achieve optimal efficiency and financial return.

The benefits of ECM implementation to an organization are best realized when ECM is viewed as part of an integrated compliance IT and management architecture versus viewing ECM and compliance as isolated—the silo perspective—or a mere repository for documents and data. Clearly, to be effective as a compliance-enhancing tool, ECM cannot operate in a vacuum, nor should it be viewed as a one-time fix. ECM-based compliance initiatives are of greatest benefit to an organization when they are implemented into an existing IT system and corporate culture with the recognition that "you must walk before you can run." Only then, by embracing deeper and more powerful elements of ECM so that it works seamlessly with other IT applications (e.g., a company's ERP, SRM, and CRM platforms), will a network of IT applications permit previously unavailable levels of control and continuity for an organization's contracts and communications. Moreover, such a compliance system offers a new and powerful ability for an organization to address and respond to compliance requirements from multiple agencies and sources in a single coherent framework.

By properly implementing ECM into a company's ongoing enterprise applications, policies, operations, and procedures, ECM can be a valuable and proactive force in positioning a company to deal effectively with the challenges of compliance today and tomorrow and in increasing the overall value of the enterprise for its stakeholders through instilling a compliance-friendly corporate culture.

# ENTERPRISE CONTRACT MANAGEMENT MATURITY MODEL

## IN THIS CHAPTER:

- The Problem Statement
- Maturity Models
- ECM Maturity Model
- ECM Maturity Appraisal Method
- How ECM Solutions Assist in Progressing to Higher Maturity Levels

## 5.1 OVERVIEW

The purpose of this chapter is to offer a comprehensive overview of the role that maturity model theory can play in the continuous improvement of Enterprise Contract Management (ECM) processes and systems within any modern organization. After extensive research, and careful consideration of this subject, the author is convinced that maturity-model-based ECM improvement initiatives offer the greatest possible opportunity for forward-looking organizations to reduce risk, increase revenues, and enhance long-term value for their stakeholders.

While some might regard the subject of an effective and efficient ECM process as arcane—and its implementation within the context of maturity model theory even more so, it is the author's belief that, in today's large, dynamic, and complex organizations, an understanding of the power and potential of this combination by managers with a view toward the future is "well worth the read." This view is held all the more strongly in this post-Enron/WorldCom era, when the importance of contracts and compliance has risen to the forefront of the corporate agenda.

A logical question regarding the title of this chapter—"Enterprise Contract Management Maturity Model"—would be: Why should ECM require a maturity model approach to be enacted effectively? Or, restated: Isn't the implementation of an efficient ECM process similar to that of any other enterprise-level process? In order to understand why the maturity model is such an important component of an effective ECM process, this chapter will build a case that only by taking into account the dynamic evolution of the enterprise—and in doing so recognizing the role that maturation plays in the life of an organization—can the fullest value of ECM be realized.

Before embarking on a discussion of the ECM Maturity Model however, it will be useful to understand the reasons behind the need for a maturity model in achieving excellence in ECM within and across an organization.

## 5.2  THE PROBLEM STATEMENT

The objective of the last section in the previous chapter was to emphasize that successful achievement of ECM improvement can be a daunting task for numerous reasons. Perhaps the most compelling reason for most failures of early ECM initiatives can be summed up as *not knowing where you are, where you want to be, and how to get there.* The absence of orientation and perspective with respect to the overall process of ECM implementation lies at the heart of many secondary reasons for failure, including lack of vision, lack of direction, lack of proper focus, and lack of alignment with other organizational objectives. Thus, for ECM initiatives to have the highest probability of success, organizations need mechanisms and a valid model, one that will enable them to accomplish the following core ECM objectives:

- Quantitatively assess the level of an organization's capabilities in the contract management function
- Identify best practices used in the ECM arena—within and across multiple industry sectors
- Identify and help prioritize key areas for improvement within ECM processes and systems

- Assist in setting the vision for excellence in ECM and the targeted optimal state of ECM processes and technology
- Communicate the ECM excellence vision, strategy, plan, changes being implemented, and benefits realized via improvements in ECM processes, tools, and techniques across the organization
- Align the ECM initiative with other organization-wide goals, objectives, and initiatives
- Define key milestones that must be achieved—from current state to the optimal state of ECM
- Chart a road map to achieve key milestones, identifying and quantifying the time, effort, cost, potential return on investment (ROI), resources, and skill sets required
- Help maintain focus on process capabilities, adherence, maturity, and performance
- Help estimate the risks associated with inaction, including implication or increased costs, reduced revenues, and fallout from noncompliance
- Assist in tracking progress against the implementation plan
- Benchmark and guide continuous improvement in people, processes, and technologies related to ECM function within the organization

The fundamental premise of this chapter is that application of the right model to ECM implementation will greatly enhance prospects for a full and successful ECM implementation. The ECM Maturity Model and ECM Maturity Appraisal Method presented in this chapter are proposed as models to assist an organization embarking on such an initiative to improve the people, processes, and technologies associated with the contract management function within and across the organization. Section 5.4 of this chapter formally introduces the ECM Maturity Model. However, before presenting the model in its own right, it will be helpful to first offer a high-level overview and define a maturity model and its components, as well as examine where maturity model theory has been successfully used in the past.

## 5.3  MATURITY MODELS

### 5.3.1  An Overview of Maturity Models

Most modern business organizations are experiencing explosive and unprecedented change. Increased globalization, ever-changing demands from customers and employees, shrinking product life cycles, decreasing response times, and paradigm-shifting advancements in technology have converged upon today's business horizon to fuel the rate of change across industry sectors and geographies. While the changes confronting modern organizations are seemingly endless and unpredictable, the capital and resources available to adjust to such changes are almost always limited. Organizations that know where to invest these limited resources in order to achieve improved performance stand a much higher probability of surviving and remaining competitive. Organizations that do not manage these resources are at perpetual risk of losing market share, operating less profitably, and losing value for stakeholders. Such organizations typically either spend very little on process improvement efforts because they are unsure about how to proceed or spend heavily on several parallel and unfocused initiatives to little or no avail in terms of long-term improvement.

Since business processes lie at the very heart of an organization's growth potential, it is not surprising that many theories and models have been developed to assist managers in optimizing such processes. One such category of business process models—maturity models—has emerged in recent years to provide an effective and proven method for an organization to gain control over, and to improve, its business processes. The underlying premise of maturity model theory is that an organization (or a division within an organization) is a dynamic entity, with differing capabilities and needs depending upon its stage of maturity. From a theoretical standpoint, the least mature organizations are those that lack the integration, vision, and sophisticated infrastructure and technology to function optimally in their environment. As an organization acquires and employs these assets, it ascends in maturity—one might say it evolves to a more mature state, until it ultimately achieves a fully mature state of ongoing excellence.

Maturity models may be applied to a wide array of situations within an organization, including:

- Supply chain management
- Software development
- Systems security
- Knowledge management
- Project management
- Product development
- Similar organizational activities and functions

Maturity models provide a framework to organizations for evolving their business functions from an ad hoc, less organized, less effective state to a highly structured, effective, and optimized state. Not surprisingly, several such models have been in use in the corporate world for over two decades. However, the recent success of the Software Engineering Institute's Capability Maturity Model (SEI CMM) has resulted in a resurfacing of attention and focus on maturity models. The benefits of models such as the SEI CMM are well documented and typically include the following:

- They are invaluable tools, as they describe the best practices that must be performed in order to improve a particular business function.
- They constitute a proven framework within which to prioritize actions and thereby manage continuous process improvement efforts.
- They provide a yardstick against which to periodically measure improvement or progress toward the optimal state.
- They provide cost savings due to less rework as a result of repeatable, predictable processes and practices.

## 5.3.2 Key Components of Maturity Models

The idea of a business process as a dynamic entity was once viewed by many as quite revolutionary—the very thought that a process could mature as opposed to being installed and static challenged many managers to rethink their approach to business process optimization. With the advent of well-developed and thoroughly tested maturity models such as the SEI CMM, the concepts of "business process life cycle" and its corollary "business process maturity" have come into broader use and acceptance. In order to provide an overview of the key components of maturity models, some basic terms and concepts need to be introduced.

The concept of "process maturity" is based on the understanding that processes have life cycles that can be assessed by the extent to which a specific process is explicitly defined, managed, measured, and controlled. Most maturity models assume that progress toward the optimal, effective, and efficient process comes in stages. There are two main components of any given maturity model:

- The measured aspect
- The maturity matrix

The measured aspect is a dimension, process, or facet of the organization. For example, in the SEI CMM, software engineering process is the measured aspect. (Note: In the ECM Maturity Model presented in the next section of this chapter, the contract management process will be used to describe the measured aspect.) The maturity matrix is a two-dimensional chart where the vertical scale represents the maturity rating of the measured aspect and the horizontal scale represents time. (Note: The maturity matrix for the ECM Maturity Model is presented in Figure 5.2 later in this chapter.)

In addition to the measured aspect and the maturity matrix, other key components of maturity models are process, process capability, process area, maturity level, common features, and base practices. Figure 5.1 shows the relationships between these components of a typical maturity model. Definitions and examples of each of these key components of maturity models are provided below:

■ **Process:** A process is a set of activities performed to achieve a given purpose. Activities may be performed iteratively, recursively, and/or concurrently. A well-defined process includes tools, methods,

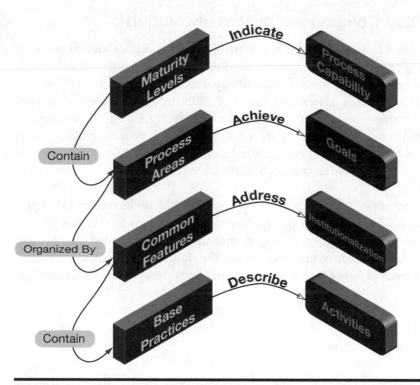

**FIGURE 5.1. The Maturity Model Structure**
(Reprinted with permission from "The Capability Maturity Model for Software: Version 1.1," Mark Paulk, Bill Curtis, Mary Beth Chrissis, and Charles Weber, *IEEE Software,* vol. 10, no. 4, pp. 18–27, July/August 1993. Copyright © 1993 IEEE.)

materials, activities, input, and output artifacts of each activity and mechanisms to control performance of the activities. Examples of process include software development, systems security, data management, supply chain management, project management, and contract management.

■ **Process capability**: Process capability is defined as the quantifiable range of expected results that can be achieved by following a certain process. The concept of process capability will be used in the ECM Maturity Appraisal Method presented later in this chapter.

■ **Maturity level**: Maturity level is the relative position of the measured aspect on a predefined maturity scale. For example, most maturity models are typically organized into five maturity levels, with each level representing an increased ability to manage and control the measured aspect or the process under consideration. Thus, each maturity level provides a layer in the foundation for continuous process improvement. Attainment of each level of the maturity framework establishes a different component in the measured aspect or the process under consideration, resulting in an increase in the process capability of the organization. Examples of maturity levels in most maturity models include ad hoc or initial, repeatable, defined, managed, and optimizing.

■ **Process area**: A process area is a defined set of related process characteristics which when performed collectively can achieve a defined purpose. If the process under consideration in a maturity model is project management, examples of process areas would be project definition, project establishment, requirements definition, project planning, project scheduling, risk management, and project monitoring and control.

■ **Common features**: The practices that describe a process area are organized by common features. Common features are attributes that indicate whether the implementation and institutionalization of a key process area are effective, repeatable, and lasting. Examples of common features employed by most maturity models include the following:

  □ *Commitment to perform*: The actions that an organization must take to ensure that the process is established and will endure

  □ *Ability to perform*: Preconditions that must exist in an organization to implement the process competently

  □ *Activities performed*: The roles and procedures required to implement the key process area

□ *Measurement and analysis:* The need to measure the process and analyze the measurements

□ *Verifying implementation:* The steps to ensure that the activities are performed in compliance with the process that has been established

■ **Base practices:** A process area is composed of base practices, which are mandatory characteristics that must exist within an implemented process before an organization can claim satisfaction in a given process area. For example, the systems security process area includes base practices such as administering security controls, assessing impact, assessing security risk, assessing threat, assessing vulnerability, coordinating security, monitoring security posture, providing security input, specifying security needs, and verifying/validating security.

Having presented the basic concepts of a maturity model, these concepts will now be applied to present a maturity model for ECM.

## 5.4 ECM MATURITY MODEL

The challenges being faced by organizations during different phases of the contract life cycle were presented in Section 2.4. The ultimate downside of inefficient processes in ECM is that they cost the organization money and increase its exposure to risk. Researchers at the Aberdeen Group estimate that a $1 billion organization with annual purchases totaling $500 million ($400 million of which is under contracts) loses $18 million every year due to lack of proper supplier contract management! A company with suboptimal contracting processes will spend additional time, effort, and expense in manually managing supplier contracts, at a cost of another $12 million annually.* In Section 3.5, we discussed the heightened interest in the field of ECM arising from the current focus on bottom-line results, increased globalization, the dawning of the era of compliance, the advent of Web-based technology solutions, and the current lack of optimal ECM processes and technology. However, organizations in the process of launching ECM implementation or improvement initiatives need tools and techniques to first create a baseline for assessing their current capabilities in ECM business processes and systems. Such organizations need to understand their current ECM status, determine where their

---

* Susan Avery, "Contract Management Is the Next Step in Smart Supply Strategy," *Purchasing Magazine,* vol. 133, no. 12, pp. 60–64, July 2004.

ECM capabilities ought to be, and identify milestones to measure their progress in the process of migration and transformation to ECM excellence. The ECM Maturity Model (ECM-MM) provides a framework to address these needs of today's contracting organizations.

The ECM-MM is a tool to assist and empower managers to drive continuous improvement in ECM processes and systems based on best practices. It is focused on the requirements for effectively and efficiently managing all stages of the contract life cycle within an organization, thereby improving an organization's interactions with its suppliers, customers, and other business partners. The ECM-MM promotes standardization and simplification of ECM business processes and systems across organizational functions, divisions, and geographies with the goal of institutionalizing ECM processes in a manner that affords predictable results, repeatable processes, consistent execution, measured performance, and continuous improvement.

The ECM-MM consists of a five-level evolutionary path comprised of increasingly organized and more mature ECM processes, designed to assist an organization's ECM migration to excellence in the following ways:

- Provide a framework to assess the organization's current ECM processes, practices, and technology
- Assist an organization in determining the desired or optimal state of ECM practices based on knowledge and experience gained from forward-thinking organizations using world-class contracting processes and systems
- Permit the definition of key milestones to chart a road map from the current state to the optimal state of ECM
- Permit the establishment of ECM process improvement goals and practices and prioritize key areas for improvement
- Offer guidance in estimating the costs and benefits associated with advancing to the next ECM maturity level, as well as the risks associated with continuing to use suboptimal ECM practices and with taking no action to improve the current state of ECM
- Create a clear structure for setting measurable benchmarks of the organization's ECM practices as compared with those of its competitors

## 5.4.1 Objectives of the ECM Maturity Model

The ultimate definition of an organization's relationships with its customers, suppliers, and other business partners is found in its contracts—those documents that codify agreements for the spectrum of activities undertaken by an organization in the pursuit of its mission on behalf of its stakeholders. It is in the best interests of all organizations to ensure that the execution of their contracts is accurate, comprehensive, defect free, and timely. While there are a number of generally accepted principles in the field of ECM, there are to date no comprehensive standards or frameworks for evaluating ECM practices, either within an organization or between organizations. By establishing such a framework, the ECM-MM provides a system for measuring and improving performance in the application of ECM principles.

The primary motivation behind developing a maturity model for ECM has been to achieve the following key objectives:

- To assist organizations embarking on implementing an ECM solution: Such organizations need to assess their current ECM processes and systems, compare their current state against the optimal state of ECM, determine areas for improvement based on the gaps identified, and define the sequence of measures that should be enacted to ensure progress toward the goal of ECM excellence.
- To help contracting organizations improve the ECM processes in a predictable, measurable, and organized way: Organizations that plan their evolution in a systematic fashion have a distinct advantage over those forced to change by events beyond their control. By proactively implementing ECM improvement on its own terms within a reasonable time frame, an organization should be able to set reasonable goals for achieving maturity in ECM processes and not be blindsided by internal and external events impacting the ECM process.
- To provide best practices, standards, and guidelines to the contracting professionals community.
- To help focus the investments of organizations in ECM tools, training, process definition, and management practices.
- To provide capability-based assurance, for example trustworthiness based on confidence in the maturity of ECM processes and practices.

Another key point to bear in mind regarding the ECM process is that what may be considered best practice today is not necessarily going to be considered best practice tomorrow. This is because as forward-thinking organizations adopt best practices, they will continue to evolve and improve their ECM processes and systems and, therefore, create new best practices in the process. Thus, the content of the ECM-MM—and for that matter of any maturity model—should be continuously updated to include new best practices in the field under consideration.

## 5.4.2  Scope of the ECM Maturity Model

So far, an overview of the ECM-MM has been provided and the objectives for building the model defined. Before providing a detailed description of the model and its components, the scope of the model will be defined. The scope of the ECM-MM presented in this chapter includes the following elements:

- The model addresses all activities involved in the complete contract management life cycle. These include contract conception and creation, internal and external collaboration, contract execution, administration, closeout/renewal, and analysis within an organization.
- The model provides requirements for application developers, system developers, integrators, and ECM vendors that develop and provide technology solutions to support the ECM processes within an organization.
- The model applies to all types and sizes of commercial as well as federal contracting organizations.

It should be noted that while the overarching concept of the ECM-MM presented in this chapter will apply to almost any type of contract, the best practices presented here deal specifically with procurement contracts. Organizations embarking on ECM improvement initiatives for other types of contracts such as sales, warranties, rental/lease, or intellectual property should identify their applicable set of best practices and use the ECM-MM as a guide for measuring and tracking progress along the ladder of maturity levels.

While the ECM-MM is a distinct model to improve and assess contract management capabilities of an organization, it is not the intent of this chapter to imply that ECM processes should be practiced in isolation from other organizational processes such as supplier relationship management (SRM), customer relationship management (CRM), traditional procure to pay (P2P), and order to cash (OTC). On the contrary, the ECM-MM promotes such integration, taking the view that ECM processes traverse multiple organizational processes. Therefore, the ECM-MM defines components that address areas where integration and coordination are critical to success.

## 5.4.3  Description of the ECM Maturity Model

Having provided an overview of the ECM-MM, followed by a discussion of its objectives and scope, it is now appropriate to formally describe the core elements. The ECM-MM (shown in Figure 5.2) provides contracting organizations

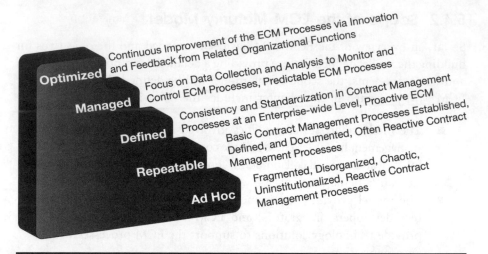

Continuous Improvement of the ECM Processes via Innovation and Feedback from Related Organizational Functions

**Optimized**

Focus on Data Collection and Analysis to Monitor and Control ECM Processes, Predictable ECM Processes

**Managed**

Consistency and Standardization in Contract Management Processes at an Enterprise-wide Level, Proactive ECM

**Defined**

Basic Contract Management Processes Established, Defined, and Documented, Often Reactive Contract Management Processes

**Repeatable**

Fragmented, Disorganized, Chaotic, Uninstitutionalized, Reactive Contract Management Processes

**Ad Hoc**

**FIGURE 5.2. Maturity Levels in ECM Maturity Model**

with guidance regarding how to gain control of contract life cycle processes while systematically evolving toward a culture of contracting excellence. The ECM-MM consists of the following five different levels of process maturity, presented diagrammatically in Figure 5.2 and discussed below:

1. **Ad Hoc:** The Ad Hoc level of ECM maturity is unquestionably the entry level, in which an organization conducts its contracting activities in an unsystematic, opportunistic, and often chaotic manner. No formal contracting processes are defined or documented at this initial level, and each contract author develops and executes contracts as he or she deems most appropriate. As such, the success or failure of a contract in serving the needs of the parties involved has little impact on future undertakings; for example, there is no internal system for self-improvement of the contract management process. The quality of contracts and the time required to author, negotiate, approve, and execute them are unpredictable. Successful completion of a contract life cycle depends on the dedicated efforts of a few motivated contracting professionals instead of the entire contracting organization. Table 5.1 provides a detailed overview of the characteristics of such an organization.

2. **Repeatable:** At the Repeatable level of ECM maturity, organizational policies for contracting processes exist, and procedures to implement such policies have been established. These procedures help contract-

**TABLE 5.1. Characteristics of an Ad Hoc Contracting Organization**

| People | Processes |
|---|---|
| ■ Success depends on the competence of individual contract authors, negotiators, or administrators in the organization and is not repeatable.<br>■ Contract authors, negotiators, and administrators follow different paths to author, execute, and manage each contract.<br>■ Contracting professionals are not held accountable for adhering to, or complying with, any contract management processes or standards.<br>■ Executives do not comprehend the extent of issues arising from poor ECM processes. | ■ Contract management processes are not defined or documented.<br>■ Processes are fragmented, disorganized, not institutionalized, and often chaotic. In times of crisis, processes are abandoned.<br>■ Fire-fighting mode: Problems are addressed as and when they arise, using manual and labor-intensive processes.<br>■ Budget is exceeded and deadlines are often missed due to long contracting cycle time.<br>■ Infrequent long-range resolution to problems. |
| **Technology** | **Risks and Rewards** |
| ■ Tools used to author and manage contracts include word-processing applications (such as Microsoft Word) and spreadsheet applications (such as Microsoft Excel). No special software is used for ECM.<br>■ Contract information is maintained separately by individual contract authors in the software of their choice, leading to outdated, inaccurate, incomplete, and duplicate contract data.<br>■ Contract monitoring and analysis is not performed because data are unavailable, not centralized, and of insufficient quality to run meaningful queries or metrics reports. | ■ Risk is extremely high due to lack of operational, contractual, and regulatory compliance and especially because no tools exist to enforce and ensure compliance.<br>■ Rewards are low. Except for the occasional success of individual contracting professionals, contracting groups and related organizational functional groups reap little benefit from contract management. |

*You have to do it before you can manage it!*

ing professionals in successfully executing the previously mastered tasks and avoiding the repetition of past failures. However, the overall contracting function is still in a reactive mode. Most processes are short and focus on addressing recently discovered problems. The ECM procedures are defined, but are applied only on either highly complex contracts or on critical/high-value contracts. The key distinguishing factor of this maturity level is that a major component of the organization's processes remains institutionalized through the experience of individual staff instead of being maintained in documented procedures. In addition to this distinguishing factor, the other main characteristics of an organization at this level of ECM maturity are provided in Table 5.2.

3. **Defined**: Organizations at the Defined maturity level have formally defined, documented, and integrated the various activities that should occur at different stages in the contract life cycle. Tools and techniques, such as clause templates and contract templates, are available to contract authors to aid them in development of contracts. Guidelines exist to assist contract authors with selection of the appropriate contract template for a particular purchase or sale, and alternate clause templates are available to provide preapproved language that can be used in place of the standard language to meet unique requirements. Approval rules and security roles are clearly defined to enable consistent internal and external collaboration and workflow across multiple contract types and divisions/business units of the organization. Exception criteria are clearly defined, along with the roles and responsibilities of individuals responsible for addressing exceptions in ECM processes. Thus, the key distinguishing factors for organizations at this ECM maturity level are the use of standard and consistent contracting processes and activities and a common, organization-wide understanding of the roles and responsibilities of individuals at different stages of the contract life cycle. Table 5.3 presents the main characteristics of an organization that has reached the Defined maturity level of the ECM-MM.

4. **Managed**: When an organization has progressed from the Defined to the Managed maturity level, a key change is evident in its focus on quantitative goals in two key areas: productivity within the contracting processes and quality of the contractual agreements. Most, if not all, organizations at the Managed level of ECM maturity employ one or more ECM solutions (discussed in detail in Chapter 3). Such ECM solutions are typically used to collect and analyze data at different stages of the contract life cycle. This focus on quantitative analysis allows organizations to better control ECM processes by defining the parameters of process performance so that they routinely fall within acceptable boundaries. The increased control resulting from employment of such ECM solutions generates desired

**TABLE 5.2. Characteristics of a Repeatable Contracting Organization**

| People | Processes |
| --- | --- |
| ■ Success depends on the competence of groups of contract authors, negotiators, or administrators in the organization and is repeatable.<br>■ Within the contracting group, individual roles and tasks are defined and documented.<br>■ Individuals are held accountable for their specific functions. However, the performance evaluation criteria are not aligned between individuals across the contracting group.<br>■ Lack of strong commitment from senior management to improve the ECM processes, procedures, and standards. | ■ Stronger ECM roles emerge, but the contracting function is still in a reactive mode.<br>■ Most processes are short and focus on addressing recently discovered problems.<br>■ Individuals create some basic ECM processes and procedures, but these are applied only on either highly complex or critical contracts or if a contract value exceeds a certain dollar threshold. |

| Technology | Risks and Rewards |
| --- | --- |
| ■ Contracts are created using a word-processing application such as Microsoft Word and tracked using a spreadsheet application such as Microsoft Excel.<br>■ In some cases, a stand-alone application (such as a document management system) may also be used to store the critical contracts in an electronic format.<br>■ Contract data are not integrated using an automated system, but are usually manually integrated by individuals in isolated areas of the organization.<br>■ Attempts to reconcile contract data require extensive effort and time because not all contracts are maintained in an electronic format, nor are data files consistent due to their residing in multiple and diverse repositories and due to inconsistency in data maintained in multiple sources. | ■ Risk is still high due to lack of operational, contractual, and regulatory compliance. Poor contract data quality and integration result in inaccurate analysis and outdated reports.<br>■ Rewards are limited. Most ROI arrives via individual processes or individuals. Little to no corporate-wide recognition of the benefits of effective contract management. |

*We are what we repeatedly do. Excellence, then, is not an act, but a habit.*
—*Aristotle*

and predictable results from each stage in the contract life cycle. Further detailed characteristics of this maturity level are provided in Table 5.4.

**TABLE 5.3. Characteristics of a Defined Contracting Organization**

| People | Processes |
|---|---|
| ■ Success depends on the competence of everyone in the contracting group and on how well the contracting group works as a team.<br>■ Senior management understands and appreciates the role of contract management in reducing costs, increasing revenues, and reducing risks.<br>■ Senior management is involved in providing guidance and direction with regard to strategy and has some visibility into contracts.<br>■ Performance of contracting professionals is evaluated using criteria that focus on adding value to the core contracting group. These are not yet aligned with those used by other organizational functional groups. | ■ ECM processes are well characterized and understood across the organization. These ECM processes are described clearly in standards, procedures, tools, and methods.<br>■ The focus of the contracting organization is on documentation, standardization, and consistency across the organization.<br>■ Contracting professionals use a set of standard ECM processes consistently across the organization on all types of contracts and improve over time.<br>■ Contracts are created using standard clause templates and contract templates.<br>■ While the ECM processes have evolved to some degree in their sophistication, when considered in isolation these processes are not sufficiently well integrated with other functions such as SRM, CRM, P2P, and OTC to provide optimal results.<br>■ The performance of the ECM processes is only qualitatively predictable. |
| **Technology** | **Risks and Rewards** |
| ■ In some cases, an application (such as an ERP system) may also be used to automate some of the ECM processes or to manage tactical ECM tasks, such as creating purchase orders in the ERP system against contracts.<br>■ Most recent versions of contracts are scanned and stored in a document repository, giving appropriate access to a subset of the organization.<br>■ Some basic reports such as number of contracts executed or number of contracts expiring in the next month are run on a periodic basis. | ■ Risk is medium due to an improvement in operational compliance resulting from well-defined processes, policies, and standards. However, risk due to regulatory compliance and contractual compliance may still continue to be high due to lack of appropriate integration of ECM processes with other organizational functional processes and lack of tools for adequate monitoring and analysis.<br>■ Rewards are observable but remain suboptimal. Except for the occasional success of individual contracting professionals, contracting groups and related organizational functional groups reap little benefit from contract management. |

**TABLE 5.4.  Characteristics of a Managed Contracting Organization**

| People | Processes |
|---|---|
| ■ Management identifies ways to adapt and adjust the ECM processes to specific unique requirements without measurable losses of quality or deviations from specifications.<br><br>■ Executive-level decision-makers begin to view effective ECM as a competitive advantage.<br><br>■ ECM initiatives receive the personnel and resources necessary to lay the foundation for a best-in-class contract management system.<br><br>■ The contracting group's goals and performance measures are aligned with those of the other organizational functions. | ■ An organization at this maturity level monitors and controls its own ECM processes through data collection and analysis.<br><br>■ Contract data are standardized, consistent, and measurable. Preventive measures are in place to ensure high quality of meta-data on contracts.<br><br>■ The performance of ECM processes is controlled using statistical and other quantitative techniques and is quantitatively predictable.<br><br>■ Basic ECM processes are integrated with other organizational core processes such as cost control, commitment management, invoice verification, schedule management, and performance management.<br><br>■ The goals of ECM shift from problem resolution to problem prevention.<br><br>■ Process improvements to address causes of ECM process variation and measurably improve the organization's processes are identified, evaluated, and deployed. |

| Technology | Risks and Rewards |
|---|---|
| ■ Sophisticated ECM solution is used which provides document management, contract authoring, resource planning, performance analysis, compliance management, and reporting capabilities.<br><br>■ ECM solution is integrated with other enterprise-wide applications such as ERP, CRM, SRM, document management system, and business warehouse system. However, the level of integration varies from basic to medium level of complexity and sophistication.<br><br>■ Contract monitoring and analysis based on a best-in-class ECM solution helps improve efficiency and effectiveness of the ECM processes.<br><br>■ Contracts are authored using clause and contract templates. | ■ Risk is medium to low due to an improvement in operational compliance, contractual compliance, and regulatory compliance achieved by adopting best practices provided by a best-in-class ECM solution.<br><br>■ Also, since the focus of organizations at this maturity level is on quantitative measures and data collection and analysis, the risks are visible and steps can be taken to mitigate these risks.<br><br>■ Rewards are medium to high. |

5.  **Optimizing**: At the highest level of ECM maturity—Optimizing, an organization's focus is on continuous improvement in ECM processes and systems. A contracting organization that has attained the Optimizing maturity level is able to continually identify and address weaknesses proactively in different phases of the contract life cycle. Contracting professionals within such organizations continually strive to increase their knowledge and improve by learning from external as well as internal resources, such as professional and research analyst organizations. Improvements occur both by incremental advances in existing processes and by innovations using new technologies such as ECM solutions and methods. Refer to Table 5.5 for detailed characteristics of Optimizing ECM organizations.

As an organization ascends from one ECM maturity level to the next, its costs and exposure to risks are reduced, while ECM process capability and adherence to organizational policies, procedures, and guidelines improve. The natural consequence of this process is a gradual but predictable increase in efficiency and an overall improvement in the organization's operations and performance. As organizations attain higher levels of maturity in ECM processes, institutionalization takes place via policies, standards, and organizational structures. This is evident from the characteristics of organizations at different maturity levels presented in Tables 5.1 through 5.5. Each of these tables describes four key aspects of an ECM maturity level:

- **People**: Who is involved and what contributions must they make?
- **Processes**: What activities must be performed?
- **Technology**: What investments in technology must be made?
- **Risks and rewards**: What risks does the organization face by staying at the current maturity level and what does it expect to gain by advancing to the next maturity level?

## 5.4.4 Progression to Higher ECM Maturity Levels

The previous section described the different levels comprising the ECM-MM and the characteristics of organizations at each of the maturity levels. In this section, we will focus our attention on what organizations can do to progress from their current level of ECM maturity to higher levels of maturity in ECM processes and systems.

**TABLE 5.5.  Characteristics of an Optimizing Contracting Organization**

| People | Processes |
|---|---|
| ■ Complete buy-in from senior management for the need to implement effective and efficient ECM processes and standards.<br>■ ECM initiatives have executive-level sponsorship and direct CEO support.<br>■ The contracting group is empowered and aligned with the business value and objectives of the organization. This leads to optimizing ECM and related organizational functional processes.<br>■ A central ECM group operates across the organization and has the support of contract authors, negotiators, administrators, change champions, and Six Sigma experts.<br>■ Contracting professionals identify opportunities to accelerate and share lessons learned, all of which, with best-practice programs, are implemented to improve the ECM processes, standards, and documentation. | ■ ECM processes are constantly being improved through both incremental and innovative technological improvements.<br>■ Procedures help the organization execute optimal contracts effectively.<br>■ Quantitative ECM process improvement objectives (such as reduce maverick spend by x%, improve operational compliance by y%, etc.) for the organization are established, continually revised to reflect changing business objectives, and used as criteria in managing ECM process improvement. The effects of deployed process improvements are measured and evaluated against the quantitative process improvement objectives.<br>■ Process improvements to address *special causes* of ECM process variation and measurably improve the organization's processes are identified, evaluated, and deployed. |

| Technology | Risks and Rewards |
|---|---|
| ■ ECM tools are standardized across the organization.<br>■ Complex ECM processes are integrated with other organizational core processes such as SRM, CRM, e-procurement, P2P, and OTC.<br>■ Data are collected from multiple systems and analyzed in unified data warehouses to routinely audit ECM processes. Deviations from optimal processes are identified, investigated, and resolved immediately.<br>■ Interfaces are bidirectional, real time, and require minimum manual intervention. | ■ Risk is low. ECM policies, processes, procedures, and technology are defined, documented, standardized, simplified, and institutionalized, allowing the organization to author and execute optimal contracts and maintain high-quality information about its contractual agreements with its suppliers and customers.<br>■ Rewards are high. Optimized ECM system leads to reducing costs, increasing revenue, enhancing visibility, and reducing risk of noncompliance with local, national, or global regulations. |

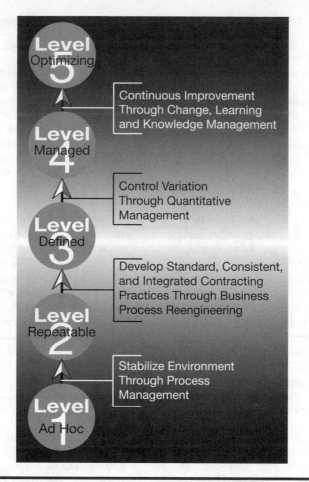

**FIGURE 5.3. Progression to Higher Levels of ECM Maturity**

As shown in Figure 5.3, in order for an organization to advance from one maturity level to the next, the following steps, actions, and initiatives must occur:

■ **From Ad Hoc to Repeatable:** In today's rapidly changing and increasingly competitive global economy, bottom-line results have been the focus at every level in virtually all organizations. The pressure from top management to continuously reduce costs and increase revenues while ensuring regulatory, contractual, and procedural compliance is usually a key driver for organizations to progress from the

Ad Hoc to the Repeatable ECM maturity level. Stabilization of the environment via good management of the underlying business processes alone can help an organization progress from a disorganized contract management state to one where the contracting professionals are not always in a brushfire management mode. Some of the key action items necessary to advance to the Repeatable maturity level include identifying and addressing key issues in the contracting process and ensuring commitment from top management to allocate appropriate resources to execute any proposed changes in organizational structure, roles and responsibilities, and task assignments.

- **From Repeatable to Defined**: The transition from the Repeatable to the Defined maturity level is often initiated when one or more members of an organization's management exercise strategic vision and can see the clear and long-range benefits of further improving the ECM process. At the Repeatable maturity level, ECM processes may be established, but they are not consistently standardized across contract types, organizational functions, or geographical units. Standardization and consistency in ECM processes and systems are the key factors that assist an organization in progressing to the Defined maturity level. Certain checks and balances need to be instituted at this stage to ensure that standard and consistent procedures and guidelines are being followed. Some of the other key activities that must occur to enable this transition include integration of ECM practices with other business processes across the organization and gathering support and commitment from senior management for implementing ECM best practices.

- **From Defined to Managed**: Since the primary focus of the Managed maturity level is quantitative assessment of business processes, most organizations rely on technology as a key enabler to progress to this maturity level. The old adage "you can't control what you can't measure, and you can't measure what you can't see" applies very well here. Technology solutions enable visibility into contracts at many critical levels, including the negotiated terms and conditions, as well as the meta-data for the contracts, such as effective start date, end date, and total estimated value of the contract. Some of the key activities associated with effective transition from the Defined to the Managed maturity level include identifying key performance metrics to be measured, setting up an automated mechanism for reporting in case of exceptions, and routinely identifying and eliminating common causes of variations in the ECM processes.

■ **From Managed to Optimizing**: By far the most complex evolutionary transition to implement within an organization, the evolution from the Managed to the Optimizing level requires fundamental change within the culture of the organization. Advancing to the Optimizing maturity level involves a deep, comprehensive, coordinated, and continuing change in people, processes, and technologies. A change of this magnitude in an organization's culture involves changes in people's attitudes and behavior, while at the same time new and better processes and technologies offer better tools and frameworks for improving ECM within and across the organization. Moreover, at the Optimizing level of ECM maturity, an organization not only brings about fundamental changes internally, but it also influences the contracting practices of its business partners. The advances in ECM made to attain the previous maturity levels provide a solid foundation for a best-in-class ECM system. These advances must be implemented continuously and consistently, primarily by documenting and replicating best practices throughout the enterprise to reach the pinnacle of the ECM-MM. To sustain these high levels of ECM maturity, it is critical to appoint one (or more depending on the structure and size of an organization) change champion to lead the ECM optimization initiative within an organization. Such an individual should be assigned the responsibility to ensure effective communication with all stakeholders, ensure effective deployment and training in the ECM solution, and provide recognition of successes achieved from continuous improvement activities within ECM.

It should be noted that the migration from one maturity level to the next may not occur immediately or continuously. At this point, the theory of smooth sailing gives way to the day-to-day realities of change that occur across divisions and levels within an organization. Different parts of a contracting organization may have different levels of maturity. For example, while the procurement contracting group already may have developed standard contract language and templates, the sales contracting group within the same organization still may be in the process of developing them. Even within the same organization, it is quite possible that two different contracting groups are using different technologies, different databases, and different procedures for authoring and executing contracts. The activities needed to facilitate the transition from one maturity level to the next will vary depending on a number of factors. These include the organizational as well as geographic structure of the organization, the commitment and leadership provided by senior management at different levels and locations of the organization, the current ECM maturity level of individual groups, and the availability of resources to support such ECM improvement initiatives within different groups or at different locations.

Also, a contracting group or multiple contracting groups within an organization may elect not to move to the next maturity level if the costs associated with the move outweigh the expected benefits. It is important to note that attempting to ascend to higher maturity levels too rapidly, or by skipping a level, can be counterproductive since each level builds a foundation from which to achieve the subsequent level. An organization must evolve through these levels in a systematic and organic manner to establish and maintain a culture of process excellence in ECM.

## 5.4.5 Shift in Focus and Improvement in Process Capability

As the processes and technologies related to ECM mature within an organization, a shift in the focus of the contracting professionals is often observed (see Figure 5.4). At lower levels of ECM maturity, contracting professionals have an internal focus as they work diligently on their respective tasks to ensure that they can complete the work assigned to them on time. Like beads on a string, the various linear elements of the contract process and life cycle are assembled and linked without the often-essential big-picture view of the entire process and its implications within and beyond the organization. This tendency to "wear blinders" changes as an organization defines and establishes repeatable processes, migrating upward toward optimal ECM maturity.

At the mid-levels of ECM maturity, contracting professionals begin to collaborate with personnel in other organizational and functional groups such as procurement, sales, finance, legal, and risk management to understand their respective requirements and expectations from the organization's contractual agreements. This focus on understanding the customer's voice helps contracting professionals improve the quality of legal documents as well as the efficiency of the contracting process, enabling them to deliver high-quality contracts for the right materials/services at the right time, all within budget.

As ECM processes mature further and reach the highest levels of maturity, contracting professionals proactively leverage best practices implemented across geographies and business units to improve the efficiency and effectiveness of the entire ECM process. At this level, the focus is not only on executing the contract life cycle but also on learning from other divisions within the organization or

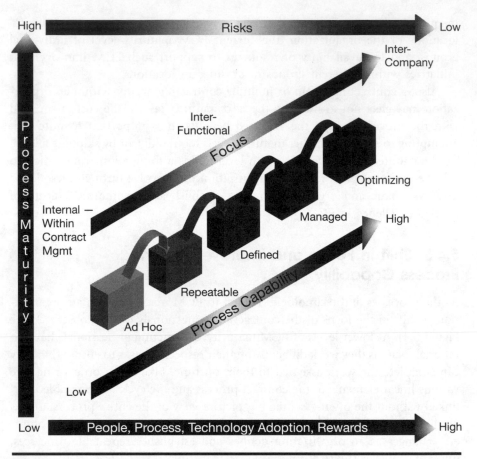

**FIGURE 5.4. The Contract Management Maturity Model**

from other organizations, thereby using lessons learned to continuously improve their own processes and systems. Moreover, instead of strictly focusing on the requirements of the personnel in other organizational functions, managers begin to view contracts as the foundation of the organization's relationships with its business partners, working collaboratively with such partners to improve the quality of the contracts both within and beyond the boundaries of the organization.

A final and added benefit accruing to organizations that achieve the highest levels of ECM maturity is the realization of higher levels of process capabilities throughout the organization (see Figure 5.4). These capabilities broadly may be defined as:

- **Process control**: The difference between expected and actual results, noting the variation around these expected results
- **Process predictability**: Measured by the variability in achieving cost and performance objectives
- **Process effectiveness**: The achievement of targeted results and the ability to raise targets

In addition, a higher capability in ECM processes also results in higher certainty, stability, accuracy, and efficiency across the contracting organization. This causes a ripple effect that results in improving efficiency through the rest of the organization as well as through the organizations of the business partners.

## 5.4.6 Summary

The ECM-MM was introduced as a powerful tool for maximizing the benefit from continuous improvement initiatives in ECM. Specifically, this section described how the ECM-MM can be a powerful tool for managers to develop performance baselines and standards against which progress toward optimal ECM processes and systems may be measured. Employing the ECM-MM to set such a baseline permits efficient identification of areas in the overall ECM process where there is greatest potential for performance improvement, reduction of cost and risk, and overall maximization of ROI. All in all, the ECM-MM is a powerful tool for managers to track progress toward excellence in ECM.

This section described in some detail the benefits of the ECM-MM, including the positive impact such a model has on enhancing predictability and elevating overall control of performance elements to acceptable levels. The model exhibits highly positive effects on overall improvement of ECM process efficiency, adherence to predetermined standards, and identification of ECM areas where capability improvement is required. Cost reduction and risk mitigation are additional benefits accruing to managers who employ the ECM-MM.

Ultimately, the net effect of the ECM-MM is to ensure that an organization's goals for ECM improvement are achieved in an orderly manner, consistent with the company's current state of ECM processes and systems, its available resources, and the degree to which its various divisions and staff are working in tandem. By ensuring that objective metrics are employed and used to routinely monitor progress in underlying ECM process capabilities, a high degree of consistency can be achieved in advancing up the ECM evolutionary ladder. The ECM-MM reinforces proactive initiatives (versus reactive responses) during ECM processes, thereby maximizing the probability that a sustained culture of ECM excellence is established and maintained both within an organization and in its dealings with the broader business community.

## 5.5 ECM MATURITY APPRAISAL METHOD

### 5.5.1 Overview

Section 5.4 of this chapter presented an overview, scope, and detailed description of the ECM-MM. This section focuses on the ECM Maturity Appraisal Method (ECM-MAM). The ECM-MAM is a tool for organizations to establish a baseline for the current state of their contracting processes and to implement systems by which future performance may be measured against the standards detailed in the ECM-MM. Such an appraisal can provide an organization valuable insight into its own ECM capabilities, enabling continuous improvement efforts within the organization. The primary goals that an organization can expect to achieve by using the ECM-MAM include:

- Determine the current overall capability of the organization with regard to ECM
- Gain an understanding of domain-related issues
- Identify opportunities for improvement
- Understand key factors influencing deployment of new organizational practices and systems
- Track the progress of ECM improvement initiatives

Before employing the ECM-MAM, an organization should identify the scope and goals of the appraisal by considering the following:

- What is the primary goal of the appraisal? Is benchmarking the primary goal, or is the appraisal being used to track progress of an ECM improvement initiative? Is the goal of the appraisal to assist in selecting the ECM solution that best meets the business requirements of the contracting organization?
- For what type of contracts, such as sales, procurement, or human resources, will the appraisal be conducted?
- Which geographic regions, business units, or divisions will be covered by the appraisal?
- Who should participate in fine-tuning the appraisal questionnaire?
- How will the results of the appraisal be presented? Who will present them, and to whom will they be presented?

- What are the potential costs and expected benefits associated with this appraisal?

The ECM-MAM groups survey questions based on key process areas within ECM, including:

- Contract conception and creation
- Contract collaboration
- Contract execution
- Contract administration
- Contract closeout/renewal and analysis

Within each key process area, these questions are arranged according to the key practices within that area. Table 5.6 provides a detailed listing of the key practices within the key process areas for procurement contracts. Similar listings may be developed by organizations using the ECM-MAM to baseline or benchmark the ECM processes and systems related to other contract types, such as sales, intellectual property, and human resources.

It should be noted that contracting areas which belong primarily to the strategic sourcing process (such as procurement planning, presolicitation planning, solicitation, and source selection) and to the traditional procurement process (such as invoice settlement) have intentionally been left out of this model because, while these business functions are very tightly integrated with ECM processes, separate maturity models should be created and used by an organization to assess its capabilities in these related functions. The ECM-MM is intended to apply to the contract conception and creation, negotiation, approval, execution, administration, and closeout processes only. It does, however, give due consideration to integration of the five key ECM process areas with other business functions.

Since one of the key challenges of most appraisals is to ensure an acceptable level of objectivity and consistency, the ECM-MAM converts the responses of individuals into a numerical score on a scale of 1 through 5, where 1 indicates "never" and 5 indicates "always." Thus, a question that is answered with a rating of 1 indicates a practice that is never used in the organization, whereas a rating of 5 indicates a practice that is well established, understood, and used extensively and consistently across the contract types and regions/divisions within the scope of the appraisal.

Also, since different practices and different process areas may have a different level of significance for different contracting organizations, the ECM-MAM accounts for such differences in business requirements by providing a weight

**TABLE 5.6. Key Process Areas and Practices for Procurement Contracts**

| Process Area | Practices |
|---|---|
| Contract conception and creation | ■ The process for authoring contracts should be established, communicated, and adhered to on all contracts.<br>■ The authoring process should involve representatives from all appropriate organizational functions, such as operations, maintenance, safety, risk management, legal, tax, and insurance.<br>■ Rules governing participation required (and the level of participation as well) from each of the related organizational groups should be clearly defined and understood by all.<br>■ The workload and skill set involved with authoring functions should be estimated and appropriate resources obtained to handle this function efficiently and effectively.<br>■ Clause and contract templates should be used as much as is possible to author contracts.<br>■ Deviations from standard or approved clause and contract language should be captured and should be reviewed by the organization's appropriate internal groups (such as legal and risk management).<br>■ There should be an ongoing effort to gather and analyze data, which should include capturing key performance indicators such as the percentage of contracts executed without requiring any change from standard language, how many—and which—clauses had to be changed in the nonstandard contracts, which clauses are most frequently modified, which vendors require modifications to standard language often, etc.<br>■ Appropriate mechanisms (automated or manual) should be in place to identify the need to update clause and contract templates where necessary, and these mechanisms should be used to keep improving the quality of the templates.<br>■ Other related business functions, such as strategic sourcing and supplier performance measurement, should also be considered when planning resources for the contract authoring process.<br>■ The end result of the contract authoring process should be a document created using standard and approved templates. |
| Contract collaboration | ■ The process for internal as well as external collaboration on contracts should be established, communicated, and adhered to on all contracts.<br>■ The collaboration process should involve representatives from all appropriate organizational functions, such as operations, maintenance, safety, risk management, legal, tax, and insurance.<br>■ Rules governing participation required (and the level of participation as well) from each of the related organizational groups should be clearly defined and understood by all. |

**TABLE 5.6.  Key Process Areas and Practices for Procurement Contracts (continued)**

| Process Area | Practices |
|---|---|
| Contract collaboration (continued) | ■ The workload and skill set involved with collaborating functions should be estimated and appropriate resources obtained to handle this function efficiently and effectively.<br>■ Standard forms and templates (such as notification templates) should be used as much as is possible to negotiate contracts.<br>■ Reasons for deviations from the standard collaboration process should be captured and should be reviewed by the organization's appropriate internal groups (such as legal and risk management).<br>■ There should be an ongoing effort to gather and analyze data, which should include capturing key performance indicators such as the percentage of contracts negotiated online versus offline, the percentage of contracts executed without going through the appropriate approval process, etc.<br>■ Appropriate mechanisms (automated or manual) should be in place to identify the need to update approval rules where necessary, and these mechanisms should be used to improve the contract quality.<br>■ Other related business functions, such as strategic sourcing, supplier performance measurement, and contract authoring, should also be considered when planning resources for the contract collaboration process.<br>■ The end result of the contract collaboration process should be a document whose language and content have been approved by both the organization and its suppliers. |
| Contract execution | ■ The process for contract execution should be established, communicated, and adhered to on all contracts.<br>■ The execution process should involve representatives from all appropriate organizational functions, such as operations, maintenance, safety, risk management, legal, tax, and insurance.<br>■ Rules governing participation required (and the level of participation as well) from each of the related organizational groups should be clearly defined and understood by all.<br>■ The workload and skill set involved with execution functions should be estimated and appropriate resources obtained to handle this function efficiently and effectively.<br>■ Standard forms and templates (such as signature blocks) should be used as much as is possible to execute contracts.<br>■ Reasons for deviations from the standard execution process should be captured and should be reviewed by the organization's appropriate internal groups (such as legal and risk management). |

**TABLE 5.6. Key Process Areas and Practices for Procurement Contracts (continued)**

| Process Area | Practices |
|---|---|
| Contract execution (continued) | ▪ There should be an ongoing effort to gather and analyze data, which should include capturing key performance indicators such as the average cycle time from initiating the contract authoring process to executing a contract online and saving appropriate documentation, the number of executed contracts that went through to the executed status using the standard defined process, etc.<br>▪ Other related business functions, such as strategic sourcing, supplier performance measurement, and contract authoring, should also be considered when planning resources for the contract execution process.<br>▪ The end result of the contract execution process should be a document whose language and content have been approved by both the organization and its suppliers. |
| Contract administration | ▪ The process for contract administration should be established, communicated, and adhered to on all contracts.<br>▪ The administration process should involve representatives from all appropriate organizational functions, such as operations, maintenance, safety, risk management, legal, tax, and insurance.<br>▪ Rules governing participation required (and the level of participation as well) from each of the related organizational groups should be clearly defined and understood by all.<br>▪ The workload and skill set involved with administrative functions should be estimated and appropriate resources obtained to handle this function efficiently and effectively.<br>▪ The process for amending executed contracts and for ensuring a four-way match between contract, purchase order, goods/service receipt, and invoice receipt is established, communicated, and developed.<br>▪ Reasons for deviations from the standard administration process should be captured and should be reviewed by the organization's appropriate internal groups (such as legal and risk management).<br>▪ There should be an ongoing effort to gather and analyze data, which should include capturing key performance indicators such as performance of supplier against contractual terms and conditions, number of modifications made to the original versions of contracts, etc.<br>▪ Other related business functions, such as strategic sourcing, supplier performance measurement, and contract authoring, should also be considered when planning resources for the contract administration process. |

**TABLE 5.6.   Key Process Areas and Practices for Procurement Contracts (continued)**

| Process Area | Practices |
|---|---|
| Contract administration (continued) | ■ The end result of the contract administration process should be an efficient and effective periodic review of executed contracts for cost, schedule, and performance evaluations. |
| Contract closeout/ renewal and analysis | ■ The process for contract closeout should be established, communicated, and adhered to on all contracts. This includes establishing a process for exercising a party's right or a mutual-agreement right of the parties to discontinue performance under a contract.<br>■ The closeout process should involve representatives from all appropriate organizational functions, such as operations, maintenance, safety, risk management, legal, tax, and insurance.<br>■ Rules governing participation required (and the level of participation as well) from each of the related organizational groups should be clearly defined and understood by all.<br>■ The workload and skill set involved with the contract closeout functions should be estimated and appropriate resources obtained to handle this function efficiently and effectively.<br>■ Standard forms, templates, and checklists should be used as much as is possible to close out contracts and to maintain complete documentation on closed-out contracts.<br>■ Reasons for deviations from the standard closeout process should be captured and should be reviewed by the organization's appropriate internal groups (such as legal and risk management).<br>■ There should be an ongoing effort to gather and analyze data, which should include capturing key performance indicators such as average cycle time from contract authoring to contract closeout, percentage of spend against contracts, etc.<br>■ Other related business functions, such as strategic sourcing, supplier performance measurement, and contract authoring, should also be considered when planning resources for the contract closeout process.<br>■ The end result of the contract closeout process should be a lessons learned and best-practices database for future use. |

factor for each question in the survey. Even before sending out the appraisal questionnaire to the participating individuals, an organization should decide on the appropriate weights to be applied to different process areas and practices. Tables 5.7 through 5.11 indicate the sample questionnaire developed to baseline ECM processes of an organization using the ECM-MAM for procurement con-

**TABLE 5.7. Assessing Capabilities in Contract Authoring**

| Practice | Process Area 1: Contract Authoring | Never | Rarely | Sometimes | Frequently | Always | Individual Score | Weight | Weighted Score |
|---|---|---|---|---|---|---|---|---|---|
| | | | | Response | | | | Score | |
| PA01.1 | The contract creation/authoring process is defined, documented, standardized, and established on an enterprise-wide level. | 1 | 2 | 3 | 4 | 5 | | | |
| PA01.2 | The contract authoring process is mandated—and adherence to the process is tracked—on all procurement contracts regardless of the criticality, confidentiality, or dollar value associated with a contract. | 1 | 2 | 3 | 4 | 5 | | | |
| PA01.3 | Most of the tasks involved in the contract authoring process, such as extracting information from RFx documents, using the contract and clause template library to initiate a document, etc., are automated. | 1 | 2 | 3 | 4 | 5 | | | |
| PA01.4 | Standard clause and contract template library is developed and appropriate usage guidelines are provided to the contract authors. | 1 | 2 | 3 | 4 | 5 | | | |
| PA01.5 | A revision history of contract documents is maintained during the contract authoring cycle for audit purposes. | 1 | 2 | 3 | 4 | 5 | | | |
| PA01.6 | The organization involves representatives from other business functions, such as legal, risk management, tax, insurance, etc., during contract authoring activities. | 1 | 2 | 3 | 4 | 5 | | | |

| Practice | Process Area 1: Contract Authoring | Never | Rarely | Sometimes | Frequently | Always | Individual Score | Weight | Weighted Score |
|---|---|---|---|---|---|---|---|---|---|
| PA01.7 | The contract authoring process is fully integrated with other contracting processes, as well as other business processes such as strategic sourcing, SRM, etc. | 1 | 2 | 3 | 4 | 5 | | | |
| PA01.8 | Automated triggers and event notifications are used to alert key stakeholders when changes are made to the standard clauses, if standard clauses are replaced or omitted from contract versions, etc. | 1 | 2 | 3 | 4 | 5 | | | |
| PA01.9 | The organization uses efficiency and effectiveness measures in periodically evaluating the contract authoring process. | 1 | 2 | 3 | 4 | 5 | | | |
| PA01.10 | Lessons learned are shared and adopted to continuously improve the contract authoring process. | 1 | 2 | 3 | 4 | 5 | | | |

**TABLE 5.8. Assessing Capabilities in Contract Collaboration**

| Practice | Process Area 2: Contract Collaboration | Response | | | | | Score | | |
|---|---|---|---|---|---|---|---|---|---|
| | | Never | Rarely | Sometimes | Frequently | Always | Individual Score | Weight | Weighted Score |
| PA02.1 | The contract collaboration process is defined, documented, standardized, and established on an enterprise-wide level. | 1 | 2 | 3 | 4 | 5 | | | |
| PA02.2 | The contract collaboration process is mandated—and adherence to the process is tracked—on all procurement contracts regardless of the criticality, confidentiality, or dollar value associated with a contract. | 1 | 2 | 3 | 4 | 5 | | | |
| PA02.3 | Most of the routine and repetitive tasks involved in the contract collaboration process, such as negotiating with suppliers until agreement is reached with regard to contract language, communicating with contract approvers to ensure financial as well as procurement approval is obtained, etc., are automated. | 1 | 2 | 3 | 4 | 5 | | | |
| PA02.4 | The contract collaboration process includes a negotiation agenda, negotiation plans and schedule, interim summary, final summary, negotiation review and approval, etc. | 1 | 2 | 3 | 4 | 5 | | | |
| PA02.5 | Electronic or hard copies of the different versions of agreements are maintained in a central repository, which allows visibility to appropriate personnel. | 1 | 2 | 3 | 4 | 5 | | | |
| PA02.6 | The organization involves representatives from other business functions, such as procurement, sourcing, engineering, etc., during contract negotiation activities. | 1 | 2 | 3 | 4 | 5 | | | |

| Practice | Process Area 2: Contract Collaboration | Never | Rarely | Sometimes | Frequently | Always | Individual Score | Weight | Weighted Score |
|---|---|---|---|---|---|---|---|---|---|
| | | | | **Response** | | | | **Score** | |
| PA02.7 | The organization involves representatives from other business functions, such as procurement, sourcing, engineering, etc., in the final decision to award a contract to a particular supplier. | 1 | 2 | 3 | 4 | 5 | | | |
| PA02.8 | The contract negotiation process is fully integrated with other business processes such as cost, engineering, project and program management, etc. | 1 | 2 | 3 | 4 | 5 | | | |
| PA02.9 | Automated triggers and event notifications are used to alert key stakeholders when changes are made to the standard language, when terms and conditions negotiated with a supplier lie outside the accepted ranges, when additional approvals are required based on predefined approval rules, etc. | 1 | 2 | 3 | 4 | 5 | | | |
| PA02.10 | Performance metrics are used that measure value added to the contracting group, to the other business functions, and to the organization as well as to the supplier's organization. Lessons learned are shared and adopted, both internally within the organization and externally with the supplier, to continuously improve the contract collaboration process. | 1 | 2 | 3 | 4 | 5 | | | |

**TABLE 5.9.** Assessing Capabilities in Contract Execution

| Practice | Process Area 3: Contract Execution | Response | | | | | Score | | |
| --- | --- | --- | --- | --- | --- | --- | --- | --- | --- |
| | | Never | Rarely | Sometimes | Frequently | Always | Individual Score | Weight | Weighted Score |
| PA03.1 | The contract execution process is defined, documented, standardized, and established on an enterprise-wide level. | 1 | 2 | 3 | 4 | 5 | | | |
| PA03.2 | The contract execution process is mandated—and adherence to the process is tracked—on all procurement contracts regardless of the criticality, confidentiality, or dollar value associated with a contract. | 1 | 2 | 3 | 4 | 5 | | | |
| PA03.3 | Most of the routine and repetitive tasks involved in the contract execution process, such as ensuring agreements follow standard contract language and any modifications to standard language have been approved by the legal group, ensuring that a contract has been signed by the appropriate person from each side, etc., are automated. | 1 | 2 | 3 | 4 | 5 | | | |
| PA03.4 | The contract execution process includes getting physical signatures or e-signatures on the final agreed-upon version of a contract. | 1 | 2 | 3 | 4 | 5 | | | |
| PA03.5 | Electronic or hard copies of the signed agreements are maintained in a central repository, which allows visibility to appropriate personnel. | 1 | 2 | 3 | 4 | 5 | | | |
| PA03.6 | The organization involves representatives from other business functions, such as procurement, sourcing, etc., during contract execution activities. | 1 | 2 | 3 | 4 | 5 | | | |

| Practice | Process Area 3: Contract Execution | Never | Rarely | Sometimes | Frequently | Always | Individual Score | Weight | Weighted Score |
|---|---|---|---|---|---|---|---|---|---|
| | | | | Response | | | | Score | |
| PA03.7 | Post-contract-award meetings are organized to keep all stakeholders informed about the key aspects of a contract. | 1 | 2 | 3 | 4 | 5 | | | |
| PA03.8 | The contract execution process is fully integrated with other business processes such as purchase order creation, commitment management, supplier performance measurement, etc. Most of this integration is enabled through automated interfaces between the organization's ECM solution and other enterprise-wide applications. | 1 | 2 | 3 | 4 | 5 | | | |
| PA03.9 | Automated triggers and event notifications are used to alert key stakeholders when milestones, such as effective start date, effective end date, etc., are approaching. | 1 | 2 | 3 | 4 | 5 | | | |
| PA03.10 | Performance metrics are used that measure value added to the contracting group, to the other business functions, and to the organization as a whole. Lessons learned are shared and adopted to continuously improve the contract execution process. | 1 | 2 | 3 | 4 | 5 | | | |

**TABLE 5.10. Assessing Capabilities in Contract Administration**

| Practice | Process Area 4: Contract Administration | Never | Rarely | Sometimes | Frequently | Always | Individual Score | Weight | Weighted Score |
|---|---|---|---|---|---|---|---|---|---|
| | | | | Response | | | | Score | |
| PA04.1 | The contract administration process is defined, documented, standardized, and established on an enterprise-wide level. | 1 | 2 | 3 | 4 | 5 | | | |
| PA04.2 | The contract administration process is mandated—and adherence to the process is tracked—on all procurement contracts regardless of the criticality, confidentiality, or dollar value associated with a contract. | 1 | 2 | 3 | 4 | 5 | | | |
| PA04.3 | Most of the routine and repetitive tasks involved in the contract administration process are automated. | 1 | 2 | 3 | 4 | 5 | | | |
| PA04.4 | A copy of the amendments to a contract is maintained and linked to the original contract so that changes made are easily visible and tracked. | 1 | 2 | 3 | 4 | 5 | | | |
| PA04.5 | The contract administration process for managing contract changes, payments, and incentive or award fees is established. | 1 | 2 | 3 | 4 | 5 | | | |
| PA04.6 | The organization involves representatives from other business functions, such as procurement, sourcing, etc., in monitoring performance against negotiated contractual terms and conditions. | 1 | 2 | 3 | 4 | 5 | | | |

| Practice | Process Area 4: Contract Administration | Response | | | | | Score | | |
|---|---|---|---|---|---|---|---|---|---|
| | | Never | Rarely | Sometimes | Frequently | Always | Individual Score | Weight | Weighted Score |
| PA04.7 | Post-award and preperformance meetings are held with new suppliers to establish processes for communication, scope change, and performance monitoring. | 1 | 2 | 3 | 4 | 5 | | | |
| PA04.8 | The contract administration process is fully integrated with other business functions such as traditional procurement, invoice verification, supplier performance measurement, etc. Most of this integration is enabled through automated interfaces between the organization's ECM solution and other enterprise-wide applications. | 1 | 2 | 3 | 4 | 5 | | | |
| PA04.9 | Automated triggers and event notifications are used to alert contract administrators if certain thresholds are exceeded or if expiry dates or review dates are approaching. | 1 | 2 | 3 | 4 | 5 | | | |
| PA04.10 | Performance metrics that measure value added to the contracting group, to the other business functions, and to the organization as a whole are used in periodic evaluations of contracts. Lessons learned are shared and adopted to continuously improve the contract administration process. | 1 | 2 | 3 | 4 | 5 | | | |

**TABLE 5.11.  Assessing Capabilities in Contract Closeout and Analysis**

| Practice | Process Area 5: Contract Closeout and Analysis | Response | | | | | Score | | |
|---|---|---|---|---|---|---|---|---|---|
| | | Never | Rarely | Sometimes | Frequently | Always | Individual Score | Weight | Weighted Score |
| PA05.1 | The contract closeout process is defined, documented, standardized, and established on an enterprise-wide level. | 1 | 2 | 3 | 4 | 5 | | | |
| PA05.2 | The contract closeout process is mandated—and adherence to the process is tracked—on all procurement contracts regardless of the criticality, confidentiality, or dollar value associated with a contract. | 1 | 2 | 3 | 4 | 5 | | | |
| PA05.3 | Most of the routine and repetitive tasks involved in the contract close-out process, such as ensuring completion of work, completing documentation, resolving any open issues, etc., are automated. | 1 | 2 | 3 | 4 | 5 | | | |
| PA05.4 | The contract closeout process includes verification that deliveries have been received, subcontracts have been settled, indirect costs have been settled, and classified documents are disposed. | 1 | 2 | 3 | 4 | 5 | | | |
| PA05.5 | A process has been established for resolving disputes and claims promptly. | 1 | 2 | 3 | 4 | 5 | | | |
| PA05.6 | The organization involves representatives from other business functions, such as procurement, sourcing, etc., during contract closeout activities. | 1 | 2 | 3 | 4 | 5 | | | |

| Practice | Process Area 5: Contract Closeout and Analysis | Response | | | | | Score | | |
|---|---|---|---|---|---|---|---|---|---|
| | | Never | Rarely | Sometimes | Frequently | Always | Individual Score | Weight | Weighted Score |
| PA05.7 | Post-closeout analysis is completed to evaluate the success of contract authoring, negotiating, execution, and administrative functions. | 1 | 2 | 3 | 4 | 5 | | | |
| PA05.8 | The contract closeout and analysis process is fully integrated with other business processes such as supplier performance measurement, commitment management, etc. Most of this integration is enabled through automated interfaces between the organization's ECM solution and other enterprise-wide applications. | 1 | 2 | 3 | 4 | 5 | | | |
| PA05.9 | Automated triggers and event notifications are used to alert contract administrators if contract closeout cannot occur due to pencing tasks, open issues around payments or supplier performance, etc. | 1 | 2 | 3 | 4 | 5 | | | |
| PA05.10 | Performance metrics that measure value added to the contracting group, to the other business functions, and to the organization as a whole are used in analysis of contracts after closeout. Lessons learned are shared and adopted to continuously improve the contract closeout process. | 1 | 2 | 3 | 4 | 5 | | | |

**TABLE 5.12. Conversion Table**

| Final Score | Maturity Level |
|---|---|
| 0.0–2.0 | Ad Hoc |
| 2.0–3.0 | Repeatable |
| 3.0–4.0 | Defined |
| 4.0–4.5 | Managed |
| 4.5–5.0 | Optimizing |

tracts. Similar questionnaires can be developed if the ECM-MAM is intended for use in evaluating the processes and systems used to manage the life cycle of other contract types, such as sales, warranties, and intellectual property.

Once the individual responses to the ECM-MAM survey have been provided, the weighted scores for individual practices within a process area can be added to calculate the total score for that particular process area. These individual scores for different key process areas should then be weighted and summed to calculate the overall score for the organization. The overall score can then be translated to the corresponding ECM maturity level using the ranges provided in Table 5.12.

## 5.5.2  Case Study

In order to facilitate understanding the ECM-MM and ECM-MAM, this section presents a hypothetical case study. To set the stage, some background information about our hypothetical organization, ABC Chemicals, Inc., is provided.

ABC Chemicals, Inc. is a specialty chemical company with two plants in the United States (ABC-US), one plant in Europe (ABC-EU), and two plants in the Asia-Pacific region (ABC-AP). Procurement at ABC Chemicals is structured so that a central procurement group, called Global Procurement Services (GPS), is responsible for defining the organization's procurement policies, procedures, standards, and guidelines across geographical regions. This group is also responsible for managing procurement of goods and services at a global level, and therefore is the primary group responsible for authoring, executing, and monitoring global contracts with suppliers. In addition to GPS, each plant also has a small local procurement group comprised of a few individuals who usually report to the local purchasing manager. These local procurement groups are comprised of buyers who specialize in purchasing specific goods and/or services, as well as contracting professionals (such as contract author, administrator, etc.) who are primarily responsible for either writing new contracts with local sup-

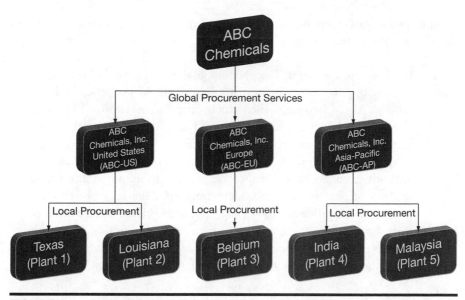

**FIGURE 5.5. Organizational Structure of Procurement Group at ABC Chemicals, Inc.**

pliers or leveraging the global contracts executed by GPS. The organizational structure for the procurement function of ABC Chemicals, Inc. is shown in Figure 5.5.

As part of the continuous improvement initiative in P2P processes, the GPS organization has decided to conduct a thorough benchmarking study of ABC's contracting function at both the global and local levels. The goal of this appraisal is to determine the current maturity level of the ECM processes and systems within the organization and, based on these results, to propose three key opportunities for improvement in ECM that promise the highest ROI. Presented below is an illustration of how the ECM-MAM can be used to conduct such an appraisal at ABC Chemicals, Inc. It should be noted that while one such solution is presented, it is not the only correct way to conduct such an analysis. If a thorough and accurate analysis is performed, the results obtained should be similar regardless of how the appraisal is structured.

### 5.5.2.1 Step 1. Planning the Appraisal

The planning phase of the appraisal establishes the framework under which the appraisal will be conducted and also prepares the logistical aspects for the execution phase. ABC Chemicals has identified the following items as a result of the discussions in the planning phase:

- **Goals of the appraisal:** The primary goal of this appraisal is to identify key opportunities for improvement in ECM processes and systems at ABC Chemicals, Inc. which offer the maximum ROI. It is also expected that the assessment will help ABC Chemicals determine the current maturity level of its ECM processes and systems.
- **Scope of the appraisal:** Only the ECM processes as they apply to authoring, collaboration, approval, execution, administration, and analysis of procurement contracts are within the scope of this appraisal. ECM processes to manage the life cycle of sales contracts, lease agreements, etc. are out of scope for this appraisal. Also, this appraisal includes all local (i.e., U.S.) as well as international locations (i.e., Europe and Asia-Pacific) of ABC Chemicals, Inc.

### 5.5.2.2 Step 2. Preparing for the Appraisal Effort

The purpose of the prepare phase of the appraisal is to customize the questionnaire provided in the previous section (Tables 5.7 through 5.11) to meet the unique setup and requirements of the organization being appraised. For example, if the GPS group within ABC Chemicals, Inc. authors and manages 75% of all contracts used by the organization worldwide, it makes sense to assign a higher weight factor to the scores of GPS than to those of the individual local procurement groups. Therefore, ABC Chemicals decided to apply weights (as shown in Table 5.13) to different procurement groups based on the number and total value of contracts executed by each procurement group.

In addition to assigning weights for the procurement groups, weights also need to be assigned to individual process areas and practices within each process

**TABLE 5.13. Weights Assigned to Individual Procurement Group Scores**

| Procurement Group | Weight |
|---|---|
| GPS | 0.75 |
| Local procurement group for Plant 1 | 0.05 |
| Local procurement group for Plant 2 | 0.05 |
| Local procurement group for Plant 3 | 0.05 |
| Local procurement group for Plant 4 | 0.05 |
| Local procurement group for Plant 5 | 0.05 |

**TABLE 5.14. Weights Assigned to Individual Process Area Scores**

| Process Area | Weight |
|---|---|
| Contract authoring | 0.2 |
| Contract collaboration | 0.2 |
| Contract execution | 0.2 |
| Contract administration | 0.2 |
| Contract closeout and analysis | 0.2 |

area. ABC Chemicals decided to put equal weight on all the process areas, as shown in Table 5.14.

The next step within the prepare phase is to assign weight factors for individual practices within a process area. ABC Chemicals determined that out of the ten practices listed in Table 5.7, practices PA01.1, PA01.2, PA01.4, PA01.7, and PA01.10 are more critical to the organization compared to the other practices within that process area. Thus, Table 5.15 shows the weights assigned by ABC Chemicals to individual practices within the first ECM process area, contract authoring. It should be noted that the weights for the practices identified as critical are much higher than the ones assigned to other practices. A similar exercise was performed to develop the customized versions of each remaining questionnaire based on Tables 5.8 through 5.11.

The prepare phase should also include other critical tasks such as orienting the group of individuals that will be asked to provide responses to the questionnaire and ensuring that they understand the expectations clearly before proceeding to the next phase.

### 5.5.2.3 Step 3. Execute the Appraisal

After assigning weights to procurement groups, process areas, and practices within each process area, the next phase in the appraisal process is the execute phase. This phase includes administering the questionnaire, collecting the responses, and calculating the weighted scores.

Table 5.16 shows how the individual scores assigned to practices within the contract authoring process area were converted to the total score for this process area for one of the procurement groups (GPS) within ABC Chemicals. The same process was followed for all remaining procurement groups as well as for all process areas. The results of this exercise are shown in tabular format in Table 5.17.

**TABLE 5.15.** Assessing Capabilities in Contract Authoring

| Practice | Process Area 1: Contract Authoring | Never | Rarely | Sometimes | Frequently | Always | Individual Score | Weight | Weighted Score |
|---|---|---|---|---|---|---|---|---|---|
| | | | | **Response** | | | | **Score** | |
| PA01.1 | The contract creation/authoring process is defined, documented, standardized, and established on an enterprise-wide level. | 1 | 2 | 3 | 4 | 5 | | 0.15 | |
| PA01.2 | The contract authoring process is mandated—and adherence to the process is tracked—on all procurement contracts regardless of the criticality, confidentiality, or dollar value associated with a contract. | 1 | 2 | 3 | 4 | 5 | | 0.15 | |
| PA01.3 | Most of the tasks involved in the contract authoring process, such as extracting information from RFx documents, using the contract and clause template library to initiate a document, etc., are automated. | 1 | 2 | 3 | 4 | 5 | | 0.05 | |
| PA01.4 | Standard clause and contract template library is developed and appropriate usage guidelines are provided to the contract authors. | 1 | 2 | 3 | 4 | 5 | | 0.15 | |
| PA01.5 | A revision history of contract documents is maintained during the contract authoring cycle for audit purposes. | 1 | 2 | 3 | 4 | 5 | | 0.05 | |
| PA01.6 | The organization involves representatives from other business functions, such as legal, risk management, tax, insurance, etc., during contract authoring activities. | 1 | 2 | 3 | 4 | 5 | | 0.05 | |

| Practice | Process Area 1: Contract Authoring | Never | Rarely | Sometimes | Frequently | Always | Individual Score | Weight | Weighted Score |
|---|---|---|---|---|---|---|---|---|---|
| PA01.7 | The contract authoring process is fully integrated with other contracting processes, as well as other business processes such as strategic sourcing, SRM, etc. | 1 | 2 | 3 | 4 | 5 | | 0.15 | |
| PA01.8 | Automated triggers and event notifications are used to alert key stakeholders when changes are made to the standard clauses, f standard clauses are replaced or omitted from contract versions, etc. | 1 | 2 | 3 | 4 | 5 | | 0.05 | |
| PA01.9 | The organization uses efficiency and effectiveness measures in periodically evaluating the contract authoring process. | 1 | 2 | 3 | 4 | 5 | | 0.05 | |
| PA01.10 | Lessons learned are shared and adopted to continuously improve the contract authoring process. | 1 | 2 | 3 | 4 | 5 | | 0.15 | |

**TABLE 5.16. Assessing Capabilities in Contract Authoring**

| Practice | Process Area 1: Contract Authoring | Response | | | | | Score | | |
| --- | --- | --- | --- | --- | --- | --- | --- | --- | --- |
| | | Never | Rarely | Sometimes | Frequently | Always | Individual Score | Weight | Weighted Score |
| | | 1 | 2 | 3 | 4 | 5 | | | |
| PA01.1 | The contract creation/authoring process is defined, documented, standardized, and established on an enterprise-wide level. | 1 | 2 | **3** | 4 | 5 | 3 | 0.15 | **0.45** |
| PA01.2 | The contract authoring process is mandated—and adherence to the process is tracked—on all procurement contracts regardless of the criticality, confidentiality, or dollar value associated with a contract. | 1 | 2 | 3 | **4** | 5 | 4 | 0.15 | **0.60** |
| PA01.3 | Most of the tasks involved in the contract authoring process, such as extracting information from RFx documents, using the contract and clause template library to initiate a document, etc., are automated. | 1 | 2 | **3** | 4 | 5 | 3 | 0.05 | **0.15** |
| PA01.4 | Standard clause and contract template library is developed and appropriate usage guidelines are provided to the contract authors. | 1 | 2 | **3** | 4 | 5 | 3 | 0.15 | **0.45** |
| PA01.5 | A revision history of contract documents is maintained during the contract authoring cycle for audit purposes. | 1 | 2 | 3 | **4** | 5 | 4 | 0.05 | **0.60** |
| PA01.6 | The organization involves representatives from other business functions, such as legal, risk management, tax, insurance, etc., during contract authoring activities. | 1 | 2 | **3** | 4 | 5 | 3 | 0.05 | **0.15** |

| Practice | Process Area 1: Contract Authoring | Response | | | | | Score | | |
|---|---|---|---|---|---|---|---|---|---|
| | | Never | Rarely | Sometimes | Frequently | Always | Individual Score | Weight | Weighted Score |
| PA01.7 | The contract authoring process is fully integrated with other contracting processes, as well as other business processes such as strategic sourcing, SRM, etc. | 1 | 2 | **3** | 4 | 5 | 3 | 0.15 | **0.45** |
| PA01.8 | Automated triggers and event notifications are used to alert key stakeholders when changes are made to the standard clauses, if standard clauses are replaced or omitted from contract versions, etc. | 1 | 2 | 3 | **4** | 5 | 4 | 0.05 | **0.20** |
| PA01.9 | The organization uses efficiency and effectiveness measures in periodically evaluating the contract authoring process. | 1 | **2** | 3 | 4 | 5 | 2 | 0.05 | **0.10** |
| PA01.10 | Lessons learned are shared and adopted to continuously improve the contract authoring process. | 1 | **2** | 3 | 4 | 5 | 2 | 0.15 | **0.30** |
| | **Total score** | | | | | | | | **3.45** |

**TABLE 5.17. Results from the Execute Phase**

| Process Area | ABC Chemicals Organizational Groups | | | | | |
| --- | --- | --- | --- | --- | --- | --- |
| | GPS | Plant 1 | Plant 2 | Plant 3 | Plant 4 | Plant 5 |
| Authoring | 3.45 | 2.00 | 2.15 | 2.05 | 2.10 | 2.40 |
| Collaboration | 2.60 | 1.85 | 2.00 | 2.05 | 1.95 | 2.50 |
| Execution | 2.80 | 2.50 | 2.45 | 2.40 | 2.50 | 2.45 |
| Administration | 2.85 | 2.00 | 2.05 | 2.00 | 1.95 | 2.50 |
| Closeout and analysis | 2.60 | 1.75 | 1.85 | 1.90 | 1.95 | 2.50 |

### 5.5.2.4 Step 4. Reporting and Analysis

In the final phase of the appraisal, results from the previous phase are reviewed, analyzed, and used to present recommendations to top management. Using the weights defined in Table 5.14, the overall score for each organizational group can be calculated. For example, the overall score for the ABC Chemicals GPS group is

$$(3.45 * 0.2) + (2.6 * 0.2) + (2.8 * 0.2) + (2.85 * 0.2) + (2.6 * 0.2) = \mathbf{2.86}$$

Thus, the maturity level of ECM processes and systems within the GPS group of ABC Chemicals is 2.86, that is, between the Repeatable and Defined levels. The overall scores for the remaining procurement groups within ABC Chemicals are shown in Table 5.18.

Also, it is possible to calculate the maturity level of an organization in a particular process area. In the case of ABC Chemicals, using the weights assigned in Table 5.13 and the results shown in Table 5.17, the maturity level of the ABC procurement organization in individual ECM process areas can be calculated. For example, the overall score for ABC Chemicals in the contract authoring process area is

$$(3.45 * 0.75) + (2.00 * 0.05) + (2.15 * 0.05) + (2.05 * 0.05)$$
$$+ (2.10 * 0.05) + (2.40 * 0.05) = \mathbf{3.12}$$

Similarly, the overall score of ABC Chemicals in other ECM process areas was calculated and is shown in Table 5.18.

Based on the overall scores calculated per group, it is easy to determine the ECM maturity level for each group within the organization and also for the organization as a whole. It is evident from the results in Table 5.18 that all the

**TABLE 5.18. Reporting and Analysis**

| Process Area | GPS | Plant 1 | Plant 2 | Plant 3 | Plant 4 | Plant 5 | Weighted Scores |
|---|---|---|---|---|---|---|---|
| | | ABC Chemicals Organizational Groups | | | | | |
| Authoring | 3.45 | 2.00 | 2.15 | 2.05 | 2.10 | 2.40 | **3.12** |
| Collaboration | 2.60 | 1.85 | 2.00 | 2.05 | 1.95 | 2.50 | **2.47** |
| Execution | 2.80 | 2.50 | 2.45 | 2.40 | 2.50 | 2.45 | **2.72** |
| Administration | 2.85 | 2.00 | 2.05 | 2.00 | 1.95 | 2.50 | **2.66** |
| Closeout and analysis | 2.60 | 1.75 | 1.85 | 1.90 | 1.95 | 2.50 | **2.45** |
| **Overall score per group** | **2.86** | **2.02** | **2.10** | **2.08** | **2.09** | **2.47** | |

individual procurement groups are functioning at the Repeatable maturity level with regard to ECM. Also, the overall ECM maturity level of the ABC Chemicals organization as a whole is 2.68, which is calculated by multiplying the overall scores of each organizational group by the weights assigned to them, given in Table 5.13.

The results in Table 5.18 provide an easy way to analyze the maturity of ECM processes and systems across an organization. Some of the key observations are:

■ The overall score of the ABC Chemicals procurement group is 2.68, which indicates that its ECM maturity level is somewhere between Repeatable and Defined.

■ The overall score of the GPS group was higher than that of all other procurement groups, which indicates that its ECM processes and systems are more mature than those used by the rest of the organization. This makes sense because ECM probably defines the primary job function and area of expertise of the GPS resources, and this is an area of core competence for them, while that is not necessarily the case for the resources working for the smaller procurement groups. ABC Chemicals' ECM initiative should therefore focus on leveraging the processes, tools, and practices used by GPS to raise the capability of ECM processes at the local procurement group level.

■ The overall score for Plant 1 was lower than that of all other procurement groups. This indicates a clear opportunity for improvement. In particular, contract closeout and analysis and contract collaboration received the lowest scores, indicating that this procurement group could benefit from implementation of an ECM solution that provides deep functionality in the areas of contract analysis/ reporting and automated workflow/collaboration.

- The weighted score of the organization in the contract authoring process area was higher than the scores in all other process areas. Thus, it appears that the contracting professionals feel confident about their use of clause templates and contract templates and the content of the contracts, which indicates a lower level of risk associated with contract authoring as compared to that associated with other contracting processes.
- The weighted score of the organization in contract closeout and analysis was lower than the scores in all other process areas. This clearly indicates a potential area for improvement that could possibly offer the maximum ROI for incremental advances.
- Since the scores in all process areas were less than 4.0, contract analysis and integration of ECM processes and systems with other enterprise-wide processes and applications offers a clear opportunity for improvement.

Some of the other key tasks involved in this last phase of the appraisal are:

- Develop a final report (i.e., finalize a findings report and develop a briefing for the ECM improvement initiative sponsor)
- Present appraisal results to the sponsor
- Report lessons learned for future appraisals

## 5.6 HOW ECM SOLUTIONS ASSIST IN PROGRESSING TO HIGHER MATURITY LEVELS

In addition to addressing challenges in the contract life cycle as discussed in Section 5.3, ECM solutions also help organizations progress to higher levels of ECM maturity in the following manner:

- **Industrialize tasks:** At the very basic level, ECM solutions help automate numerous tasks in the contract life cycle, such as contract creation, internal and external collaboration, approval, execution, monitoring, and analysis. Such solutions industrialize contract management processes and enable organizations to progress from the Ad Hoc maturity level to the Repeatable maturity level.

■ **Ensure adherence:** ECM solutions help organizations enforce and ensure adherence and compliance to organizational policies, procedures, standards, and business conduct guidelines. An effective and efficient ECM solution implements an organization-wide contract creation, approval, execution, monitoring, and analysis system with appropriate templates for clauses, contracts, and notifications/alerts to monitor and bring to the surface any exceptions in the processes. This enables an organization to reduce and prevent defects and variability in the contracting process, thereby leading to the establishment of defined ECM processes within and across the organization. ECM solutions are a key tool for organizations that are trying to progress from the Repeatable to the Defined maturity level.

■ **Embed a culture of continuous improvement:** As an organization begins using an ECM solution to author and manage its worldwide contractual agreements, one of the key benefits realized is enhanced visibility into the contracts. This visibility allows the organization to efficiently and accurately measure its performance against key indicators such as total number of contracts; number of contracts with one supplier or customer; spend by commodity code or by type of service, vendor, or region; and average cycle time for each contracting activity. Standard reports generate information which can then be analyzed and used to monitor and control ECM processes, helping to drive consistency and predictability in the ECM processes and enabling an organization to progress from the Defined maturity level to the Managed maturity level. This enhanced visibility also provides a basis for driving continuous improvement in underlying contracting processes, minimizing error-prone manual tasks, and solidifying the effectiveness of internal controls. The overall effect of ECM is to reduce cycle time, risk, and rework and to help embed a culture of continuous improvement in ECM processes and systems across the organization.

■ **Leverage lessons and best practices:** High-quality ECM solutions are designed and developed based on best practices observed in forward-thinking organizations across industrial sectors and geographics. ECM vendors such as Contiki, Emptoris, I-many, Nextance, and Upside Software collaborate with research organizations such as Gartner Research, Aberdeen Group, and AMR Research and professional organizations such as the National Contract Management Association and International Association for Contract and Commercial Management to understand the key challenges and core requirements of member organizations with regard to ECM. These research and professional organizations also gather and share lessons learned by member organizations that either have already launched ECM initiatives or are in the process of doing so, which in turn assists ECM vendors in identifying new functionality to be added to their ECM solutions. This can also help identify changes required to existing functionality of an ECM solution that could plug the holes in the contracting processes at different organizations. ECM solutions provide a mechanism to leverage best practices and lessons learned from other organizations, which enables an organization to continuously improve and optimize its ECM business processes and systems and thus progress from the Managed to the Optimizing maturity level.

■ **Institutionalization**: ECM solutions provide a framework and an infrastructure to contracting professionals through which they can share their knowledge and experiences with other contracting professionals within an organization. A contract author can view the documents written by others and use the language in certain clauses to drive negotiations based on prices and terms developed and negotiated by other contract authors and managers within the organization. ECM solutions retain corporate knowledge and establish methods, practices, and procedures in instances where experienced contracting professionals leave the organization. Best contracting practices become ingrained within the corporate culture as all contracting professionals routinely follow defined processes and learn from the experience of others.

## 5.7 SUMMARY

Modern enterprises are emerging—either willingly or by force of competition and law—into a world where the contract is the central force for determining survival and success. With many organizations operating with tens of thousands of agreements in effect simultaneously, the risks of noncompliance, inefficiencies, and cross-compatibility are higher than ever. Therefore, the approaches and tools to enable a migration to higher levels of ECM expertise must be increasingly sensitive, sophisticated, and attuned to both the minutest details and broadest visions of a company, its people, and its stakeholders.

ECM is rapidly emerging as a powerful approach to stay ahead of the game in today's rapidly evolving business world. In order to implement truly efficient, effective, and sustainable ECM processes and systems, however, the very implementation and improvement process itself must be viewed evolutionarily, taking into account the current stage of a company (or its target divisions), the dynamic nature of the contract life cycle itself, and the fact that the process of ECM implementation and improvement must occur while "the train is moving down the track."

This chapter presented a new tool kit for ECM implementations and improvement initiatives to address the above-stated challenges—the concept of the ECM-MM, an approach which employs the latest in maturity model theory to the process of ECM implementation and improvements. By approaching ECM initiatives with this dynamic gestalt, it becomes possible to account for the many idiosyncratic aspects of the ECM evolutionary process, through which an enterprise migrates from lower and ineffective levels of ECM to the highest level of ongoing improvement and cultural integration of ECM as the norm.

# SECTION II.
# IMPLEMENTATION

# IMPLEMENTATION METHODOLOGIES

## IN THIS CHAPTER:

- Six Sigma
- Should ECM Implementation Be a Six Sigma Project?
- The ECM Solution Implementation Road Map Using Six Sigma
- Alternate ECM Solution Implementation Methodologies

## 6.1 OVERVIEW

In the previous chapters of this book, a compelling case for Enterprise Contract Management (ECM) solutions was presented. ECM solutions—when properly deployed—offer a number of core capabilities that enable organizations to meet a wide range of challenges, both within and beyond the contract life cycle. In addition to their positive impact on compliance and the bottom line, ECM solutions provide an essential road map to ensure that modern organizations remain in control of their contractual futures.

The process of implementing a major ECM solution in an existing organization may seem daunting on first consideration. In point of fact, this process is a fundamental one in which the very legal fabric of an organization is affected. The sheer depth and nature of ECM solution implementation suggest its power to bring about positive and lasting change within an organization. Many implementation methodologies have been utilized for ECM solution implementations in the past. However, it is the opinion of the author that Six Sigma methodologies and principles offer a superior approach and present the maximum probability for a successful ECM solution implementation, one that is both comprehensive and sustainable. The combined use of the traditional Six Sigma DMAIC methodology and the relatively newer DFSS methodology offers the best prospects for maximizing the potential benefits for ECM solution implementation.

At the outset of this chapter, however, it is important to clear the air about the applicability of Six Sigma methodologies for ECM solution implementation initiatives. In today's complex and dynamically changing business community, the use of Six Sigma approaches has taken on a multitude of varied forms and applications, oftentimes resulting in multiple Six Sigma projects being undertaken simultaneously within a single large organization. This might lead some to presume that the use of Six Sigma methodology for ECM implementation might require some preexisting frame of reference or context into which it would need to fit in order to be of true value to an organization. Fortunately—and especially for many small to medium-size organizations, this is not the case. The Six Sigma approach is equally applicable on a large-scale integrated basis (as described above) or on a freestanding basis for use solely to assist in ensuring maximum benefits from ECM implementation.

In this chapter, we will explore how the principles and concepts of Six Sigma can be applied to ensure success in an ECM solution implementation initiative. A road map for implementing an ECM solution using Six Sigma concepts will be provided and compared with ECM solution implementation road maps using two alternate implementation methodologies. However, before delving into the details of how a Six Sigma initiative might be of true value in ECM solution implementation, it may be useful to first review the origin, basic concepts, and methodologies of Six Sigma.

## 6.2  SIX SIGMA

### 6.2.1  Origin of Six Sigma

Contrary to popular belief, Six Sigma is not just about quality. It is true that the origin of Six Sigma was in the field of quality control. The quest to achieve Six Sigma began at Motorola in 1979 when the company launched a Total Quality Management (TQM) initiative to improve the quality of its products. At a time when most American organizations believed that quality costs money, Motorola realized through its TQM initiative that, if done correctly, the improvement of quality could actually reduce costs. In 1985, Bill Smith, an engineer at Motorola, presented a paper that concluded that if a product was found to be defective and corrected during the production process, other defects were inevitably missed and found later by the customer during early use of the product. However, if a product was manufactured error-free, it rarely failed during early use by the customer. Smith's findings were greeted with skepticism, but they ignited a fierce debate within Motorola because customer dissatisfaction with products that failed shortly after purchase was very real.

Through further research, Motorola realized that if hidden defects caused a product to fail shortly after purchase, something needed to be done to improve the manufacturing process. Thus began the quest to improve quality and simultaneously reduce production time and costs by focusing on the design and development of a product. This link between higher quality and lower cost led to the development of Six Sigma—an initiative headed by Bob Galvin, Motorola's CEO at the time. This initiative first focused on improving quality through the use of exact measurements to anticipate problem areas, not just react to them. Essentially, Six Sigma would allow a business leader to be *proactive*, rather than *reactive*, in addressing quality-related issues.*

By 1986 Six Sigma had become the major business process methodology at Motorola, and in 1988 Motorola received the first Malcolm Baldrige National Quality Award from the U.S. government for its improvement record based on its Six Sigma program. Within four years, Six Sigma had saved Motorola $2.2 billion. Six Sigma methodology began to quickly spread to other organizations, such as IBM, Texas Instruments, and Kodak, across industry sectors and beyond manufacturing. General Electric embraced Six Sigma in 1995, when Jack Welch, GE's CEO at the time, became enthusiastic about Six Sigma and decreed that 40% of every senior manager's bonus would depend on his or her achieving Six Sigma results. Welch was determined to show customers that Six Sigma was making GE products better and mandated that 70% of all GE Six Sigma projects must be in nonmanufacturing areas. This mandate led GE to work hard toward developing concepts that would make Six Sigma useful outside engineering and operational domains. It is a well-known fact that GE profited by about $7 to $10 billion from Six Sigma over a period of five years.

Over the last decade, organizations that have adopted Six Sigma have realized staggering successes. Some of the well-known examples in this respect are:

---

* Mikel Harry and Richard Schroeder, *Six Sigma: The Breakthrough Management Strategy Revolutionizing the World's Top Corporations,* Currency Doubleday, New York, 2000.

- DuPont added $1 billion to its bottom line in the first two years of initiating its Six Sigma program and increased this to $2.4 billion in four years.
- Honeywell achieved record operating margins and savings of more than $2 billion in direct costs.
- Bank of America saved hundreds of millions of dollars within three years of launching Six Sigma, cut cycle times by more than half, and reduced the number of processing errors by an order of magnitude.
- Allied Signal Inc. reported that the cumulative impact of Six Sigma over a period of five to six years was a savings in excess of $2 billion in direct costs.

It is apparent that, unlike older quality approaches such as TQM, Six Sigma has broken out of the narrow focus of quality control and grown over time to represent a number of different, yet linked, concepts. Subject matter experts and leading practitioners, therefore, describe it in several different ways:

- Six Sigma is a problem-solving methodology geared toward dramatically reducing organizational inefficiencies that translates into bottom-line profitability.
- Six Sigma is a disciplined, data-driven approach to process improvement aimed at the near elimination of defects from every product, process, and transaction.
- Six Sigma is about selecting the right people to drive and lead systematic improvement in a prescribed, disciplined, measurable, and repeatable manner.
- Six Sigma is a comprehensive statistics-based methodology that aims to achieve nothing less than perfection in every company process and product.
- Six Sigma is not an improvement program. It is instead a business philosophy that employs a step-by-step approach to reducing variation, increasing quality, customer satisfaction and, in time, market share.—Mikel Harry, CEO, Six Sigma Academy

Whether it is described as a philosophy, vision, initiative, goal, method, or tool, Six Sigma today is really all about *improving profitability,* that is, helping organizations make more money by improving efficiency and customer value. In short, the benefits of Six Sigma go straight to an organization's bottom line. Unlike mindless cost-cutting programs which also reduce value and quality, Six Sigma identifies and eliminates costs which provide no value to customers by focusing on customer requirements, defect prevention, cycle time reduction, and cost savings. Six Sigma concepts help organizations gain breakthrough knowledge on how to improve processes to do things better, faster, and at lower cost.

In addition to the impact on the bottom line of an organization, Six Sigma has also proven to be a key management tool in the arsenal of senior managers for responding to critical organizational needs and integrating proactive, customer-focused management into the daily routine. As a management tool, Six Sigma is not owned by senior or middle management. Instead, it tends to merge leadership and employee energy and involvement by empowering those at the front lines of the organization to discover true customer requirements and develop efficient business processes, ideas and solutions, meaningful measures, and powerful improvement tools, resulting in improving every facet of the business from production to human resources and from order entry to accounts receivable.

Before proceeding further in explaining the key themes and methodologies of Six Sigma, it makes sense to first understand the basic concepts behind it. The next section, therefore, focuses on providing this information at a high level.

## 6.2.2 The Basics of Six Sigma

At the heart of Six Sigma methodology is the concept of measuring a process in terms of its defects or nonconformance with customer requirements. Statistically speaking, achieving a Six Sigma performance level implies that an organization's processes are performing nearly perfectly, which in statisticians' terms means delivering only 3.4 defects per million opportunities.

The Greek letter sigma ($\sigma$) stands for standard deviation. Standard deviation is a statistical way to describe how much variation exists in a process, a set of data, or a group of items. It is thus used to measure defects in the outputs of a process and show how far the process deviates from perfection. Table 6.1 lists the defects per million opportunities and percent of satisfactory output per sigma level.

It is evident from Table 6.1 that a $1\sigma$ process produces 691,462.5 defects per million opportunities, which translates to a percentage of satisfactory outputs of only 30.854%. If the performance of this process is improved to a $3\sigma$ level, the process will produce 66,800 defects per million opportunities, and if performance is further improved to a $6\sigma$ level, only 3.4 defects per million opportunities are produced. This is also depicted graphically in Figure 6.1.

As can be seen in Figure 6.1, a $3\sigma$ process is wider than customer specifications, resulting in waste and cost of poor quality. However, a Six Sigma pro-

**TABLE 6.1. Defects per Million Opportunities at Different Sigma Levels of Performance**

| Capability Index | Defects per Million Opportunities | Percent of Output Defect-Free |
|---|---|---|
| 0.5$\sigma$ | 841,000 | 16% |
| 1$\sigma$ | 690,000 | 31% |
| 1.5$\sigma$ | 500,000 | 50% |
| 2$\sigma$ | 308,000 | 69.2% |
| 2.5$\sigma$ | 159,000 | 84.1% |
| 3$\sigma$ | 66,800 | 93.3% |
| 3.5$\sigma$ | 22,800 | 97.72% |
| 4$\sigma$ | 6,210 | 99.40% |
| 4.5$\sigma$ | 1,350 | 99.865% |
| 5$\sigma$ | 230 | 99.970% |
| 5.5$\sigma$ | 32 | 99.9968% |
| 6$\sigma$ | 3.4 | 99.99966% |

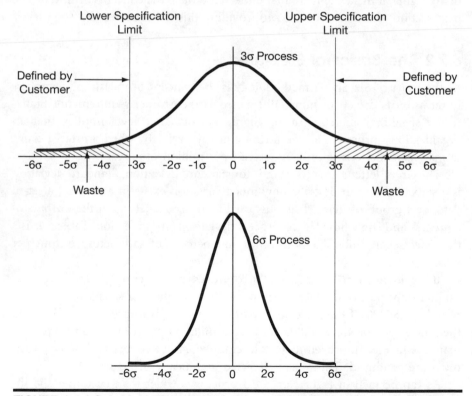

**FIGURE 6.1. Graphical View of Variation and Six Sigma Performance**

cess fits within the customer specifications, so that even if the process shifts a little, the majority of the resulting products will still meet customer expectations.

Thus, the central idea of Six Sigma is if the defects in a process can be identified and measured, the root causes of such defects can be identified and systematically controlled or eliminated to approach a quality level of zero defects. In the following section of this chapter, we will examine some of the key themes of Six Sigma philosophy.

## 6.2.3 Key Themes of Six Sigma

There are six key principles or themes in Six Sigma methodology, all of which, when working in concert, yield the optimal results of the Six Sigma process. These principles are:

1. **Genuine focus on the customer**: In Six Sigma methodology, the customer is the alpha and omega—the core focus in terms of the ultimate determination of value. The impact of any Six Sigma initiative within an organization should ultimately be evaluated in terms of its perceived effect on the customer and on that customer's assessment of the value and quality of the products or services being offered.

2. **Data driven and fact driven**: The Six Sigma approach is not subjective and does not rely upon the intangible assessments of participants, customers, stakeholders, or management. The Six Sigma approach begins and ends with data, measurement, metrics, and quantification. Six Sigma helps managers determine the information they need to evaluate the process under study, and it helps them determine how best to utilize that information for maximum benefit.

3. **Focus on process management and improvement**: Six Sigma establishes business processes as the key vehicles of success. It requires that leaders and managers develop mastery over processes, not just as a necessary evil but actually as a way to build competitive advantage in delivering value to customers.

4. **Proactive management**: Six Sigma encompasses tools and practices that replace habits with a dynamic, responsive, and proactive style of management: defining ambitious goals, reviewing them frequently, setting clear priorities, focusing on problem prevention versus fire-fighting, and questioning why things are done rather than blindly defending the status quo.

5. **Boundary-less collaboration**: Six Sigma creates an environment and management structure that support true teamwork. It expands op-

portunities for collaboration as people learn how their roles fit into the big picture, empowering them to recognize and measure the interdependence of activities in all parts of a process.

6. **Drive for perfection and tolerance for failure**: The Six Sigma philosophy blends an ongoing pursuit of perfection—based on the customer's ever-changing definition of perfection—and an acceptance of the reality that, in such a pursuit, occasional setbacks will occur.

## 6.2.4  DMAIC: The Key to Six Sigma Methodology

Beyond the philosophy and principles of Six Sigma is the process itself—or more accurately, the process series by which Six Sigma principles are applied to an organization's target objective. The Six Sigma methodology is based on a five-step process whose acronym is DMAIC, which stands for **D**efine, **M**easure, **A**nalyze, **I**mprove, and **C**ontrol. Briefly, these steps can be defined as follows:

- **Define**: Set the context and objectives for the improvement project. Ensure that the Six Sigma team shares a common understanding of the problem, the objective, and the process.
- **Measure**: Determine the baseline performance and capability of the process or system being improved. Ensure that the Six Sigma team has a clear grasp of the quantitative process by which the problem will be defined, progress measured, and results assessed.
- **Analyze**: Employ classical analytical techniques and tools to distill the underlying meaning behind the data and results being measured. Seek to understand the cause-and-effect relationships in the process or system under study.
- **Improve**: Utilize the results of the analysis to consider, propose, develop, and test process modifications that lead to a validated improvement.
- **Control**: Establish and adhere to plans and procedures to ensure that true improvements—once validated—are sustained beyond the scope of the initial Six Sigma process.

## 6.2.5  Benefits of Six Sigma

Thus far in this chapter, we have discussed the historical evolution and application of Six Sigma in the modern business landscape. We have reviewed the underlying principles and processes involved and discussed in general terms the benefits of a well-managed and well-executed Six Sigma methodology. In the following section, the benefits to be gained from the Six Sigma approach will be outlined in specific detail, and then we will begin to investigate the specific application of Six Sigma methodologies to ECM implementation.

While the case has been made above that Six Sigma leads to an improvement in process, we have not yet defined what such specific processes might be, nor have we alluded to the depth of the success and improvement that might be realized from a Six Sigma approach. It should be emphasized at this point that success as defined in a Six Sigma context means "*sustained success*"—that success which endures the changes within an organization and which is founded upon the solid underpinnings of a truly refined process enhancement.

A second fundamental benefit of Six Sigma is that it provides a "unified and performance-based goal" for everyone in the organization. This leads to a truly integrated approach to process improvement, one which supports the sustained success referred to above.

A third benefit of Six Sigma, which was alluded to earlier in this chapter, is the "enhancement of customer value" that results from a successfully administered and executed Six Sigma process. At the heart of the measurement is customer activity—purchasing, repurchasing, satisfaction, and long-term affiliation with the organization and its products and services. In a successful Six Sigma program, a corollary to customer value is an organization's being equipped to respond to customers' increasing and varied demands. This enables the organization to not only offer value in the near term, but to be fundamentally equipped and prepared to respond to customer demands and changing purchasing habits based upon as yet unknown factors in the economic, demographic, and regulatory landscapes.

While process improvement is a de facto objective of Six Sigma initiatives, improvement at a static rate is not viewed as acceptable under the tenets of Six Sigma—the goal of a Six Sigma process is to identify those underlying rate-limiting steps to process improvement and to attack them at their source. The resulting effect is an acceleration of not only the quality of the improvement at hand, but an acceleration of the actual rate at which future improvements are realized.

At the heart of Six Sigma is the acknowledgment that process changes do not occur in a vacuum. By definition, the Six Sigma process is multidisciplinary, team driven, and integrated in its approach. As such, it fosters a great deal of cross-pollination of ideas and exchange, thereby accelerating the rate of improvement and creating a culture of enhanced awareness of the interdependence of otherwise seemingly disparate or unrelated functions within the organization.

Finally, Six Sigma is not simply a theory, an exercise, a drill, or a topic for discussion around boardrooms and management meetings. It is designed—at its very core—to produce true strategic and functional change within an organization. Herein lies the "Measure" function—which literally requires that results move off the drawing board and across the cash register.

Having now dealt in somewhat more detail with the specific benefits of a Six Sigma approach to an organizational process challenge, we will turn attention to the specific application of Six Sigma principles to ECM solution implementation. The remainder of this chapter focuses on the methods, benefits, and strategies through which Six Sigma may be effectively used as a tool for successful ECM solution implementation.

## 6.3 SHOULD ECM IMPLEMENTATION BE A SIX SIGMA PROJECT?

Many factors should be considered in evaluating if a Six Sigma approach is appropriate for an ECM implementation. By way of example, in a typical large organization with complex and interrelated programs under review, often multiple Six Sigma programs are launched simultaneously. Even in large companies with abundant resources and well-qualified staff, this simultaneous launch can place high demands on organizational resources. A key challenge at the outset of any Six Sigma initiative, therefore, is to determine which programs to undertake immediately and which to defer, or queue, until essential manpower and other resources are available. In this manner, the overall quality and integrity of each individual Six Sigma initiative—as well as the composite benefits of the combined initiatives—may be fully realized. A case in point would involve the sequential launching of Six Sigma cost-cutting initiatives versus simultaneous launch of all such initiatives. By sequencing the launch and subsequent analysis of each of the initiatives, the analysis of benefits, errors, and areas for further refinement becomes much more feasible.

A second critical question to be asked at the outset of considering the appropriateness of a Six Sigma initiative for ECM implementation is the cost-benefit analysis question: Is the initiative of sufficient importance and potential impact to yield benefits that would justify its implementation in the first place? Subquestions surrounding this issue are:

- ■ Does ECM present an area of tremendous opportunity, or is it likely to be of only marginal benefit?

- Is there sufficient pain in the target area of implementation to warrant a Six Sigma approach?
- Is there a significant gap between the current and desired/needed performance in contract management?
- How serious are the challenges the organization faces in the following areas?
  - ☐ Fragmentation (disconnect) of critical procedures
  - ☐ Labor-intensive (expensive, time-consuming) processes
  - ☐ Poor visibility into contracts (lack of key intelligence)
  - ☐ Ineffective monitoring and management of compliance
  - ☐ Inadequate analysis of contract performance

Having cited these and many other questions that must be asked and answered by managers considering a Six Sigma approach to ECM implementation, one might ask if there is any systematic way to approach this complex process. Fortunately, there are three criteria that may be used as guidelines in evaluating whether or not the ECM implementation should be a Six Sigma project:

1. Results or business benefits
2. Feasibility
3. Organizational impact

## 6.3.1 Results or Business Benefits Criteria

At the outset of considering the benefits of a Six Sigma approach to ECM solution implementation, managers must ask how beneficial or important contracts are to the organization as a whole and to paying customers or key external audiences (for example, shareholders, regulators, and supply chain partners). Put another way:

> What value will a state-of-the-art ECM solution have in helping you realize your organization's business vision, implement your marketing strategy, or improve your competitive position in the market?

There are additional questions within this single question:

- How might a Six Sigma project, directed at implementing an ECM solution, affect your organization's mix and capabilities in your areas of core competency?
- What is the short-term dollar gain likely to be?

- What would the long-term gain look like and over how many years would that extend?
- How accurately can you expect to project such performance?

Other questions regarding the net results and benefits of Six Sigma include the lead time required to address the challenges facing ECM implementation, the nature and scope of regulatory issues that demand urgent action, and the need to preempt or mitigate some other risks facing the organization at the outset of the ECM implementation initiative. The timing of the ECM initiative and the timeliness of a Six Sigma approach are often essential considerations in an organization, especially when human and financial resources are already stretched and near-term deadlines, performance targets, and goals often take high priority in relation to longer range strategic enhancement initiatives. What might be the consequences of delaying the initiative at the present time? If there is a negative impact, how great will it be, and when might it be felt?

Rounding out the list of initial benefit questions includes addressing whether or not there are other projects or opportunities dependent on resolution of challenges with the ECM processes and systems. A case in point might be the need to conduct a spend analysis or implement a state-of-the-art supplier relationship management system within the organization. Finally, does the ECM solution implementation project under consideration depend on the successful completion of other projects (e.g., does the organization need to address a customer data or supplier issue before it can start identifying what contracts need to be considered)?

## 6.3.2 Feasibility Criteria

Once an organization's management has resolved the issue of the overriding benefits to be gained from a Six Sigma approach to ECM solution implementation, the entire question of tactical and operational feasibility should be addressed. Typical questions voiced by management at this stage of consideration concern the level and type of resources, time and money that will be required, and the level and availability of people, systems, knowledge, skill, and expertise required. If these resources are not available, at what level (and cost) will outside expertise need to be sought? In short, senior management needs to gain a clear level of vision and comfort that the process about to be undertaken not only offers theoretical benefits, but that such benefits can be realized because the organization is appropriately equipped and ready for the process to be initiated.

Some additional critical questions need to be answered as well, such as the degree of complication and difficulty that might be encountered in mapping various contractual processes and data into the target ECM solution, the actual feasibility of the implementation process itself, and the rollout of implementation processes across different business units and geographical regions.

Finally, as with any major consideration, the issue of timing remains a key unknown:

- Based on what you know, what is the likelihood that the ECM solution implementation will be successful in a reasonable time frame?
- How much support for this project should you anticipate from key groups within the organization, and will they be available when you will need them?

In the last analysis, managers would like to know if they can truly create and justify a solid business case for undertaking the ECM solution implementation.

## 6.3.3 Organizational Impact Criteria

Beyond the benefit and feasibility dimensions of the ECM solution under consideration, some fundamental questions about its impact upon the organization—both as a whole and in terms of its constituent operating parts—need to be addressed:

- What new knowledge about the company's business, customers, procurement/sourcing processes, quotation/sales processes, etc. might be gained from the project?
- To what extent will the project, once complete, help break down barriers between groups in the organization and create better contracting process management?
- What are the true risks, costs, and potential benefits of approaching ECM solution implementation from a Six Sigma perspective?

As can be seen from the above discussion, there are many issues and unknowns facing managers as they consider whether or not a Six Sigma approach is appropriate for their ECM solution implementation. Fortunately, there exists a broad base of case history, data, and real-world results to provide support for this critical period of inquiry and assessment.

Once a decision has been made to proceed with a Six Sigma approach, the process of implementation commences. The following section addresses the major elements of this implementation process and describes the issues, challenges, and potentials of various approaches.

## 6.4 THE ECM SOLUTION IMPLEMENTATION ROAD MAP USING SIX SIGMA

The popularity and widespread use of Six Sigma over the past several decades have led to the development and utilization of many variations on the classical Six Sigma theme. Today, many different versions of Six Sigma exist, referred to by acronyms such as DMADV, DMADOC, DMCDOV, DCOV, DCCDI, DMEDI, and DMADIC. However, the best-understood and still most widely used Six Sigma methodology is known by its acronym—DMAIC.

Later in this section of the chapter, one other Six Sigma methodology especially well suited for ECM implementation will be introduced. This second methodology—referred to as DFSS—will be discussed in some detail after further introduction of DMAIC as the foundational methodology upon which the Six Sigma implementation is based.

### 6.4.1 The DMAIC Process: Key to Six Sigma Methodology

At this point, it will be useful to examine the elements of DMAIC in more detail, especially as they relate to the application of Six Sigma methodologies to ECM solution implementation. Figure 6.2 illustrates the five steps involved in the DMAIC process. These steps are described in detail below.

#### 6.4.1.1 D—Define

The purpose of the Define phase of DMAIC is to ensure that, at the outset, a fundamental knowledge base has been established regarding the vision, goals, and strategy of the initiative and that this knowledge is shared by all stakeholders who will play a role in the success of the initiative. Beneath this broad-based set of definitions reside a variety of definitions key to the success of the initiative, the first of which is to define the actual ECM process which is to be implemented. This includes its subprocesses, its enabling processes, and how information (in the form of contracts) flows through the organization from inception to conclusion of the contractual relationship. Key to the Define phase is clearly identifying the customer (internal as well as external to the organization), the

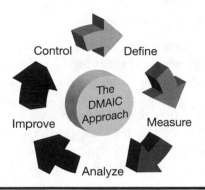

**FIGURE 6.2. The DMAIC Process**

customer's needs and requirements, and how these needs and requirements are—or are not—currently being met.

Tied closely to the measurement phase of DMAIC is the definition of the critical measures for each of the subprocesses in the initiative process, including how such measures are aligned with the customer and the customer's needs and requirements. Definition of any gaps between the process outputs and customer requirements is key during this stage, as is the clear identification of how improvements in ECM processes will position the organization vis-à-vis other organizations both within and beyond its core industry sector.

Lastly, the Define phase requires a clear definition of what benefits may be expected as a result of the ECM solution implementation and what level of resources will be required to achieve these benefits.

Key tasks/deliverables of the Define phase that correspond to the above-mentioned efforts include:

- Creation of a project charter
- Identification and delineation of the process, and subprocesses, in an as-is process map
- Clear identification of each type of customer and each customer's requirements
- Identification of critical-to-success (CTS) or critical-to-satisfaction factors
- Linkage of customer requirements to process outputs
- Identification of internal and external resources
- Securing internal organizational approval for the project
- Development of the project plan with milestones and deliverables

### 6.4.1.2 M—Measure

Although the issue of measurement has been discussed briefly in previous sections of this chapter, its central role in Six Sigma methodologies warrants further elucidation. The Measure phase of DMAIC in the Six Sigma world means much more than mere quantification per se. Measurement affords true validation of the definition of an initiative, and it offers an underlying framework for gathering, organizing, and presenting the results that will ultimately determine the efficacy of the initiative. The measurement process begins with a search for those facts, data elements, and metrics that offer clues about the causes of problems and insight into where processes may be influenced, tracked, and measured. Finally, measurement enables the actual absolute and comparative review of results, at the process and subprocess levels—results which, once determined, lead to further knowledge about how to better collect data, measure, and analyze future results.

Key tasks and deliverables of the Measure phase of DMAIC include:

- Development of detailed process maps (as-is and to-be processes) with clearly defined outputs and inputs, as well as roles and responsibilities for individual tasks in each process
- Clear definition of output and performance measures
- Development of a data collection plan and document-based performance measures
- Development of methods to validate the measurement system itself
- Description of process capability and entitlement
- Development of a quantifiable system for assessment of the control plan
- Creation of a cause-and-effect matrix to determine focus within processes
- Creation of a Failure Mode and Effects Analysis (FMEA) to assess and prioritize process risks

### 6.4.1.3 A—Analyze

Implicit in the Six Sigma approach to process improvement is analysis—the process by which measured events and data are assessed in light of the goal of any given study. It is by the process of systematic and objective analysis that sources of variation are identified, quantified, and assessed in light of their impact upon a predetermined set of results criteria. In the case of an ECM solution implementation, for example, analysis would be used to determine how a given contract management system handles exceptions to the norm (e.g., unusual contractual terms for payment or conditions for default). Conversely, analysis under a Six Sigma approach might be applied to an ECM solution implementation by first starting from a functional division (procurement, for example) and assessing how it might best be staffed in relation to coordinated efforts in other divisions. A third example of analysis in an ECM solution setting might involve determining by comparison the levels of knowledge and expertise that are in place within differing levels or divisions and assessing how these resources might either complement one another or limit achievement of the end goal.

Since identification of variation is one of the key goals of Six Sigma analysis, a strong focus is placed on identifying the underlying causes for variation—exploring the procedures, techniques, methods of contract negotiation (for example), measurement criteria, and human resources that are brought to bear upon a given ECM program under analysis. An obvious prerequisite of this level of analysis is to first establish the expected outcome of the ECM solution (i.e., what its capabilities and potential are and how these might best be measured). Once the performance standards and objectives have been defined at both the technical and functional levels, the key input variable in the process may be linked to the expected output.

The actual process of analysis begins by integrating the actual experience of the process being measured into an analytical framework, gathering resulting measured outcomes, then formulating a theory about the basis for observed variation. This hypothesis, generated with the input of the Six Sigma team, may then be used to propose additional tests of the process that would provide additional data either in support of or refuting the proposed hypothesis. This cycle of systematic testing, data gathering, assessment, and hypothesis formulation and refinement continues until it is evident to the Six Sigma team that either there is adequate support for the hypothesis or it cannot be supported and must be replaced with one more consistent with measured outcomes.

Key deliverables during the Analyze phase of DMAIC are:

- Develop and prioritize a list of sources of variations/exceptions in the process
- Systematically and consistently collect data to validate sources of variations
- Determine relationships between different sources of variations
- Identify key input variables that affect the output(s)

### 6.4.1.4  I—Improve

The fruits harvested during the Analyze phase are those causal elements that are deemed to be directly or substantively linked to variations in the process. Secondly, the underlying relationship between the causal elements and the variation is made evident as a result of the Analyze phase. Once the limits of variability and tolerance of a given element are known, the Six Sigma team can focus on how to best redefine tolerance levels or how to otherwise optimize the conditions under which the affected phase of the process must operate.

This phase, referred to simply as the Improve phase, represents the turning point in the Six Sigma methodology, whereby the results of the team's work begin to actually influence the process in question. Logical tasks and deliverables during the Improve phase are:

- Systematically experiment with key performance indicator variables
- Determine optimum to-be process and propose operating tolerances
- Develop a new process performance baseline and capability
- Validate significance of improvements

### 6.4.1.5  C—Control

The main goal of this phase is to ensure that improvements resulting from the Six Sigma approach to process improvement have enduring impact and that people and processes do not revert to previous conditions. In order for Six Sigma to be deemed truly successful, there must be a long-term positive impact on the way people work and on the impact of such work on the products and services ultimately valued by customers.

The Control phase of Six Sigma, therefore, focuses upon creating a process for monitoring implemented changes and for developing and utilizing a plan of response when problems with reversion arise. This process is as much psychological as it is operational; the need to sell the successes achieved by ECM solution implementation is critical to the overall sustained realization of benefits for the organization. A second aspect of control is to focus senior management's attention on those relatively few critical measures that will provide true indications of the ECM processes and subprocesses and in particular on their ongoing efficiency and effectiveness.

By selling the successes, and by focusing senior management on efficient monitoring, the Six Sigma DMAIC approach can ensure ongoing support throughout the organization for the original goals and subsequent outcomes of the initiative. At this point in the maturation of the process, many of the responsibilities originally under the watchful eye of the process champion and his or her supporters may be handed off to others for more routine monitoring and reporting.

The key deliverables during the Control phase of a Six Sigma ECM solution implementation are:

- Create an approved control plan that encompasses documentation required to maintain improvements
- Lock in optimum key performance indicators (KPIs)
- Monitor and control KPIs
- Meet CTS factors consistently—sustainable results
- Document project and process improvements

## 6.4.2 Design for Six Sigma Approach

As mentioned earlier in this section, the needs of ECM implementation vis-à-vis Six Sigma are somewhat unique and require consideration of a supplemented approach to DMAIC. Whereas DMAIC methodology is suitable for situations where products or services already exist and are not performing up to expectations, the Design for Six Sigma methodology, referred to as DFSS, is more suitable in situations where the product/service does not exist and needs to be designed or redesigned from the ground up. Such is the case with most ECM implementations, in which there are typically no formal processes or systems for evaluation and measurement. In the very best of situations, an organization's ECM systems have relatively poorly defined methods and processes in place for capturing data, establishing and monitoring processes via metrics, and evaluating theories about process improvement. In this respect, ECM solution implementations offer an outstanding opportunity to apply DFSS as an adjunct to the Six Sigma DMAIC approach.

DFSS is a systematic Six Sigma methodology that uses tools, methods, training, and measurements to enable the design of products, services, and processes that meet customer expectations at Six Sigma quality levels. What is unique about the DFSS methodology—and what makes it work particularly well in ECM implementation—is that DFSS is best suited to application with processes for which there have been little—if any—prior optimization system in place.

DFSS optimizes the design process to achieve Six Sigma performance (i.e., a defect rate of 3.4 defects per million opportunities) and integrates characteristics of Six Sigma at the outset of new product development with a disciplined set of tools. The central idea here is that when Six Sigma principles and quality are integrated into the design of a product, process, or service, high-level customer satisfaction is assured because design process methodology transitions from a reactive, build-and-test mode to a predictive, balanced, and optimized progression. By focusing on improving the design of products, services, and processes, DFSS helps reduce the time and material costs of poor quality—scrap, rework, repairs, inspections, delays, customer complaints, returns, recalls, and lost sales or accounts. Also, the better the design in terms of meeting and exceeding customer requirements, expectations, and priorities, the easier it is to provide service and support (maintenance, repairs, and troubleshooting).

DFSS initiatives vary dramatically from company to company but typically start with a project charter linked to the organization's strategic plan, an assessment of customer needs, a functional analysis, an identification of critical-to-quality (CTQ) characteristics, concept selection, a detailed design of products and processes, and control plans.

The classical or traditional approach to designing products, services, and processes generally involves several functional departments working in *series*. DFSS, on the other hand, is a *parallel* activity with all relevant areas of the organization represented within a cross-functional team. Furthermore, decisions are based on data rather than judgment. Thus DFSS offers the following advantages over traditional approaches to product, service, and process design:

- Provides a structure for managing development projects
- Adds value and improves customer satisfaction
- Enables anticipating problems and addressing/mitigating the risk associated with them
- Minimizes the need for design changes
- Reduces development cycle time
- Reduces total life cycle cost
- Reduces manufacturing cycle times and time to market
- Improves product quality, reliability, and durability
- Improves communication among an organization's functional groups or departments
- Reduces costs of after-sale service and support

The key advantages of DFSS can be summed up in four major categories, the first of which is customer satisfaction. This is the ultimate measure of success, since it ultimately determines the conversion of all improvement efforts into sales and earnings. A second category of advantage is in the area of quality of product, service, or process. Time and cost advantages round out the key areas, which in combination with customer satisfaction and quality result in a completely integrated and optimized improvement methodology for an organization.

Similar to traditional Six Sigma which employs the DMAIC process, DFSS employs a four-step process called IDOV (**I**dentify, **D**esign, **O**ptimize, and **V**alidate). Briefly defined, these steps involve the following functions and goals:

- **Identify**: Listen to the customer to select the best product concept.
- **Design**: Build a thorough knowledge base about the product and its processes.
- **Optimize**: Achieve a balance of quality, cost, and time to market.
- **Validate**: Demonstrate with data that the voice of the customer has been heard and that customer expectations have been satisfied.

### 6.4.2.1 I—Identify

The focus of the Identify phase is to define the requirements of the ECM solution based on customer requirements. The team identifies the customer, the CTQ or CTS specifications, the technical requirements, and the quality targets.

The process of identifying begins with a core definition of who the customers are—both internally and externally—on the buy-side and sell-side contracting processes. Another dimension of customer definition involves identification of key stakeholders in the purchase/sale decision, subsequent use of the product or service in question, and ultimately the repurchase or expansion of the customer/supplier relationship.

Each of these subgroups of the identified customer has specific requirements that must be met in order to optimize the process under scrutiny and review. Data regarding such customer requirements might be obtained from a variety of sources, including reviewing customer complaints, surveys and focus groups, one-on-one interviews, and deeper inquiries (such as field reports and large-scale data analyses) into the issues surrounding the purchase and use decisions of customers.

Once customer requirements are identified, they may then be employed in a series of stages and steps, including identification, prioritization, and documentation of the CTS factors that set technical requirements, performance targets, ranges of acceptability, benchmarking standards, competitive parameters, and specification limits. Establishment of CTS metrics, design of scorecards, and selection of design concepts are part of this process. Once these elements are in place, it is possible to analyze the impact of CTS factors on technical requirements, including use of Quality Function Deployment to translate customer CTS factors into technical specifications.

The net result of this Identify process is to develop innovative alternatives to satisfy customer functional requirements, supplemented by appropriate risk analysis and consideration of means for error-proofing new concept designs in accordance with predicted Sigma Six levels of quality.

### 6.4.2.2 D—Design

The purpose of the Design phase is to build a thorough knowledge base about the ECM solution, including its functionality, configuration options, and capabilities to support the ECM processes. During the Design phase, the team translates the customer CTS factors into functional requirements and alternative configuration options; through a selection process, the team evaluates the alternatives and reduces the list of alternatives to one—the best-fitting concept.

During the Design phase, the conceptual design is formulated, primarily for precontract processes such as RFQ, RFI, RFP, or quotes and contracting processes such as authoring, negotiation, approval, execution, administration, and renewal or termination. Post-contract processes (e.g., purchase/sales orders, receipts/issuance of goods, and invoices) are also given due consideration during the Design phase.

Beyond the fundamental design elements, a variety of supporting aspects of contract design must be considered and developed. These include the naming and data tracking of contracts, the design of core contract templates, the design of contract notifications, specific requirements of custom fields, security model design, and master data conversion protocols (for use with vendors, customer products, price lists, etc.).

### 6.4.2.3 O—Optimize

The purpose of the Optimize phase is to achieve a balance of quality, cost, and time to market. The team may use advanced statistical tools and modeling to predict quality level, reliability, and performance. It also uses process capability information and a statistical approach to tolerances to develop detailed design elements and to optimize design and performance.

In the Optimize phase, a key priority is to employ pilot and small-scale implementations and test runs to evaluate performance of new prototypes and processes. The focus during this phase should not be to test out new designs, but rather to finalize designs that have already been through sufficient analysis and refinement to warrant optimization. Once a design has successfully passed small-scale pilot implementations, it can be engineered and refined to increase its robustness; in the case of an ECM solution, it should be relatively impervious to natural or unavoidable variations in inputs, processes, components, and materials.

### 6.4.2.4  V—Validate

The purpose of the Validate phase is to demonstrate that the ECM solution satisfies the voice of the customer and to ensure that the design will meet the customer CTQ/CTS factors. This phase consists of testing, verifying, and validating the design, as well as assessing performance and reliability. The team tests prototypes, and the design goes through iterations as necessary.

Key elements of the Validate phase include ensuring that the ECM solution is appropriately configured to support the agreed-upon to-be practices, to demonstrate reliable and reproducible processing capability, and to withstand the limits of tolerances determined to be necessary. It must also be sufficiently amenable to statistical process controls and monitoring to ensure ongoing quality control.

Once the design has met the team's specified requirements, it may be stabilized and prepared for go-live implementation and maintenance. The final step in this process, documentation, duly updates and validates scorecards for the design in question.

The DFSS method, whether the IDOV approach outlined above or its variants, extends the power and discipline of Six Sigma to the project start, where it makes the greatest difference in terms of time and money.

Most opportunities for successful implementation of ECM solutions exist when both DMAIC and DFSS methodologies and principles are applied in concert with one another. The more thorough the design of new ECM processes and systems, the less rework required, the lower the total cost of ECM solution ownership, and the higher the customer satisfaction attained (see Figure 6.3).

As indicated above, a combined approach using DMAIC and DFSS during an ECM solution implementation is proposed, tailoring the use of each methodology to its best-suited application and outcome. Most certainly, however, when applied to the goal of implementing an ECM solution for an organization, both DMAIC and DFSS methodologies have their place. As shown in Figure

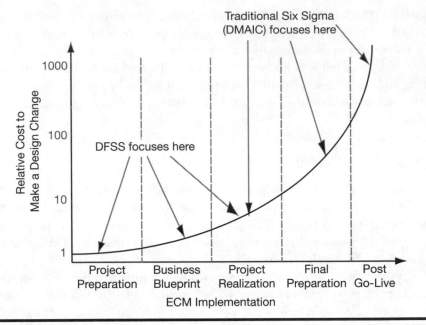

**FIGURE 6.3. Why DFSS?**

6.4, the DMAIC process should be used as the overall approach to guide, implement, integrate, and improve the ECM systems and processes across an organization.

At the same time, the DFSS methodology should be used within each phase of the ECM solution implementation so that the design/configuration of the ECM solution is continuously improved in order to best fit and support the desired business processes. If customer requirements change during the process, the DFSS tasks within successive DMAIC phases will help ensure that the ECM implementation team refines the design of the ECM solution to better meet the current set of customer requirements. As the ECM solution implementation team progresses through successive phases of the DMAIC methodology, team members gain a better understanding of the capabilities and limitations of the chosen ECM solution. Planning and scheduling DFSS tasks within successive DMAIC phases provides the team members with an opportunity to revisit and fine-tune the design of the ECM solution based on this enhanced understanding. By selectively utilizing DFSS to focus with greater clarity on design of the ECM solution during all stages of the implementation project, there is greater assurance that gaps between as-is and to-be processes will be minimized. It also ensures that fewer unforeseen issues will be encountered after go-live and less

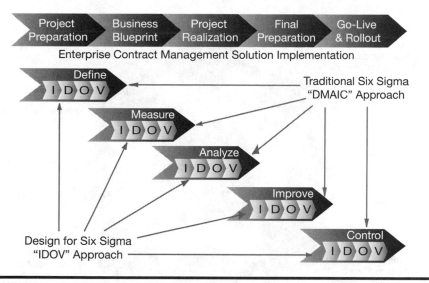

**FIGURE 6.4. Implementing an ECM Solution the Six Sigma Way**

overall rework will be required. It should be noted, however, that the recommendation to focus on design during all stages of the ECM solution implementation project should not be interpreted as an excuse to fall into a vicious circle of designing and redesigning the ECM solution. As illustrated in Figure 6.4, through the decreasing size of the IDOV elements in different phases of the DMAIC methodology, the effort and time involved in DFSS tasks should continue to decrease as the project progresses from one DMAIC phase to the next.

Beyond the initial implementation of the ECM solution, the organization may once again employ the DMAIC approach to sustain excellence, continue improving its contract management processes, maximize the return on investment from its investment in the ECM solution, reduce the total cost of ownership of the ECM solution, and instill a culture of continuous change and learning across the organization.

## 6.4.3 The ECM Six Sigma Team

Success in an ECM solution implementation initiative is heavily dependent on successfully putting together the right team, with the right resources and the right knowledge, skills, and attributes. The ECM Six Sigma team should be comprised of one or more resources in a variety of roles (as shown in Figure 6.5) and associated responsibilities. A detailed description of each role, along with the associated responsibilities, is provided below.

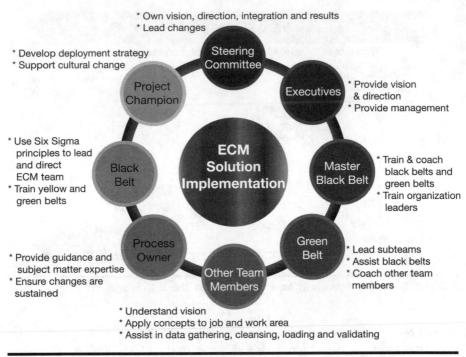

**FIGURE 6.5. The ECM Six Sigma Team: Roles and Responsibilities**

### 6.4.3.1 ECM Project Champion

Success in ECM solution implementation starts at the top, typically with a "champion" of the entire ECM implementation process and a "steering committee" to offer support, guidance, and authority. The champion serves as the leader, mentor, and coach, supporting the project teams and ensuring the necessary resources to achieve successful implementation. The champion promotes the Six Sigma methodology throughout the organization, particularly in key functional groups such as contract management and procurement.

Typically, the champion exhibits the following attributes:

- Scopes, prioritizes, and aligns the ECM solution implementation initiative to business strategy and goals
- Selects Black Belts, Green Belts, and Yellow Belts (see below) and ensures they are appropriately trained, tasked, and deployed
- Supports Black, Green, and Yellow Belts through the removal of organizational barriers, securing necessary resources, coaching, and reviewing project implementation status

- Holds team members accountable for project goals, ensures that the team is on track, and reports progress against target metrics
- Promotes best-practices sharing, and leverages solutions and improvements across organizational boundaries

### 6.4.3.2 Master Black Belts, Black Belts, Green Belts, and Yellow Belts

Levels of expertise in Six Sigma are designated in terms of martial arts mastery, with the highest level of attainment being the Master Black Belt. Master Black Belts provide the highest level of essential technical leadership to the ECM implementation team. They are also the experts responsible for leading the ECM implementation project teams. These key agents are fully dedicated to the implementation initiative and are thoroughly trained in Six Sigma tools and techniques.

Master Black Belts are characterized by the following qualities and capabilities:

- Highly proficient in Six Sigma tools and techniques to achieve tangible business results
- Scope, prioritize, and align the ECM solution implementation initiative to business strategy and goals
- Focus on identifying and defining projects, teaching, mentoring, and actively working to institutionalize Six Sigma thinking
- Ensure that the necessary infrastructure for Six Sigma is in place, by coaching and mentoring project teams, training Black Belts, and helping train employees

Support to the Master Black Belt is often provided by Black Belts, Green Belts, and Yellow Belts—usually high-performing members of project teams with sufficient functional expertise in relevant areas to provide valuable specific support. The key attributes of these three groups are:

- **Black Belts**
  - ☐ Mentor or coach others in applying Six Sigma methods and tools
  - ☐ Lead complex departmental, business unit, or cross-functional process improvement projects such as an ECM solution implementation
  - ☐ Disseminate new strategies and tools via training, workshops, and case studies
  - ☐ Manage risks, help set direction, coordinate activities, break through barriers, and keep project scorecards

- **Green Belts and Yellow Belts (in accordance with expertise and seniority)**
  - ☐ Lead ECM initiative at business unit or geographical level
  - ☐ Help Black Belts collect and/or analyze data
  - ☐ Work closely with other continuous improvement leaders to apply formal data analysis approaches to the ECM solution implementation initiative
  - ☐ Teach local teams and share knowledge of Six Sigma

### 6.4.3.3 *The Steering Committee or Leadership Council*

In support of the champion and the functional team, it is essential for a steering committee, or leadership council, to lead and support every project from beginning to end and to inspire commitment throughout the organization. The steering committee lends broad-based credibility, support, and guidance to the implementation effort, by offering perspective across divisions within the organization and ensuring that company-wide goals and policies are adhered to during the implementation process.

Key roles and responsibilities of the steering committee are to:

- Agree upon, drive, and sustain the vision and set goals for the ECM solution implementation initiative
- Ensure that the goals of the ECM initiative are linked to enterprise goals
- Align process excellence across the organization
- Serve as sponsors and local champions for the ECM solution implementation
- Enable the quantification of the impact of the ECM solution initiative on the company's bottom line
- Establish the roles and infrastructure of the ECM solution implementation initiative
- Identify, allocate, and authorize resources
- Periodically review the progress of the project, offer ideas, and assist as required
- Act as a roadblock remover when teams identify barriers
- Ensure that the project team gets the training, resources, information, and cooperation necessary to succeed
- Celebrate successes, and provide recognition, rewards, and other incentives for employees who contribute to the success of the initiative
- Share best practices throughout the organization

Rounding out the Six Sigma team are functional experts in each of the varying divisions or levels in the organization. These individuals have the unique skills and experience to ensure successful introduction of new policies and procedures by securing essential buy-in and offering the grass roots support required as the ECM implementation begins to take effect. In a typical ECM solution implementation effort, cross-functional team members should be recruited from all essential areas and divisions within the company, including but not limited to contract management, procurement, sales and distribution, maintenance, warehouse/storeroom, customer service, accounting, engineering, and information technology.

A final note on the Six Sigma team: in addition to internal expertise and organizational resources, some input should also be sought from supplier, customer, and other business partner organizations. This external input helps ensure that the Six Sigma approach to ECM solution implementation achieves its fullest success both within and beyond the organization.

## 6.5 ALTERNATE ECM SOLUTION IMPLEMENTATION METHODOLOGIES

So far in this chapter, we have seen how the principles and processes of Six Sigma can be utilized in ensuring successful ECM solution implementations. However, this is not intended to imply that Six Sigma principles and processes offer the only methodology that will ensure a successful ECM solution implementation. Many other methodologies have been tried and tested in various IT solution implementations over the last three to four decades. Any of these methodologies can be used to implement an ECM solution, provided they recognize and address the issues, risks, and change management considerations unique to ECM solution implementations. In this section of this chapter, a high-level overview of two such methodologies is presented.

The first one, called the *IDEAL^{SM} Model*, was first developed by the Software Engineering Institute to guide development of a long-range, integrated plan for initiating and managing software process improvement initiatives. However, the same concepts may be applied to ECM solution implementation initiatives within an organization. Since most ECM solution implementation initiatives are complex projects and have far-reaching effects, organizations embarking on such initiatives require a specialized and systematic approach not only to manage the initial configuration and implementation but also to ensure ongoing adoption of the ECM solution by end users.

The second methodology was developed by the author based on his experience in managing over fifty successful ECM solution implementations. It is based on proven methodology that has been used for over two decades to successfully implement and upgrade large and complex software applications, such as enterprise resource planning (ERP) applications, across the world. It can be customized to meet the specific needs of organizations embarking on an ECM solution implementation initiative. Let us begin with a description of the IDEAL^SM Model first.

## 6.5.1 The IDEAL^SM Model*

The goal of the IDEAL^SM approach is to institutionalize a philosophy of continuous improvement by evaluating the current status of business processes, making improvements, analyzing, and repeating the process. As illustrated in Figure 6.6, the five phases of the IDEAL^SM approach are:

| | |
|---|---|
| Initiate | Lay the groundwork for a successful improvement effort |
| Diagnose | Determine where you are relative to where you want to be |
| Establish | Plan the specifics of how you will reach the optimal state |
| Act | Do the work according to the plan |
| Learn | Learn from the experience and improve your ability |

The activities within each phase are described at a high level in the following sections.

### 6.5.1.1 I—Initiate Phase

In this phase, critical groundwork for the ECM process improvement initiative needs to be completed. This usually involves putting together a business case and aligning the ECM improvement initiative with organizational goals, objectives, and other organizational initiatives that may already be in progress or due to be launched. Some of the critical tasks within this phase are as follows:

- **Stimulus for change**: The need for change can be brought about by unanticipated events or circumstances, an edict from top manage-

---

* IDEAL^SM is a service mark of Carnegie Mellon University. The IDEAL^SM model graphic and portions of *The IDEAL^SM Model: A Practical Guide for Improvement* by Jennifer Gremba and Chuck Myers, copyright ©1997 by Carnegie Mellon University, are used in this publication with special permission from the Software Engineering Institute.

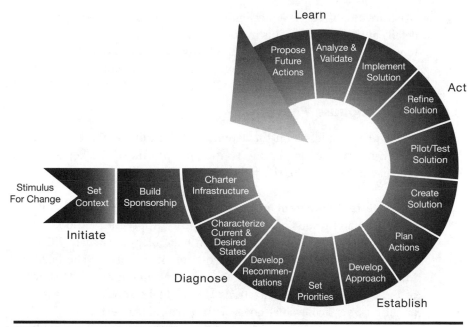

**FIGURE 6.6. The IDEAL<sup>SM</sup> Approach**

ment, or information gathered from previous or current benchmarking activities, such as the use of the ECM Maturity Model and
Appraisal Method. Regardless of the stimulus for change, it can have
a major impact on the visibility and success of an ECM improvement initiative within an organization. When the reasons for change
are evident, known, and agreed upon by key stakeholders, there is
greater buy-in and therefore greater possibility of success.

■ **Setting context**: Once the reasons for change have been identified,
an organization should set the context for the work that will be done
as part of the ECM improvement initiative. For example, if the ECM
process improvement initiative is part of a larger procure-to-pay or
order-to-cash process improvement initiative, then this needs to be
communicated clearly to key stakeholders, thereby ensuring that they
understand the dependencies between different organizational initiatives aimed at achieving business goals and strategies. The setting
of context goes a long way toward promoting the need to participate
in the ECM improvement initiative.

■ **Charter infrastructure:** Once the reasons and context for change are
understood and communicated, organizations need to charter infra-

structure, that is, set up a mechanism to manage the implementation details of the initiative. This includes identifying a team of resources to work on the initiative, as well as clearly communicating the roles, responsibilities, and accountability of each team member.

### 6.5.1.2 D—Diagnose Phase

The Diagnose phase builds upon the activities of the Initiate phase to develop a specific path forward for improving contracting practices. The key activities during the Diagnose phase are the following:

- **Characterize the current and desired states**: Using the ECM Maturity Model and results of the ECM Maturity Appraisal Method, the current state of people, processes, and technology related to ECM can be characterized within and across the organization. The ECM Maturity Model should then be used to determine the desired state of the organization. Organizations should make sure that they set ambitious, yet achievable, goals with a realistic time frame, given their current state and available resources. It is not necessary for all organizations to target the Optimizing maturity level in ECM, because the costs of achieving such a maturity level need to be weighed against the benefits. Only if the cost-benefit analysis for achieving the next maturity level indicates potential benefits higher than expected costs should organizations proceed with the next steps.

- **Develop recommendations**: Having identified the current and desired states of ECM, organizations should perform a gap analysis to identify all changes needed in organizational structure, staffing levels, skills, training, and technology to progress to the next ECM maturity level. This should be followed by defining the scope of the ECM initiative. Will it focus only on procurement contracts or on other types of contracts as well? Will an ECM solution be implemented and rolled out as part of this initiative? Will this be a "big-bang" implementation, or will the ECM solution be rolled out in small waves or phases by geographical regions or organizational functions? Will the organization begin using all the functionality offered by the ECM solution, or will it first focus on only the functionality critical to its effective and efficient operations? Recommended changes should be prioritized so that an organization can focus on those that promise the greatest return on invested time, effort, and resources.

### 6.5.1.3 E—Establish Phase

The recommendations developed in the previous phase are prioritized in the Establish phase. This is then used to develop a detailed action plan comprised of tasks, dependencies between tasks, milestones, deliverables, and responsibilities. The key activities in this phase are:

- **Set priorities:** Priorities are set for recommended actions based on resource availability, dependencies between different tasks, external factors, and other organizational initiatives that may demand the time and attention of the same resources that will be involved with the ECM improvement initiative.
- **Develop an approach and an implementation plan:** Using the scope defined for the ECM improvement initiative, along with the priorities set for different objectives, an approach can be developed. This approach should include, at the very minimum, an implementation plan with details such as the tasks involved, the interdependencies between these tasks, resources required for each task, a risk management plan, and a change management plan. The change management plan should consider the organization's culture and readiness to change and should identify key stakeholders so that a communication plan can be developed to address each stakeholder's specific requirements. Other critical factors are likely sources of resistance, sponsorship levels, and other organizational initiatives that may be placing demands upon the same resources needed to make the ECM improvement initiative a success.

### 6.5.1.4 A—Act Phase

Most of the work that was conceptualized and planned so far is implemented during the Act phase. Solutions that address the areas for improvement discovered in the previous phases are created, piloted, refined, and implemented throughout the organization. Plans are developed to execute pilots to test and evaluate the new and improved ECM processes and solutions. After successful piloting of the new ECM processes, and determination of the organization's readiness for organization-wide adoption, deployment, and institutionalization, concrete plans to accomplish the rollout may then be developed and executed.* Typical activities in this phase include the following:

---

* Bob McFeely, *IDEAL*[SM]: *A User's Guide for Software Process Improvement*, Carnegie Mellon University, Pittsburgh, 1996.

- **Create the solution**: The initial solution developed is usually a best-guess solution, and it may address improvements in one or more key elements, such as existing tools, processes, knowledge, and skills.
- **Pilot the solution**: The solution developed is tested on a smaller scale first so that any kinks in the process may be ironed out before rolling out the solution at an enterprise-wide level.
- **Refine the solution**: Based on the knowledge, lessons, and experience gained from the previous step, the solution is continuously refined until a satisfactory solution is reached.
- **Implement the solution**: Once a satisfactory and workable solution is reached, it can be rolled out to different organizational functions or geographic regions using a rollout team and a rollout plan. Depending on the magnitude of the changes involved and the size of the organization, this step may require substantial resources and time.

### 6.5.1.5 L—Learn Phase

This phase, the last one in the IDEAL<sup>SM</sup> approach, is, as its name suggests, concerned with the review of the entire ECM improvement initiative. This includes measuring, monitoring, and analyzing KPIs to determine if the expected benefits were realized, to identify what worked and what did not, and to ensure that the gains made as a result of the ECM improvement initiative have not been lost over a period of time. This phase involves a self-examination by the organization to continually update its own procedures and keep pace with changes in the organization and its outside business and regulatory relationships, in order to ensure that the newly implemented ECM solution provides value to the organization for an extended period of time. Two key activities are performed in this phase:

- **Analyze and validate**: This task includes gathering, analyzing, summarizing, and documenting lessons learned. It also includes answering questions such as: In what ways did the ECM improvement initiative serve its intended purpose? Did it achieve the objectives set by the organization at the beginning of the initiative? What worked well? What could have been done more efficiently and effectively?
- **Propose future actions**: Based on the lessons captured in the previous step, future actions should be proposed to appropriate levels of management for consideration.

It should be noted that there is no one correct approach to ensure continuous improvement in ECM within any organization. Continuous improvement is not dependent on a tool or technique, but is a way of life. Organizations embarking on an ECM improvement initiative should select and use whatever approach works best within their culture, but focus on instilling a culture of continuous learning and improvement to ensure sustained excellence in ECM.

## 6.5.2  Generic ECM Solution Implementation Methodology

Similar to the IDEAL[SM] Model, the generic ECM solution implementation methodology (shown in Figure 6.7) is broken down into five major phases. Certain project threads or work streams (such as process, integration, data readiness, project management, change management, and training) run across each phase of the project. This indicates that tasks associated with these work streams need to occur through all phases of the project; for example, project management and change management tasks need to begin even before a complete team is put in place and will continue even after some of the core team members are reassigned at the end of the implementation.

The objectives and tasks associated with each phase of this methodology are described in the following sections.

### 6.5.2.1  Preproject Preparation Phase

This phase of the project is focused on the activities that occur prior to assembling the ECM solution implementation team and includes initial analysis and design work. This phase allows the organization and its ECM solution implementation partner to identify, schedule, and mobilize appropriate resources for

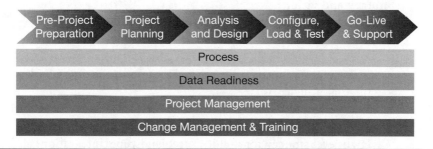

**FIGURE 6.7.  Generic ECM Solution Implementation Methodology**

the project. During this phase of the project, the following main tasks are usually completed:

- Physical deployment architecture and component layout diagrams are developed.
- Equipment specifications for the server hardware are developed.
- System sizing/capacity planning and usage/utilization requirements are identified.
- Acquisition and configuration of hardware and software, including operating system, ECM solution, and any non-ECM software components, are completed.
- ECM solution is installed.
- Security requirements are documented and the appropriate solution is implemented.
- The organization identifies contract templates that are most commonly used in the organization.
- Existing contract management processes are documented.
- Team members are identified and mobilized.
- Work spaces and location for project team are secured.

### 6.5.2.2 Project Planning Phase

This phase of the project is focused on the activities that assist the ECM solution implementation team in developing a plan to implement the ECM solution selected, lay the technical and functional foundation for the initiative, and better understand the current maturity level of processes, tools, and techniques associated with ECM within the organization. During this phase of the project, the following main tasks are usually completed:

- **Strategy and vision**
  - □ Business vision of the conceptual design is developed.
  - □ Preliminary business models that support the vision are developed at a high level.
  - □ ECM solution functionality needed to support the vision is identified at a high level.
  - □ KPIs to be used to measure the organization's post-go-live and ongoing success in ECM are identified.
  - □ High-level strategy for architecture, landscape, integration, and data is developed.

- **Project management**
  - ☐ The ECM solution implementation team and resources are mobilized.
  - ☐ A project kickoff, planning, and process meeting is planned and scheduled.
  - ☐ Project approach, scope, and assumptions are confirmed with key business stakeholders.
  - ☐ The project plan, key milestones, delivery dates, resources, and dependencies are presented to key business stakeholders, and consensus is reached with regard to the general approach for the initiative.
- **Change management**
  - ☐ Key stakeholders, including change champions, are identified.
  - ☐ A communication plan is developed to facilitate activities and processes needed to manage timely and appropriate generation, collection, distribution, and storage of project information.
  - ☐ Key responsibilities are assigned and communicated to team members.
  - ☐ Opportunities for process standardization, data gathering, harmonization, normalization, and cleanup are identified.
  - ☐ The contract management processes affected are identified, documented, and discussed with key stakeholders to get their buy-in.
  - ☐ Training approach for core team, extended team, and end users is defined. This includes identifying different user roles relevant for training, as well as developing a training plan that describes who will be trained, what training will be provided to which users, when the training will be offered, where it will be offered, and what media options will be used.
- **Risk management**
  - ☐ Dependencies between tasks and potential risks associated with execution of the tasks are documented and addressed, where required.

### 6.5.2.3 Analysis and Design Phase

The key objectives of this phase are to:

- Understand the environment in which the organization operates.

- Gain a good understanding of the organization's current processes, including performance, goals and objectives, short- and long-term challenges, and initiatives currently under way.
- Align the contract management process with the organization's overall business strategy, goals, and objectives.
- Define the requirements for the future state and use of the ECM application selected, thereby establishing the basis for the overall success of the ECM solution implementation.

During the Analysis phase of the project, the following main tasks are usually completed:

- Analyze and document "as-is" business processes, such as the contract initiation process, contract collaboration (internal and external) process, contract approval process, contract execution process, contract termination process, and contract renewal process.
- In addition, business requirements of organizational structure, security roles and permissions, integration with ERP and non-ERP applications, reporting, and administrative options are also captured.

As opposed to the Analysis phase where the focus is primarily on current processes and systems, the focus of the Design phase is on future contracting processes, systems, organizational structure, and KPIs. Some of the main tasks completed during the Design phase are:

- Future contracting processes are identified and documented.
- Gaps in the current versus desired capabilities of the ECM solution selected are identified and addressed.
- The organization's infrastructure needed to support the new business processes may be redesigned; workforce changes, training requirements, and key issues for each site included in the project scope are identified.
- Functional specifications for interfaces, reports, conversions, and system enhancements are developed and reviewed.
- Accountability for business benefits and a benefit tracking mechanism are established.
- Key components of contract and clause templates, such as tracking, sorting, searching, and reporting fields, are defined. While specific terminology varies slightly from one ECM solution to the next, it is

during the Design phase that the team designs the contract/clause template library, the security model, and reports.

■ A key part of the Design phase of most ECM solution implementations is developing the design for loading contracts that were executed by the organization in the past. This activity is commonly referred to as legacy data load. Depending on the maturity level of an organization's current ECM system, this activity may involve gathering and cleansing data, scanning executed contracts, and loading the contracts into the ECM solution.

In addition to the activities described above, some change management tasks are also executed in the Analysis and Design phase of an ECM solution implementation project. These include the following:

■ Benefits of the ECM solution are confirmed with change champions.
■ Impact of process and technology changes on individuals, jobs, and roles is assessed.
■ A plan to conduct tests within the new ECM solution is developed. This is critical to ensure that the ECM solution selected satisfies business requirements. During the Design phase, test scenarios are identified, test scripts and data are developed, and end users who will execute these tests are also identified.

### 6.5.2.4 Configure, Load, and Test Phase

The purpose of this phase is to configure the ECM application based on the design developed in the previous phase and to test the application. The following key activities are usually completed in this phase:

■ Administrative options within the ECM solution are configured.
■ A library of contract and clause templates is built.
■ User accounts and roles are configured.
■ Appropriate configuration is put in place to enable controlled access to contractual information by authorized users.
■ Legacy contract data are loaded into the ECM solution.
■ Other items, such as interfaces with other applications, e-mail notification events and templates, interviews/wizards to guide users through the steps to create and execute contracts, and reports, may also be configured depending on the capabilities of the ECM solution selected.

- The ECM solution configuration, as well as reports, interfaces, conversion programs, enhancements, and forms, are tested.
- **Change management**
  - ☐ Change champions and other key stakeholders are involved in developing test cases, entering test data, and testing the application.
  - ☐ Change champions are involved in developing and validating the training agenda, content, and schedule.
  - ☐ A deployment plan is developed and communicated.
  - ☐ A plan is developed to provide adequate support for the application post-go-live.

### 6.5.2.5 Go-Live and Support Phase

The final phase of an ECM solution implementation includes "going live" with the solution selected, training end users, and turning over the application to ongoing maintenance and support groups. Key activities usually completed in this phase include:

- **Change management**
  - ☐ End-user training is conducted.
  - ☐ Application support liaison contacts are identified and trained.
  - ☐ Knowledge transfer occurs from the core project team to the support group.
- **Project management**
  - ☐ Data conversion plan for the future is developed, if required.
  - ☐ High-level planning for additional work beyond the scope of the implementation is completed.
  - ☐ A plan is developed to secure sustained leadership commitment to the use and rollout of the application beyond the scope of the initial implementation.
- **Project closeout**
  - ☐ The core team develops documentation for future reference.
  - ☐ Project success is measured through benefits realization tracking. Post-go-live surveys and management questionnaires are used to quantify the success of the project.
  - ☐ Lessons learned from the implementation and rollout are gathered and shared across the organization for future implementations.

## 6.6 SUMMARY

An organization considering implementation of an ECM solution is faced with many unknowns, not the least of which is the best methodology by which the ECM solution in question might be implemented and validated as successful. This challenge can appear particularly daunting in light of the fundamental subject of the implementation—every legal contract currently in place and all future contracts to be entered into—as well as the fact that ECM solution implementation involves, ipso facto, every division, person, and aspect of a company.

Clearly, proven methodologies are required to minimize the risks of suboptimal implementation and to maximize the potential benefits that may be derived from ECM solutions. This chapter presented three such proven methodologies. However, it is obvious from the discussion presented that the most comprehensive and proven of such methodologies is one that is based on Six Sigma principles and processes. Six Sigma is a time-tested and highly quantitative approach to process optimization that is clearly based in metrics and analytics, but it recognizes the human, intuitive, and philosophical elements that are critical to the success of any complex initiative. In this chapter, an attempt was made to focus specifically on those aspects of Six Sigma which are optimally suited to and required for successful and sustained ECM solution implementation. The role of two Six Sigma approaches—DMAIC and DFSS—was dealt with in considerable detail, as were the composition of the Six Sigma team and the roles of its members.

A recurring theme in Six Sigma ECM solution implementation is the focus on the customer and the impact of the implementation on the value placed by the customer on an organization's future products and services. With this as the guiding principle, a well-formed Six Sigma team in control, and the principles of Six Sigma as a map, the probability of a successful and sustainable ECM solution implementation is greatly enhanced. In the next chapter, we will dive deeper into the change management considerations that should be kept in mind during all phases of an ECM solution implementation to ensure success.

# CHANGE MANAGEMENT CONSIDERATIONS*

## IN THIS CHAPTER:

- The Change Champion
- Organizational Change Management Elements: Key to Success in ECM Solution Implementations

## 7.1 OVERVIEW

Were this topic being discussed strictly with top physicists, it might justifiably be dedicated to Archimedes, the great Greek mathematician to whom is attributed the now-famous quote: "Give me a lever…and I can move the world" (see Figure 7.1). Fortunately, Archimedes' observations regarding the principles of leverage apply not only in the physical world but also in organizations, where,

---

\* The author gratefully acknowledges John P. Kotter and Harvard Business School Press, whose definitive texts *Leading Change* and *Managing Change and Transition* provided much of the conceptual underpinning for this chapter's focus on key organizational change management elements that help ensure success in Enterprise Contract Management solution implementation projects.

189

**FIGURE 7.1.  Archimedes' Lever**

as in mechanics, we observe how otherwise minor events can exert powerful effects far out of proportion to their size.

Against the backdrop of major organizational initiatives and priorities, the process of implementing an Enterprise Contract Management (ECM) solution may appear to be a relatively modest element of a company's overall development and growth. However, the impact of such an initiative can extend to the furthest reaches of an organization's operations and financial performance. Much like Archimedes' lever, it is not the size of the ECM initiative but the placement of the organizational fulcrum in relation to the load that determines its ultimate effect.

This chapter recognizes that ECM solution implementations do not occur in a vacuum, but rather they are part of—and exert a positive influence on—the very evolution of an organization. Like trying to use a lever when there is no fixed point, attempting to effectively implement an ECM solution without fixing certain points of reference within the organization would likely have very little lasting effect. By understanding the dynamics of organizational change, and by using these dynamics for maximum positive effect, lasting benefits may be derived from ECM solution implementation initiatives.

As with any complex process, initiatives such as the implementation of ECM solutions may be broken down into constituent dimensions or elements—those key cause-and-effect relationships which have proven to be most critical to successful ECM solution implementations in the past. This chapter identifies eight such organizational change management elements which, if considered proactively, permit the greatest value to be obtained from implementing an ECM solution both within and across an organization.

## 7.2  THE CHANGE CHAMPION

At this point, it is prudent to explain the critical role of the ECM change champion. The ECM change champion—that single person inside an organization with a vision of the full benefits to be derived from an ECM solution implementation—first and foremost creates a team and consensus to ensure success. He or she translates the vision and specific knowledge of these benefits into enhanced awareness of the organization's need for an ECM solution. Moreover, the change champion instills a sense of urgency within the organization to embrace the ECM solution implementation initiative and ensures that the organization possesses the infrastructure to utilize, measure, and analyze the resulting changes in organizational performance. In truth, a change champion is but one person and is incapable of personally implementing the ECM solution and driving its adoption across the organization alone. By definition, the implementation of an ECM solution requires active involvement and endorsement from all key divisions and operating units within an organization. It is the ECM change champion's first goal to identify, recruit, and educate the members of a team—that core coalition required to achieve the critical path to success in implementation and adoption of the chosen technology solution throughout the organization. Each organization needs a different group of members forming this coalition, but the core functions are easily identifiable across organizations such that specific team members may be contacted, engaged in the process, and incorporated into the broader "team of champions."

While it is the ECM change champion's responsibility to create and forge this coalition, ensuring that there is a clear goal before the team as a whole and each team member, this is just the beginning of the coalition-building process. In many organizations, the decision to implement an ECM solution is made at the corporate level. This decision is then mandated from upper management to individual business units, often including business units with few and limited resources to support the new initiative. Moreover, at the time a new ECM initiative is being mandated from the top, individual business units are very likely already being pulled in different directions due to current corporate initiatives. Thus, it is critical for an ECM change champion—and the implementation team as a whole—to build powerful links and support systems not just at the central/corporate level but at the level of individual business units as well.

This process is made even more complex when an organization's business units are geographically dispersed, especially if they are distributed around the world. While U.S.-based divisions may face pressures from one set of regulatory bodies, and therefore be required to comply with one set of constraints and controls, the business units in the Asia-Pacific region and European continent often address other critical issues and compliance with another set of regulatory bodies. Thus, not all business units will necessarily understand and share the same sense of urgency for an ECM solution as the corporate office. Anticipation of such inherent obstacles to unity is one of the key responsibilities of the ECM implementation team; as the saying goes, "an ounce of prevention is worth a pound of cure."

A final area where coalition building is essential is in regard to the maturity level of ECM processes and systems prior to beginning the ECM solution implementation. Since different groups within an organization may be employing different business processes and tools/methods (such as Microsoft Excel spreadsheets, Microsoft Word documents, Microsoft Access databases, enterprise resource planning applications, or some custom-built applications) for managing ECM processes, there is good likelihood that these groups will be at different levels of ECM maturity. Incongruity in ECM maturity levels within an organization may prove a stumbling block to deploying common ECM business processes and systems across that organization. Oftentimes, those business units already employing advanced ECM systems and processes will resist another investment of time, money, and resources in implementing an ECM solution if they feel that their current processes are already effective and efficient. It is the duty of the ECM change champion to help these business unit managers understand the benefits of implementing an ECM solution across the organization and standardizing the business processes, tools, and techniques used to manage the contract life cycle across the organization.

## 7.3 ORGANIZATIONAL CHANGE MANAGEMENT ELEMENTS: KEY TO SUCCESS IN ECM SOLUTION IMPLEMENTATIONS

Having defined the overall goal of this chapter—setting forth key organizational change management (OCM) elements to drive an ECM implementation to success—and having discussed the need for a change champion and a team, we now turn to the specifics of OCM elements needed to ensure a successful ECM solution implementation. In doing so, some of the common pitfalls that can impede this success will be illustrated.

If Archimedes' lever provided an image of the impact that effective ECM implementation can have on an organization, another fundamental invention—the wheel—will offer us a valuable model to describe the role played by key OCM elements in the ECM implementation process. The effectiveness of a

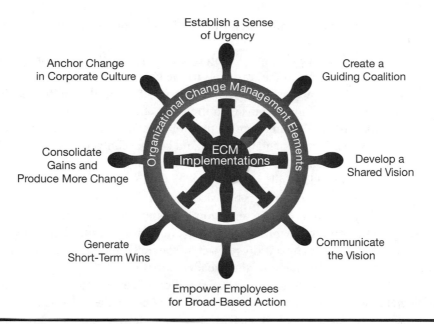

**FIGURE 7.2. OCM Elements Are Key to Success in ECM Implementations**

wheel depends to a great extent upon the strength, balance, and effectiveness of the individual spokes between the outer rim of the wheel and the hub around which the wheel revolves. Likewise, the elements of OCM function like spokes in the "ECM implementation wheel" (see Figure 7.2), all pointing toward the central goal or hub, with maximum efficiency and effectiveness achieved when all spokes are actively engaged and balanced.

## 7.3.1 Establish a Sense of Urgency

First and foremost, there must be an awareness of a need for a change. An ECM implementation in an organization of any level of size and maturity can be a time-consuming and complex process. ECM solution implementation benefits do not magically appear the day after the application is installed and ready for use. ECM solutions are not programs that provide instant gratification—quite the contrary; the very processes they manage are so integral to the core of the organization that it requires time to realize the fullest benefits of such solutions. Given this aspect of ECM implementation, it is understandable that those unfamiliar with the process would wonder, "What's the rush? Why should it matter if a component of the ECM implementation is enacted today, tomorrow, or for that matter next month? Aren't there higher priorities on the corporate agenda?"

It is the ECM change champion's job to clearly define the need for change and to communicate this to the team and to the key stakeholders in a way that both mobilizes them and engenders their personal commitment to change. Building the case for change begins with the ECM change champion and his or her vision for what ECM can mean to the organization. In concert with each member of the ECM implementation team and key stakeholders, and in concert with each other as team members, key issues which if solved by implementing an ECM solution would result in true benefits for the organization should be jointly identified. Since the changes being considered will have an (often initially unknown) impact upon the organization, assessing the company's level of maturity and flexibility to embrace new ECM initiatives is critical at this stage to ensure that team members do not act unilaterally and without sufficient forethought, to the detriment of the broader initiative.

The lack of a sense of urgency can be a significant detriment to effective ECM implementation and can result in largely operating below the radar as elements of the initiative do not receive the priority they deserve. Perhaps the most effective method an ECM change champion can use to instill a sustainable sense of urgency about the initiative is to thoroughly inform stakeholders and educate them in the steps, benchmarks, and stages of the ECM solution implementation process itself.

## 7.3.2 Create a Guiding Coalition

At the core of any successful ECM implementation is the team—a *guiding coalition* of essential members of an organization who possess the intellectual and motivational resources to support the initiative and see to its permanent installment within the company. By definition, the process of coalition building involves crossing borders between divisions and levels of authority in a company, with relationships needing to be forged between varied functions, profit centers, IT systems, and divisional cultures.

Identifying the right people to comprise such a heterogeneous team is part of the art of being a truly effective ECM change champion. Team members should—by definition—be team players, but should also have sufficient independence, experience, and convictions to stand up for their respective needs and rights within the organization. These should be people of sufficient authority, capability, and credibility to deliver their constituents to the fully implemented ECM process.

Once core team members are identified, a coalition identity, based upon common vision and mutual trust, needs to be established. This can be accomplished through clear and open communications, sharing experiences, and giving appropriate levels of credit for jobs well done.

The importance of a unified goal for the coalition cannot be overemphasized. This goal—the embodiment of the underlying vision—is the single common and guiding force that will knit together the otherwise disparate activities of the team as it fans out into the broader organization. If the individual members of a coalition are like states in the Union, the goal and underlying vision may be likened to the Constitution, binding all parties to a common creed.

### 7.3.3  Develop a Shared Vision

By definition, the vision for ECM solution implementation will become as big as the vision of its change champion. It is crucial for the ECM change champion and the coalition to fully develop and communicate their vision for successful ECM implementation. Taking the big-picture/long-term view and infusing the vision with its possibilities are essential to inspiring people with that which otherwise might seem like a procedural exercise with little relevance to their daily lives or careers. Such inspiration can greatly enhance the possibility for buy-in on the part of those new to the process in the weeks and months following launch of the initiative.

Since a full-scale ECM solution implementation involves a multiplicity of subinitiatives across geographies, divisions, and levels of authority, there is always a tendency for stratification of the process, whereby communications and integration suffer. The ECM team must be proactive in countering this tendency, by forging cross-linked alliances and communications, literally bringing together those who are essential to the success of the initiative and thereby connecting the dots so that the underlying image of success becomes visible.

### 7.3.4  Communicate the Vision

"The devil is in the details," and nowhere is this saying more relevant than in the world of contract management. But there is a hidden danger in this message when applied to ECM implementation—rushing too fast into the step-by-step process can lead to a loss of common vision on the part of the team and ultimately the organization as a whole. Arguably, the ECM change champion's primary function is one of communication. Like any good leader (or cheerleader, for that matter), the champion must be a quintessential spokesperson, ambassador, and proponent of the initiative. To be effective in this capacity, the champion must have a clear grasp of the communications tools at his or her disposal, must identify the key stakeholders in each target group, and must develop a clear plan for how, what, when, and where to communicate to others the plans and progress of the initiative.

The following is an actual case history, directly quoted from a senior executive at an ECM solutions implementation firm:

> One of my clients decided to launch the ECM solution implementation project with the primary goal of attaining global visibility into its worldwide contractual agreements. However, in the rush to implement the ECM solution, this goal was forgotten immediately. The first business unit to utilize an ECM solution decided to maintain full confidentiality of its contractual agreements from the other business units within the organization. The plan was that if one of the other business units wanted to see one of that unit's contracts, a formal request form would have to be filled out and approved by appropriate personnel before the contract in question could be shared. This obviously was not in alignment with the initial goal of attaining global visibility, but no one questioned it initially. After a few business units were "live" on the ECM system, some people started questioning where the benefit was from implementing all business units on this ECM system when everyone still had to go through a manual and long approval process to view contracts of another business unit. This made the implementation team and the steering committee rethink and reevaluate their original goals and objectives behind ECM solution implementation, and they redesigned/ reconfigured the ECM system to enable people from different business units to search for, share, and view each other's contracts.
>
> Thus, the problem was fixed, but the rework could have been avoided to begin with if proper attention was paid to details initially and the original goals and vision behind the ECM project were always kept in mind during all the phases of the implementation project.

All of the standards of good communication apply to this process, including keeping a clear, simple, and consistent message; engaging in a dialogue rather than preaching from the pulpit; using multiple means and channels to get the word out; and reinforcing the message to drive home its relevance and import.

When problems or conflicts arise, clarity of communication often can be the key to resolution. A champion must be able to think on his or her feet at such times in order to explain delicate and often complex issues with accuracy, diplomacy, and authority.

## 7.3.5 Empower Employees for Broad-Based Action

Vision is a great thing, but in the absence of empowerment, it is of little value. Beyond infusing the coalition with the vision for the ECM initiative, the champion must equip the team to act in an effective and coordinated manner to accomplish both near-term and long-range goals.

This empowerment begins by instilling a shared sense of purpose in the team and a clear understanding of how each member fits as an essential member of the overall ECM implementation engine. Structuring communications, team hierarchies, and functional roles consistent with this fit is crucial, as is providing necessary training for all members throughout the launch, enactment, monitoring, and transferal processes. Core elements of the organization must be aligned such that success is assured and rewarded. When problems arise—even those that involve deliberate resistance to the initiative, there must be a system in place to address them proactively, unequivocally, and with the broadest view toward organizational unity and success.

## 7.3.6 Generate Short-Term Wins

What use is a vision if it is not known, heard, spoken, and shared? Periodic reminders of the ECM implementation vision, including reflections upon short-term victories and their implications, are essential during all stages of the ECM implementation process. These communications may be informal or formal, verbal or written, one on one, or in group settings; the weaving of the vision as part of the ECM fabric can, and should, occur at all levels in the process. ECM implementation requires endurance before attainment of the sought-after goal. This is not a sprint to the finish line. Those team members not prepared to go the distance may need to be buoyed by occasional short-term victories along the way—reminders, if you will, of the progress which, though seemingly minor on the surface, is part of attainment of a much larger goal for the entire organization.

The strategy of infusing a long-term ECM implementation with short-term victories is perhaps best initiated from within the rank and file of a company, rather than dispensed from the top down. In this way, the mid-term achievement of goals may truly be claimed by those who most need to be recognized for their achievement and those who most need to be reminded that the near-term sacrifices and transitions are well worth the effort and present discomfort. Such victories along the way should be accompanied by overt recognition of specific achievements made by team members, with inclusive reference made to the whole team upon achievement of key milestones. We all thrive on intermittent reinforcement, especially when the task is long and the goal seems far away. ECM solution implementation is no different. Examples of short-term wins in ECM solution implementation projects can include:

- Implementing ECM in a business unit or a division with a small number of contracts
- Implementing a few contract templates within the ECM solution, instead of all desired templates
- Implementing the most critical (by contract value or by exposure to risk) contract instances within the ECM solution, instead of all active contract instances

These occasions also may be used to reflect upon the progress made to date toward the longer range goals of the ECM implementation, permitting exchange of views and strategies, which may result in valuable refinements of the strategies about to be enacted. Consistent reinforcement of the progress being made will also serve to silence cynics and detractors, giving less and less oxygen to their resistance. This also provides a clear example to senior management that the ECM champion and his or her core team are well suited to lead the organization to a successful ECM solution implementation. Much as a pump creates positive pressure, so do the recognition of near-term milestones and the resulting team building create momentum that further enhances the prospect for success of an ECM implementation.

The final element involved in generating short-term wins is to ensure that adequate systems are in place to measure performance, identify suboptimal results, and quantify progress in objective terms. The ECM change champion's first objective in measuring progress should be to identify what will be measured and to ensure that the targets of measurement are directly related to progress of the implementation. Encouraging the organization to embrace such quantification is facilitated by impressing upon all involved that without measurement there is no basis to assess progress. A second step in creating an environment of quantification is to ensure that the measurement goals and methods are purely objective and balanced—not predetermined or predisposed to a specific subgroup or set of results. Lastly, by linking attainment of specific goals to measurable benchmarks, the entire team retains a clear vision of its progress toward the interim short-term wins that will sustain it along the often lengthy road to complete ECM implementation.

## 7.3.7  Consolidate Gains and Produce More Change

It is critical that the ECM change champion stay the course until ECM implementation has been completely accomplished and its true benefits measured and communicated. Given the length of an ECM implementation process, it is tempting to declare an early victory, which might easily lead some to rest on their laurels and resume business as usual. By establishing objective metrics and systems for measuring the effectiveness and efficiency of ECM processes and systems at the outset of the program, the ECM change champion will have a well-grounded fulcrum against which to measure the degree of change being attributed to the ECM solution as it comes online.

As the ECM implementation process begins to bear fruit, gain momentum, and become part of the organizational culture and framework, it becomes possible to consolidate team progress, focus upon areas where true gains have been made, and refocus efforts on those areas that remain to be addressed. Obviously, this level of dynamic adjustment in the process is only possible when the team monitors progress and rapidly adjusts its strategies, approaches, and resources to address areas of greatest need. In some respects, the stakes get higher as ECM implementation approaches completion—the dynamically changing organization has invested much in its new approach to contract management; therefore, much is now expected. This is all the more reason why, as ECM implementation approaches full attainment of its objectives, management must be even more responsive to change, more willing to assist team members in need, and more willing to solicit support from senior managers and their employees. At this stage of ECM implementation, it is crucial that the organizational engine be in top running condition, with as few unnecessary interdependencies as possible.

## 7.3.8  Anchor Change in Corporate Culture

Back to our friend Archimedes for a moment. Anyone who has ever tried to push or move a heavy object without being firmly grounded knows the sinking feeling of failure when you—not the object—start to move. This can happen with poorly grounded ECM initiatives just as easily as with physical objects. Only when the true resistance of the object is overcome will the firmness of the foundation be critically tested. It is, therefore, essential for the ECM change champion to recognize the depth with which ECM implementation must be embedded within the infrastructure, data systems, and culture of an organization for it to truly be effective. In the absence of such grounding, ECM initiatives may be cast aside at the very point in time when they are most needed to protect the company from risk or to take full advantage of an opportunity for growth and future success.

The final OCM element required for successful ECM implementation is to solidify and institutionalize the changes made through a comprehensive retooling of the organization's policies, systems, and infrastructure. This process—*anchoring change in the company culture*—will ensure that progress made during the implementation process will survive and flourish as the organization faces new challenges and opportunities.

While it might seem that anchoring change within the company's culture would be relatively straightforward, this can be a very sensitive and delicate process to successfully achieve. Those with vested interests in the old way of contract management will likely make a last stand before capitulating, and turnover of some staff may be the result. By focusing on the long-term benefits of an ECM solution implementation across the entire enterprise, and by instilling a continuous top-down-up flow of feedback and communication, the potentially negative impact of anchoring change may be mitigated and the fullest positive potential may be realized.

## 7.4  SUMMARY

As demands for increasingly sophisticated and powerful ECM solutions present themselves to corporate managers, the challenges of effective implementation of such solutions require greater attention to ensure success. A fundamental challenge to ECM implementation is the unique, dynamic, and often unpredictable environment of change that occurs within an organization itself. This very factor raises both potential risks and opportunities for successful ECM implementation. As increasingly powerful ECM solutions are designed, developed, integrated, and implemented, they inevitably affect larger, heterogeneous groups of people and more organizational areas. The challenges in such technology implementation initiatives are often more behavioral than technical. Some senior managers mistakenly assume that once an ECM solution is procured and installed, everyone in the organization will simply fall in line behind the changes accompanying such an initiative. Such managers, not surprisingly, grow increasingly frustrated when the ECM solution chosen is not adopted with open arms by the organization or when the benefits from the initiative do not meet the original expectations.

To implement an ECM solution successfully and ensure maximum adoption by the target user population, senior management must internalize the changes from the beginning of the ECM initiative, so that others will follow. The transformation in business processes, functions, and systems must permeate through the organization, with the ECM change champion and other influential business unit or functional leaders doing their part to create a cascade of positive changes throughout every level of the organization. Only when the eight elements of OCM presented in this chapter are followed during and after an ECM implementation effort will an initiative of this magnitude achieve its fullest potential.

# RISK MANAGEMENT CONSIDERATIONS

## IN THIS CHAPTER:

- Types of Risk
- Risk Management Process

## 8.1 OVERVIEW

Ultimately, the future benefits of an Enterprise Contract Management (ECM) implementation have to be weighed against both the real and perceived risks associated with this major change in an organization's contract management processes. Real risks, while for the most part known and quantifiable, must nonetheless be anticipated and minimized to the extent possible. Perceived risks, while in some cases nonexistent, can still represent a real impediment to the buy-in needed to build a coherent and forward-looking ECM implementation team.

## 8.2 TYPES OF RISK

As illustrated in Figure 8.1, there are six major types or levels of risk in ECM implementation, from broad organizational program issues to highly specific technical elements of the process.

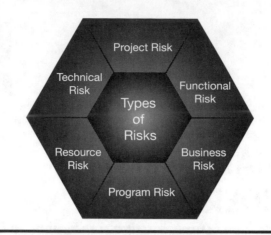

**FIGURE 8.1. Types of Risk**

## 8.2.1 Program Risk

In order for ECM to be successfully implemented, there needs to be a broad-based commitment in favor of its benefits and an acknowledgment that the changes involved in the transition will be worth the effort. The absence of such a program-level commitment throughout the enterprise represents a serious risk to success of the project. One reason such a commitment might be lacking is that the objectives of ECM implementation might be perceived as running counter to the goals and initiatives of others in the organization, thereby eroding the support that is derived for a unified effort. The lack of a broad-based sponsorship in support of the project and its champion represents a fundamental risk to the overall success of an ECM implementation.

## 8.2.2 Project Risk

Beyond its perceived impact to the organization as a whole, ECM implementation has certain inherent internal risks as a project in and of itself. Of primary concern: Is the project headed by a capable and committed leader, one both knowledgeable and focused, with the team-building skills required to keep the project on course? Has the project been adequately planned, with input from all relevant sources, and scenarios tested thoroughly before proceeding? Another risk at the project level is that the architects of the ECM implementation misread the scope of the project, either over- or underestimating its cost or its impact on other aspects of the organization's operations. Obviously, the project is at risk in the absence of solid monitoring systems and controls to ensure that problems are identified early on and adequately addressed to stay the course. In general, most key risks at the project level can be traced back to the quality and depth of key decision making.

## 8.2.3 Functional Risk

Despite management skill, planning, and organization-wide buy-in, a successful ECM implementation relies heavily upon certain key functional elements, including operational and administrative support, adequate business process controls, reliable delivery of promised functionality, and bolt-on applications from other sources. The overall reliability and usability of the functional infrastructure of the broader organization are key to ECM implementation success, right down to the "handshake" required to integrate the new ECM application with an organization's enterprise resource planning system.

## 8.2.4 Resource Risk

Ultimately, the success of ECM implementation boils down to the adequacy and timing of resources, whether human, financial, or operational. Are key people "on the team" and available when needed? What resources are truly critical path? Has there been adequate planning and authorization to create the budget for the project, and if so, do the decision-makers have authority to free up funds when needed? Ensuring that critical resources are available when needed and that they have been dedicated to the process by a broad-based network of support and authorization are critical to the success of an ECM implementation program, especially in an organization where many other priorities compete for the very resources required for success of the project.

## 8.2.5 Business Risk

An often-overlooked dimension of risk deals with the organizational alignment of ECM implementation with other business divisions and ongoing activities in the organization. Due to the fundamental nature of ECM, numerous business processes are impacted during implementation, and often people's roles in management and support will undergo unexpected shifts. Against the backdrop of this shifting situation, it is always possible that there will be miscommunication, which may lead to secondary problems in terms of teamwork, morale, and project unity. The impact of go-live upon numerous other business elements within an organization is often unknown and must be anticipated with appropriate communications, controls, and training. All in all, ECM implementation involves risk to the overall continuity of business operations.

### 8.2.6 Technical Risk

The final area of risk to be covered is in the technical underpinning of the implementation process from start to finish. Inappropriate, inadequate, or malfunctioning hardware and software are at the top of this critical list, including issues such as scale, architecture, and data conversion capabilities. Beyond the isolated systems and applications themselves are risks associated with networking both within and beyond the organization, reliability and speed of performance, and data and access security, as well as robustness, which includes disaster recovery and redundant file structure.

## 8.3  RISK MANAGEMENT PROCESS

The type, magnitude, probability, and impact of risks faced in the process of implementing an ECM solution are unique to every organization depending on several factors, including but not limited to the following:

- Project size, scope, schedule, and complexity (especially as related to customization and integration with other software applications)
- Current state of contract life cycle management business processes, tools, and technical landscape
- Knowledge, experience, and skills of core team members
- Breadth and depth of commitment from top executives to the ECM initiative
- Other initiatives competing for the resources that are also required for the ECM initiative
- Experience/capabilities of the consulting/implementation partner
- Capabilities of the ECM vendor

It is, therefore, appropriate to outline a systematic process for addressing risks associated with a typical ECM implementation project. In its broadest sense, ECM risk management involves five key stages (as shown in Figure 8.2):

1. **Risk identification**: This is accomplished by drilling down both within and outside the organization to specifically identify those elements of

**FIGURE 8.2. Stages in Risk Management**

present and future risk. Typically, this involves creating specialized risk task forces within the organization whose members possess the specific skill sets to thoroughly, and efficiently, identify risks of each type and at each level.

2. **Risk analysis and assessment**: Once a set of risks has been identified, it needs to be evaluated in terms of its degree of severity, critical path implications, and relative impact upon the ECM implementation process. This process of analysis and assessment is typically an iterative one, involving succeeding layers of the organization, as the details of a specific risk become apparent.

3. **Plan for risk mitigation**: Having identified and assessed the risks to ECM implementation, it is now possible to develop a proactive plan for either eliminating each risk in question, circumventing it, or mitigating, to the extent possible, its impact upon the overall process.

4. **Monitoring risk profile**: Since risks, by definition, are often unexpected and unpredictable, the process of managing ECM implementation must include establishing systematic reporting and monitoring systems for all ongoing and uncovered risks. This can and should include standard reporting systems and routine meetings and communications, coupled with objective metrics.

5. **Control of risk environment**: The ultimate goal of risk management is not to eliminate all risks from the ECM process—that is impossible,

since any process of change involves some degree of risk. The goal of risk management is to control the risk environment within tolerable levels so that the core elements of the ECM implementation process are achieved.

## 8.4 SUMMARY

There are risks associated with any organizational change as sweeping as an ECM solution. Early identification and continuing management of true, as well as perceived, risks are vital to a successful ECM implementation. Risk management is a circular process; for example, the more thorough risk management is from the beginning of the process, the more buy-in is created in stakeholders. An organization with complete buy-in creates an atmosphere in which fewer potential risks will come to fruition. The more planning that is done to mitigate known risks, the better an organization will be able to react to the unanticipated. In risk management for ECM solution implementation, "an ounce of prevention is worth a pound of cure."

# INTEGRATING AN ENTERPRISE CONTRACT MANAGEMENT SOLUTION

## IN THIS CHAPTER:

- The Business Imperative for an Integrated ECM Solution
- Building a Business Case for Integrating ECM Solutions
- ECM Solution Integration Approaches
- Ten Steps to Integrate ECM Solutions
- Vision of a Fully Integrated ECM Solution

## 9.1 OVERVIEW

Just as a skeleton provides the structural framework for the human body, contracts have evolved in today's modern organizations to provide the support, stability, and informational infrastructure that enable an entire organization to function—indeed, to survive and prosper—in today's ever-changing business climate. Without contracts, there would be no modern organizations as we know them. Certainly, there would be no mid- to large-scale enterprises operating across the nation and the world, conducting thousands of transactions simultaneously and positioned to respond—legally and competitively—to un-expected changes in the financial, social, and political spheres in which they must operate.

It is a maxim that organizations with sound contracts stand to prosper while others fail. Well-crafted agreements between an organization and its employees, partners, vendors, and customers lie at the very core of a company's success. Such agreements once crafted, however, would stand lifeless were they not negotiated, administered, monitored, executed, and at times enforced with the highest levels of professionalism and accuracy. Given the essential role that contracts play in today's business environment, a logical question is: How can modern organizations rise to the task of managing such a huge and complex challenge as their "contract universe"? Obviously, individual human effort and expertise go only so far in addressing such an enormous and complex array of relationships, documents, and compliance requirements, especially in some of today's larger organizations which operate under literally tens of thousands of contracts on a daily basis. Clearly, the need for state-of-the-art applications, such as Enterprise Contract Management (ECM) solutions, is called for to ad-dress this critical and growing need.

This chapter covers one of the final stages of ECM solution implementation by focusing on its integration within, throughout, and beyond the organization. A case is built to show that only through such an integration of ECM solutions can modern organizations fully expect to realize a maximum return on their ECM investment. The many challenges facing managers in today's mid-size to large enterprises are outlined in the context of the benefits made available through ECM solution integration, including:

- The impact of effective ECM solution integration on the extended enterprise
- The impact of such integration on an organization's agility in a competitive marketplace
- The role of ECM solution integration in a global business environment
- The impact of technology advances, outsourcing, and today's in-creasing era of compliance on the role that ECM solution integration can play in enhancing an organization's prospects for survival and success

This chapter seeks to build a compelling case that the benefits of ECM solution integration far outweigh the risks. Considerable space and content are devoted in this chapter to address this issue in hopes of providing the reader with an objective and comprehensive assessment of the pros and cons of ECM solution integration. Building upon the premise that ECM solution integration makes sound business sense, this chapter describes the major integration approaches, including:

- Information oriented
- Business process oriented
- Services oriented
- Portal oriented

Beyond the specific perspective or approach taken to ECM solution integration, the ten major steps involved in the process are outlined in considerable detail, from understanding business goals and objectives to measuring success and supporting continuous improvement. The chapter concludes with the author's vision of a fully integrated ECM solution and the role that it might play in the successful organizations of the future.

## 9.2 THE BUSINESS IMPERATIVE FOR AN INTEGRATED ECM SOLUTION

From the discussion in the previous chapters, it is evident that an ECM solution offers significant benefits to an organization. However, as shown in Figure 9.1, implementation of an ECM solution can come in many colors, ranging from cursory and one dimensional to fully integrated. It is the underlying premise of this chapter that only through a fully integrated approach can an organization expect to reap full benefits—benefits that span both the organization itself as well as across organizations.

Like any systems integration initiative, an ECM solution integration initiative is usually driven by goals of increased efficiency, effectiveness, and compliance and reduced cost, errors, and rework. Other key business drivers behind the need for integrating an ECM solution within as well as across organizations are discussed in the following sections.

### 9.2.1 The Extended Enterprise

Organizations traditionally were built around the link-and-node type of supply chain models in response to the sequential nature of tasks, where results from one task are handed off to the next task in the production process. However, success in today's business environment demands a much higher level of integration and collaboration in a complex web-like pattern to enable efficient,

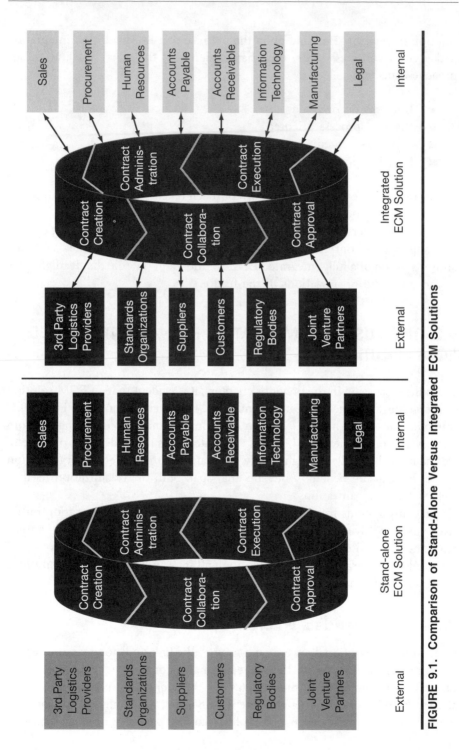

**FIGURE 9.1. Comparison of Stand-Alone Versus Integrated ECM Solutions**

effective, and fast flow of products, services, and information within an organization and with its business partners. Today, leading organizations operate as extended enterprises instead. An extended enterprise is the entire set of collaborating companies, both upstream and downstream, from raw material to end-product consumption, that work together to bring value to the marketplace.* The member organizations of an extended enterprise are bound by a shared set of norms and social contracts that emphasize a win-win philosophy so that each shares equitably in the gains and the risks inherent in any form of the competitive arena. Members view their destinies to be interdependent.

The fact that success in modern business is now a function of the collective performance of the extended enterprise—and not of individual organizations—represents a significant change from traditional business relationships. This change is reflected in the highly complex contracts being authored, executed, and administered and in the need for speed, accuracy, and visibility in the contracting processes across organizations. This need is fulfilled by an ECM solution that is integrated not only with other enterprise-wide applications within an organization, but is also integrated with the applications of the extended enterprise's member organizations. This ensures that each member organization has access and full visibility to the contractual terms and conditions, the effective dates and other contractual meta-data, and performance to date of each member organization against contracted terms. A fully integrated ECM solution generates automated notifications that are sent to all appropriate members of an extended enterprise in case of exceptions, thus speeding up the discovery, analysis, and collective decision-making process necessary to address such exceptions.

## 9.2.2 The Agile Enterprise

An agile enterprise is one that responds with relative rapidity to changes in the business environment. These changes can be regulatory, competitive, market, or customer driven. To respond with agility to such opportunities or threats, an organization needs the ability to respond rapidly in a variable, efficient, and resilient manner. However, an organization cannot achieve or demonstrate such agility in isolation. Agility can be achieved only when the extended enterprise is able to reorganize and synchronize its many component businesses through real-time collaborative processes, executed in concert to derive value for all participants. Since contracts lie at the core of an extended enterprise, business agility in such organizations is enabled via ensuring that their contracts permit:

---

* Edward Davis, *The Extended Enterprise: Gaining Competitive Advantage through Collaborative Supply Chains,* Financial Times Prentice Hall, Upper Saddle River, NJ, 2003.

1. Seamless integration of the planning (through contractual relationships) and execution needed for efficient, stable processes
2. The ability to detect, analyze, monitor and respond to changes
3. Learning how the extended enterprise operates (contract analysis and reporting)
4. Learning how the operations of the extended enterprise can be adjusted to improve efficiency and effectiveness (contract renewals, negotiations, amendments)

It is important to note that contracts in an extended and agile enterprise are no longer the static documents they once were. They have evolved into dynamic relationship blueprints that require attention to identify opportunities for improvement (through negotiating better rates) when business partners may not be fulfilling commitments (through capturing the quality, quantity, and time of delivery of products and/or services rendered) or to recognize when partners are doing an excellent job.

A stand-alone ECM solution enables contract life cycle management capabilities within an extended enterprise, but does not foster business agility, nor does it take advantage of the full team of participants involved in the contracting process. The net result of a stand-alone approach, therefore, is to restrict the ability of an extended enterprise to function as an agile enterprise. Only through integration of an ECM solution within and across all parties involved can an organization dynamically manage its contractual agreements in real time, leverage the true capabilities of the ECM solution, and realize its transformation into a truly extended and agile enterprise.

## 9.2.3  Globalization

Globalization is not a new trend. It has been a much-debated topic since the early 1980s and has been used as an umbrella term for a complex series of political, economic, social, and technological changes occurring around the globe. This is due to the increasing interdependence and interaction between people and organizations and is fostered by technological advances such as the rise of PCs and full-scale platforms and Internet-based real-time transactions. However, for the purposes of this chapter, globalization refers to the growing economic interdependence of organizations in countries worldwide through increasing volume and variety of cross-border transactions in goods and services, international capital flows, and rapid and widespread diffusion of technology. Globalization is both a cause as well as a result of the extended enterprise model described above.

The trend toward globalization has had a significant impact on the number, type, size, and complexity of contractual agreements entered into by organizations. Organizations entering into global contracts frequently face unique challenges such as country-specific laws, regulations and business guidelines, taxes, immigration laws and requirements, currency exchange, multiple languages, and cultures. Not all of these issues can be addressed directly by an integrated ECM solution. There is no doubt, however, that such a solution is best suited to bring visibility to such issues and to effectively automate, completely or partially, their resolution through the consistent application of business rules and data.

## 9.2.4 Technology Advancements

Products and systems within the information technology sector are changing rapidly. Computer power and speed are doubling every year, costs are coming down, and the capabilities of hardware, software, middleware, and networks are improving dramatically. However, no other technology invention has had a bigger impact on the corporate world than the Internet. The advent and increased use of the Internet has led to the rise of e-business, e-commerce, e-mail, e-banking, e-learning, and countless Web-based applications. It would not be an overstatement to say that the Internet has transformed the way business is conducted in the Digital Age.

In today's networked economy, the focus of organizations has shifted from internal to external, centralization to decentralization, growth in size to growth in value, brick-and-mortar organization to virtual organization, predictability to continuous change, and integration to core competencies. Buyers and sellers are interacting directly over the Internet via e-marketplaces or trading networks. Supply is matched with demand instantaneously. Product pricing is moving from seller determined to buyer determined, from fixed to flexible, from previous-sale based to this-moment based, and from occasional discounts to continuously changing prices. There is a general trend toward real-time transactions and real-time information in every aspect of business. This adds another dimension to the complexity of the contractual agreements of business partners. These agreements have to address the terms and conditions governing transactions that occur in the brick-and-mortar world as well as the *virtual* world. Also, information and audit trails of all transactions, whether manual or automated, need to be shared in real time or as close to real time as is possible, and any exceptions should trigger automated alerts/notifications so that corrective action is taken immediately. Supplier performance against contracted terms and conditions as well as an organization's performance against its own contracts with its customers must be measured, and appropriate actions should be taken proactively to address inconsistencies and areas for improvement. Since a stand-alone ECM solution is not able to deliver the expected results in such scenarios, internal and external integration of a company's ECM solution is not an option—it is an imperative.

## 9.2.5 Outsourcing

Similar to the trend of globalization, outsourcing is not new. Several decades ago, organizations began to outsource functions (such as IT) for which they had no internal competency. The cost-cutting measures of the 1990s continued the trend of outsourcing functions (such as human resources, data processing, mail distribution, security, and housekeeping) that were necessary to run an organization but were not related specifically to its core business. The concept of outsourcing has evolved over the last decade to the point where it is now considered to be the development and establishment of strategic partnerships. Outsourcing in today's corporate world is no longer limited to delegation of responsibility for noncore, nonstrategic functions. The focus today is less on ownership and more on developing strategic partnerships to bring about enhanced results. Today, companies enter into outsourcing agreements in order to gain access to world-class capabilities, reduce and control operating costs, improve the host company's focus, free up the organization's internal resources for more strategic activities, and share risks with the partner organization.

Outsourcing, as an approach to doing business, reflects the continuing evolution of corporate structure. The traditional, centralized, static, link-and-node type of business model is being replaced by a dynamic, networked environment where the ability to manage change and enable innovation is of paramount importance. The strategic partnership, which is at the foundation of an outsourcing relationship, is defined, negotiated, executed, and managed through a contract or service-level agreement. An organization's ability to effectively and efficiently manage the life cycle of its contracts in real time lies at the heart of every outsourcing agreement. While a stand-alone ECM solution adds significant value to an organization's contracting processes, most of these benefits are dependent on the end users manually entering data captured in another application as a result of related tasks and processes. Integration of an ECM solution internally and externally eliminates this dependency to a great extent and adds the benefit of maintaining an automated audit trail to provide backup documentation in case of an audit or dispute.

## 9.2.6 Era of Compliance

The last decade has ushered in the so-called "era of compliance," in which modern business enterprises rework their practices and values in an attempt to minimize risk in the wake of corporate and national disasters such as Enron, WorldCom, and 9/11. Characterized by strict codes and guidelines, the era of compliance places unprecedented demands on organizations, which must embrace compliance as an essential factor in their survival, growth, and success. This new emphasis on compliance has placed increasing demands on corporate executives and corporations themselves, as increasing regulatory and compliance demands spur the movement toward ECM solutions.

ECM solutions occupy a unique place in the spectrum of IT tools available to compliance managers. Since the information most critical to compliance is virtually always contained in contracts, the tools by which such contracts are managed become an essential link between an organization's operations and its ability to sustain a compliant status. ECM solutions come in a wide array of shapes and sizes, but in most cases they offer compliance managers numerous fundamental benefits both to implement change toward a culture of compliance and to achieve the highest level of sustained compliance. As has been pointed out in previous chapters, the process of implementing and integrating an ECM solution into an ongoing organization's compliance environment is a complex and multifaceted process, one which requires considerable planning and communication, continuous monitoring, and appropriate outside expertise. By integrating a proactive approach toward ECM implementation and integration, and setting a goal of long-term sustainable compliance, managers can maximize the value of ECM for their organizations and ensure that it serves their compliance needs fully, both now and in the future.

The driving forces mentioned above represent a pressing need for organizations to reach beyond the traditional means of setting up, executing, and administering business partnerships and relationships. Contract development, execution, and administration need to occur in as real time as is possible, with as little unnecessary human intervention as possible. Companies must author and manage their contractual relationships in an automated manner to improve responsiveness to changing market, customer, and regulatory demands and to stay competitive in an ever-changing corporate environment. Integrating an organization's ECM solution internally (within the organization) and externally (with applications of business partners or allowing business partners access through an extranet, a supplier portal, or a customer portal) is a major step in this direction.

## 9.3  BUILDING A BUSINESS CASE FOR INTEGRATING ECM SOLUTIONS

By the end of the twentieth century, organizations had identified continued investment in IT as a necessary business element to stay competitive. However, at the outset of the twenty-first century—and due to increased globalization, more competition, political and economic instability, and technology advancements, further investment in IT is no longer viewed as desirable or even as merely critical. It is now viewed as absolutely essential for any organization hoping to survive and prosper. Despite this dependence on IT for survival, investments in new technology solutions still must be justified in terms of return on investment (ROI). Understandably, most chief information officers (CIOs) and chief financial officers (CFOs) today are demanding a detailed financial justification for every IT project—whether large or small, and every project is expected to add to the bottom-line performance of the organization.

Unlike some prospective investments in IT, the business case for implementing an ECM solution is straightforward. According to AMR Research, "ECM implementations take two to three months—and achieve a 150% to 200% payback within one year."[*] The Aberdeen Group reported that "the ROI for an organization with $750 million in annual revenue and $200 million in annual spend from an ECM implementation is more than 3X in the first year!"[**] It is interesting to note that some of these estimates are based on implementation of a stand-alone ECM solution. Thus, it seems obvious that an integrated ECM solution is bound to have an even better ROI than a stand-alone ECM solution. There are well-documented costs of workers and business partners (suppliers and customers) having the wrong information, incomplete information, too much information, or simply no information at all. However, the financial justification for an ECM solution integration initiative is tougher to put together than that for an ECM solution implementation. This is because:

- Unlike an ECM solution implementation initiative, its integration initiative is usually not launched to address a specific event or situation.
- The integration initiative affects the organization as a whole, impacts daily business processes, and its cost is usually considerably higher when compared with other IT initiatives.

---

[*] The Compelling ROI of Contract Management, AMR Research, Boston, February 2003.
[**] The Contract Management Solution Selection Report, Aberdeen Group, Boston, June 2005.

■ The investment required to integrate an ECM solution with other enterprise-wide applications is in addition to the investment made in the ECM solution.

It is no surprise to find that CIOs and CFOs today are concerned about investing further in integrating a chosen ECM solution until the following questions are answered:

■ What are the costs associated with the ECM integration effort?
■ What are the benefits of ECM integration, and how can the benefits be quantified?
■ Will integrating the ECM solution lead to positive ROI in a reasonable time frame?
■ What are the risks associated with the ECM integration effort, and how can these risks be quantified and addressed/mitigated?
■ How can investments made in enterprise resource planning (ERP), ECM, supplier relationship management (SRM), customer relationship management (CRM), business intelligence (BI), portals, middleware, and other enterprise-wide applications be leveraged in the ECM integration effort?

Given the complex nature of ECM solution integration, there are no easy answers to the questions above. When addressing the decision whether to integrate an ECM solution, the business case should provide a clear assessment of the costs versus benefits and risks versus opportunities of integration versus using the solution in a stand-alone mode, as shown in Figure 9.2. This section of the chapter discusses these different aspects of the ECM solution integration business case.

## 9.3.1 Costs

Identifying the cost components of an ECM solution integration initiative is usually straightforward. The following types of cost components are involved:

■ **Architecture costs**: These are capital costs related to the initial deployment and include:
   □ Software license costs (such as for middleware, adapters, operating systems, and databases)
   □ Hardware costs (such as the cost of the development environment, testing environment, and production environment)
   □ Architectural hardware and software implementation costs

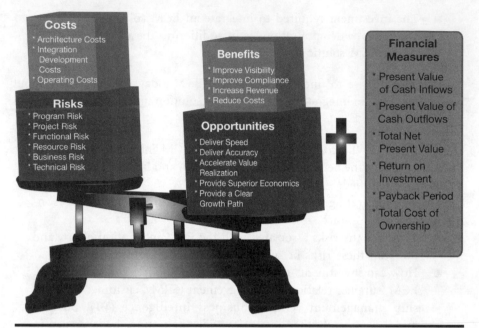

**FIGURE 9.2. Business Case for ECM Solution Integration**

- **Integration development costs**: These costs are variable, dependent on the number of interfaces being developed, and often capitalized. They include:
  - □ Cost for development of interfaces
  - □ Cost for development of collaboration between different applications
- **Operating costs**: These are expensed costs and include the following:
  - □ Maintenance and support costs for hardware and software
  - □ Labor costs for operational staff

## 9.3.2 Risks

An ECM solution integration initiative faces six major classes of risk, from broad organizational program issues to highly specific technical elements of the process as described in Chapter 8:

- Program risk
- Project risk
- Functional risk

- Resource risk
- Business risk
- Technical risk

The type, magnitude, probability, and impact of risks faced in the process of integrating an ECM solution are unique to every organization depending on several factors, including, but not limited to, the following:

- Size, scope, schedule, and complexity of the desired integration with other software applications
- Capabilities of the ECM solution and other software applications within the scope of the integration initiative
- Current state of ECM business processes, tools, and technical landscape
- Breadth and depth of commitment from top executives to the ECM solution integration initiative
- Other initiatives competing for the resources that are also required for the ECM solution integration initiative
- Knowledge, experience, and skills of core team members
- Experience/capabilities of the consulting/implementation partner

A systematic process for identifying and addressing risks associated with a typical ECM solution integration project must be put in place. This should be similar to the one described in Section 8.3.

## 9.3.3 Benefits

The benefits associated with implementing an ECM solution were discussed in detail earlier. However, the following are key benefits that can be expected from integrating an ECM solution with other enterprise-wide applications:

- **Improve visibility**: An ECM solution improves visibility into an organization's contracts by acting as a single repository of all the contracts executed by the organization. In addition, when an ECM solution is integrated with other enterprise applications that store key information such as spend data, supplier data, goods receipt data, and invoice receipt data, it improves visibility into critical areas. These include organizational spend against contracts, organizational performance against regulatory and procedural compliance policies and guidelines, supplier performance against contractual terms, and the workload of contracting professionals.

- **Improve compliance**: Integrated ECM solutions facilitate improved regulatory, procedural, and contractual compliance. They also significantly enhance automation in these three categories of compliance. For example, actual goods received and goods invoiced data from an ERP application can be integrated with contractual data in the ECM solution and compared automatically. Any exceptions can trigger an automated notification to the contract administrator, who can then take suitable action to address the noncompliance.

- **Increase revenue**: As mentioned earlier, an ECM solution helps contracting professionals to focus their time and efforts on negotiating better contracts for an organization and identify an increased number of up-selling and cross-selling opportunities. However, when integrated with an organization's accounts payable/accounts receivable application, events can be configured in the ECM solution to trigger an automated reminder or alert that notifies accounts receivable personnel to invoice for all services rendered and collect penalties and charges where applicable.

- **Reduce costs**: Integrating an ECM solution can help reduce costs due to improvement in process efficiency and reduction in maintenance cost. For example, typical cost savings include:
  - Reduction in data entry and duplication
  - Reduction in manpower costs
  - Reduction in transaction processing costs
  - Reduction in the number of errors and thus reduction in error handling costs
  - Reduction in overpayments via integration with the ERP application supporting the accounts payable function
  - Reduction in audit-related costs
  - Reduction in reporting costs

## 9.3.4 Opportunities

Integrating an ECM solution across an enterprise is a strategic initiative with an impact beyond cost savings. ECM solution integration shortens the decision-making process within an organization, as shown in Figures 9.3 and 9.4. These figures depict the three components of latency (data latency, analysis latency, and decision/action latency) between the time when a business event occurs (such as a supplier not meeting contractual terms and conditions) and when an informed decision is executed.*

---

* Richard Hackathorn, "The BI Watch: Real-Time to Real-Value," *DM Review,* January 2004.

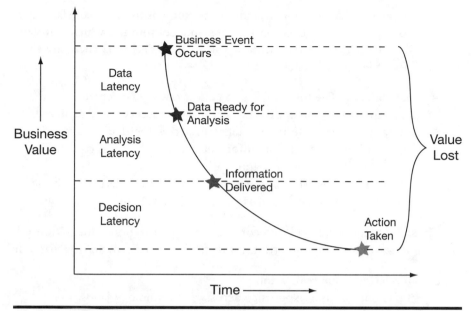

**FIGURE 9.3.  Components of Latency in a Stand-Alone ECM System**

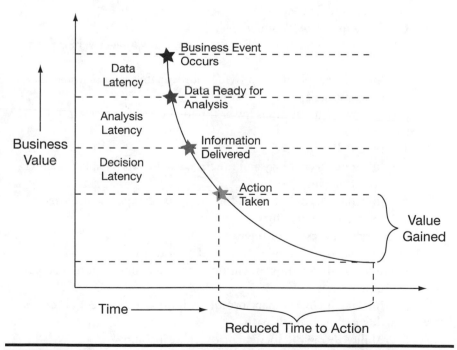

**FIGURE 9.4.  Components of Latency in an Integrated ECM System**

Integrating an ECM solution provides opportunities to reduce the latency at one or more points in the decision-making time continuum, which translates into a dramatic increase in the business value of the decision. There are three major types of levels of latency:

- **Data latency**: The time it takes to collect raw data, prepare the data for analysis, and store the data where it can be accessed and analyzed.
- **Analysis latency**: The time it takes to access the data, analyze the data, transform the data into information, apply business rules to the data, and generate alerts if appropriate.
- **Decision latency**: The time it takes to receive an alert, review the analysis, decide what action is required (if any), and take action.

Thus, if designed and deployed correctly, an ECM solution integration initiative offers the following opportunities to further transform an organization:

- **Accelerate value realization**
  - ☐ Common user experience across the technology landscape
  - ☐ Reduce change management issues
  - ☐ Better control over resources
  - ☐ Increase efficiency
- **Provide superior economics**
  - ☐ Integrated applications have economic advantages versus point tools
  - ☐ Integrated applications provide more capability for a similar class of investment
  - ☐ Integrated applications lower the total cost of ownership for the organization
- **Improve delivery speed**
  - ☐ Integrated technology and functional landscape enable faster decision making
  - ☐ Integrated technology and functional landscape enable faster response to competitors
- **Delivery accuracy = confidence**
  - ☐ Integrated data model ensures data integrity
  - ☐ Integrated environment eliminates manual integration of stovepipe tools
  - ☐ Integrated environment promotes improved business processes
- **Provide a clear growth path**
  - ☐ Ability to rapidly increment overall capability
  - ☐ Ability to add new services

## 9.3.5 Key Financial Metrics

As mentioned earlier, the business case for ECM solution integration should address the associated costs and benefits, as well as risks and opportunities. Once these have been quantified as accurately as possible, the next step in the development of the business case is the calculation of some key financial metrics:

- **ROI**: ROI analysis is a de facto requirement in the IT industry today. According to a recent *Information Week* study, more than 82% of all IT decisions in today's business environment require ROI analysis. Quantitatively defined, ROI is the benefit of an investment divided by the cost expressed in percentage terms, normally over a period of three years:

$$\text{ROI} = \frac{\text{(Benefit from integrating ECM solution)}}{\text{(Total cost of integrating ECM solution)}} \times 100$$

  Thus, if the total cost of integrating an ECM solution is $100,000 and the benefit expected from it is $40,000 per year, the ROI is 40% in the first year. ROI analysis is fairly simple once the estimates of benefits and costs are determined. However, ROI does not communicate an entire story. It identifies the percentage of return, but does not give an indication of how long it will take to break even on an investment or the overall profits that investment will bring in.

- **Payback period**: This is a measure of the time it will take for an investment to break even. It is calculated by dividing the initial cost of investment by the net annual cash flows it will bring back into the business and results in a number of years. Payback period calculation assumes that benefits accrue steadily over a period of time. For example, if an ECM solution integration initiative requires an investment of $100,000, increases revenue by $25,000 per year, and decreases cost by $15,000 per year, then:

$$\text{Payback period} = \frac{\text{(Cost of ECM solution integration initiative)}}{\text{(Increase in revenue/year} + \text{Decrease in costs/year)}}$$

$$= \frac{(\$100,000)}{(\$25,000 + \$15,000)}$$

$$= 2.5 \text{ years}$$

- **Total cost of ownership (TCO):** TCO is the life cycle cost view of the ECM solution integration initiative. It includes direct costs (such as the cost of hardware and software acquisition, setup, integration development, training, ongoing maintenance, upgrades, and all operating expenses) and indirect costs (such as interruption to regular work of employees due to hardware/software downtime). The main insight offered by TCO is the understanding that initial integration development costs could be a very small portion of the TCO.

## 9.4  ECM SOLUTION INTEGRATION APPROACHES

Integrating enterprise-wide solutions (such as an ECM solution) requires a strategic approach to coordinating many technology solutions at both service and information levels, in order to support the ability of such solutions to exchange information and leverage business processes in real time. The resulting information and business process flow between internal and external systems provides organizations with the capability to do business in real time based on predefined rules. Therefore, before proceeding with a discussion of the steps required to integrate an ECM solution with other enterprise-wide applications, it would be useful to first discuss the different approaches available to technically implement and deploy such a deep and broad level of integration. These approaches can be classified into four general categories, as explained below.

### 9.4.1  Information-Oriented Integration Approach

The primary focus of integration with this approach is at the database level or at information-producing application programming interfaces (APIs). Thus, with this integration approach, data may be replicated from one enterprise-wide solution to the ECM solution or vice versa. For example, as shown in Figure 9.5, an ERP application may be the system of record for supplier, user, and material information, and this data can be replicated in the ECM solution. This prevents duplication of data and enables maintaining data consistency and quality across technology systems.

In addition to data replication, this integration approach can also be used to set up a data federation, that is, integration of multiple databases and database models into a single, unified view of the databases. For example, as shown in Figure 9.6, if an ECM solution is built on an Oracle database, such a database can be virtually integrated with other physically separate databases of other

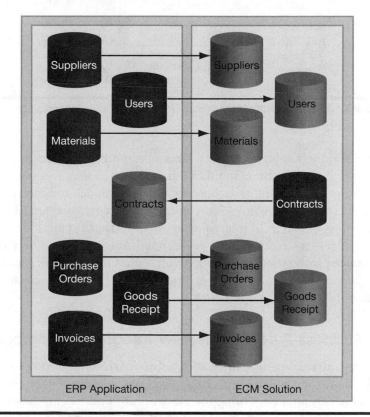

**FIGURE 9.5. ECM Solution Integration Using Data Replication**

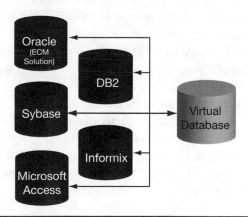

**FIGURE 9.6. ECM Solution Integration Using Data Federation**

**FIGURE 9.7. ECM Solution Integration Using Interface Processing**

enterprise-wide technology solutions. This is a more elegant approach compared to the data replication approach, as it does not require changes to the ECM solution or to the other technology solutions under consideration.

Finally, as shown in Figure 9.7, the information-centered approach can also be used to integrate an ECM solution with other packaged applications through interface processing (i.e., by using well-defined APIs). This is a very efficient mechanism for integrating an ECM solution with different applications. However, such integration usually includes little regard for business logic and methods within the source or target systems.

## 9.4.2  Business-Process-Oriented Integration Approach

The business-process-oriented integration approach refers to the process of managing the movement of data between applications that may be internal or external to the organization, during the execution of business processes such as procure to pay, order to cash, hire to retire, etc. This movement is triggered by the occurrence of predefined events within specific business processes. The primary goal here is to integrate an organization's relevant business processes, in order to gain end-to-end visibility of critical processes and maximize ROI while supporting information flow and control logic.

To the uninitiated, it may seem like business process integration is the same as traditional application integration, where two or more systems are integrated based on information exchange. However, the truth is that, whereas traditional application integration projects are more tactical in nature, a true business process integration effort is usually strategic in nature. It leverages business rules to determine how systems should interact and better leverage the business value from each system—internal or external—via a common abstract business model that defines the sequence, hierarchy, events, execution logic, and information movement between systems.*

---

\* David S. Linthicum, *Next Generation Application Integration: From Simple Information to Web Services,* Addison-Wesley, Boston, 2004.

This integration approach lends itself very well to the ECM solution integration problem due to the fact that contracting processes typically fall between strategic sourcing processes and traditional procurement processes. For example, to gain end-to-end visibility of the procurement processes within an organization, one needs to look at the following high-level activities:

1. Request for materials and/or services originates
2. Sourcing strategy is determined
3. Qualified or approved suppliers are identified and notified of the need
4. If no contract exists, the contract process (creation, negotiation, approval, and execution) is executed
5. Purchase order is created with reference to the contract and transmitted to the supplier
6. Supplier ships the goods or performs service(s) at the requestor's facility
7. Supplier sends corresponding invoices
8. Buying organization issues a payment

As can be seen from the list of activities above, the contract process (activity 4) is preceded by traditional procurement (activity 1) and strategic sourcing processes (activities 2 and 3) and followed by traditional procurement processes (activities 5, 6, and 7). Traditional financial processes (activity 8) further follow the traditional procurement processes. To further develop this example, let's assume that the organization under consideration uses the following systems (as shown in Figure 9.8):

- A best-of-breed strategic sourcing application (for RFx processes)
- A custom-built contract management application (for contracting processes)
- An ERP application (for traditional procurement processes)

Using the business-process-oriented integration approach, the following integration can be designed, developed, and executed:

- A requisition is created in the ERP application.
- The creation of a requisition in ERP triggers an event in the strategic sourcing application. This prompts the buyer to execute the RFx process. Assuming several suppliers bid on the materials requested, the buyer compares the bids and awards the bid to one of the suppliers.

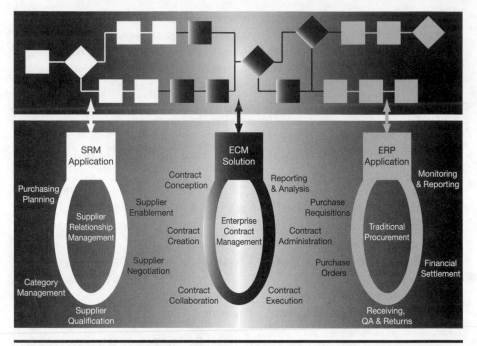

**FIGURE 9.8. ECM Solution Integration Using Business Process Integration Approach**

- Awarding the bid to a supplier triggers an event in the contract management application that notifies a contract author of the need to execute a contract with the selected vendor. Key information from the bid in the sourcing application may also be transferred to the contract in the contract management application.
- The contract author executes a contract in the contract management application.
- The execution of the contract triggers an event in the ERP application. The traditional procurement processes of purchase order creation, transmission, receiving goods, entering and validating invoices, and sending payment to the vendor are executed in the ERP application.
- Issuing a payment to the supplier from the ERP application triggers an update of the contract in the contract management system indicating spend against the contract to date.

This is a very simple example of the concept of the business-process-oriented integration approach. In real life, such integration typically involves several instances of data replication or data federation (i.e., information-oriented integration) and several instances of services-oriented integration.

Another way to view the creation of a business process integration model is by defining the hierarchy of processes across business partners or across multiple functional areas within an organization. For example, the business process of creating a contract requires smooth functioning of subprocesses such as creation of supplier records, materials/services, price lists, and discounts. An organization can gain great value by linking its critical higher level contracting business processes with subprocesses (such as master data creation and maintenance) that may be scattered across its technology landscape.

## 9.4.3 Services-Oriented Integration Approach

The services-oriented integration approach allows integration between multiple applications based on linked, repeatable business tasks or services. This integration approach enables users to build composite applications that draw upon the functionality from multiple sources (i.e., systems/applications) within and beyond the enterprise to support horizontal business processes. As shown in Figure 9.9, such integration is accomplished either by defining application services that can be shared or by providing an infrastructure for sharing application services. Application services can be shared by hosting them on a central server or by accessing them interapplication, such as through distributed objects or Web Services.* Web Services allow organizations to not only move information from application to application but also to create composite applications, leveraging several application services found in local or remote applications.

Most best-of-breed ECM solutions today offer a set of standard Web Services that can be used to enable integration with ERP, supply chain management (SCM), SRM, CRM, BI, or legacy applications. Consider the following scenarios as examples:

- **Configuration data or master data related**: ECM solutions typically use configuration data elements (such as company code, purchasing organization, plant codes, purchasing groups, material groups) and master data elements (such as suppliers, customers, users, products, price lists) in the process of contract creation and execution. The system of record for most of these data elements is usually an ERP application. Web Services can be used to retrieve information dy-

---

* David S. Linthicum, *Next Generation Application Integration: From Simple Information to Web Services*, Addison-Wesley, Boston, 2004.

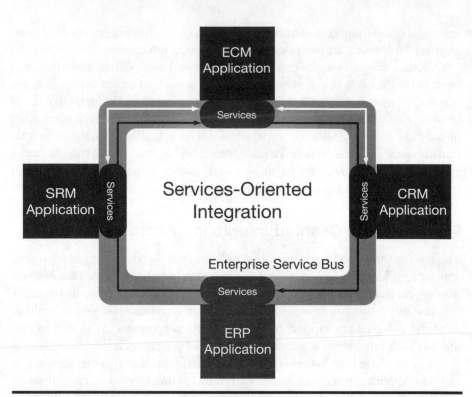

**FIGURE 9.9. ECM Solution Integration Using Services-Oriented Integration Approach**

namically for these data elements from the ERP application at the time of creating a new contract within the ECM application. Such interfaces can also be used to update information in the ECM solution (such as a supplier record) when a corresponding record is updated in the ERP application. These updates can be configured to occur in real time or on a predetermined schedule.

■ **Transactional data related**: The services-oriented integration approach can be used to trigger transactions in an ECM solution based on events occurring in other enterprise-wide applications. For example, posting a supplier invoice in an ERP application for a purchase order created against a contract stored in an ECM solution should invoke a Web Service that triggers the update of actual spend information on the contract in the ECM solution. The approach can also be used to trigger transactions in other enterprise-wide applications based on a transaction that originated in an ECM solution.

For example, on contract execution, the ECM solution can be configured to publish an event to an integration broker/ERP application, which can then use the Web Service in ECM to retrieve contract data and push the same to the ERP application.

■ **Business reporting and analytics related**: Last but not least, services-oriented integration also provides the capability to combine information from multiple applications (including an ECM solution) for business reporting and analysis. For example, running a report to view actual spend against contracts could invoke multiple Web Services: one that retrieves relevant contract meta-data from the ECM solution and another that retrieves corresponding purchase order and invoice data from the ERP application.

While the services-oriented integration approach is clearly the way of the future, it should be noted that this approach is also the most expensive one. Services-oriented integration usually necessitates changing source and target applications. In some cases, it may even necessitate the creation of a composite application, further adding to the cost of integration. Most leading ECM solution vendors have, therefore, recently focused significant development efforts on providing a set of standard out-of-the-box Web Services in order to enable services-oriented integration, should an organization choose to use this approach.

## 9.4.4 Portal-Oriented Integration Approach

A portal is a Web site or gateway that provides a broad array of services, resources, and tools such as search engines, e-mail, forums, and discussion groups. A portal-oriented integration provides a graphical user interface (GUI) in the form of a Web application through which multiple applications, internal and/or external to the organization, are aggregated and can be accessed. This enables workflow and collaboration based on a set of business events that may occur within one or more applications accessed via the portal. Portals (as shown in Figure 9.10) are examples of a best-in-class composite application interface, as they save users the trouble of having to learn and use multiple applications. Instead, users can focus on executing business processes via a single, simple, familiar, easy-to-use, role-based Web interface that enables information integration, business process integration, and people integration behind the scenes.

With regard to ECM solution integration, the portal-centered integration approach offers great opportunities and benefits. Access to an ECM solution can be embedded within an employee, supplier, or customer portal for employees, suppliers, and customers, respectively. Embedding an ECM solution within an

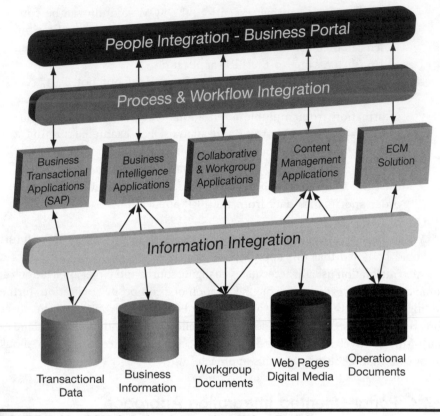

**FIGURE 9.10. ECM Solution Integration Using Portals**
(Adapted with permission from Colin White, Business Integration: Enterprise Portal Evaluation, October 2005, http://www.b-eye-network.com/view/1762.)

employee portal can provide a complete one-stop information shop for all employees. If access to other applications (such as an RFx application or ERP application) is also provided through such a portal, it is possible to integrate key transactions across applications, such as using supplier bid data to prepopulate a contract inside the ECM solution. Once contracts are executed within an ECM solution, it is possible to seamlessly export this data to an ERP application, where the end user can execute follow-on transactions, such as creating purchase orders against these contracts. Also, once goods receipts and invoices are posted against purchase orders in the ERP application, this data can be transferred to the ECM solution, enabling the end user to view the spend against a contract within the ECM solution.

One of the beauties of portal-oriented integration is that if single sign-on is set up, end users are not required to continually log on or off between applications. They also do not need to know which application to use for a particular transaction or to get specific information. Since a portal GUI can be customized to meet the specific requirements of a work role, it is possible to guide a user via hyperlinks from one application to the next automatically, depending on the user's requirements. The transition from one system to the next is not visible, and this keeps the end user focused on executing the business process, rather than logging on and logging off multiple systems to enter data manually or get data from one system to enter into another system.

Similar to integration with an employee portal, integration of an ECM solution with supplier or customer portals also offers an organization and its business partners many advantages. Once this integration is enabled, a business partner may be directed to a single portal where all information relevant to the supplier/customer/trading partner is made available. The business partner can access the ECM solution via the portal and review existing contracts with the organization. The supplier/customer may also collaborate on new contracts online, make edits to contracts presented by the organization, or add information such as rates, quantities, and materials/services offered. Since the entire contract process (including creation, negotiation, approval, and execution) occurs online in this scenario, this integration approach has great potential to improve the efficiency and effectiveness of an organization and its business partners in contract management.

It should be noted that any organization would likely implement a hybrid of two or more of the integration approaches described above. There is no one correct approach that applies to all organizations. When developing a strategy to integrate an ECM solution, each organization needs to carefully consider its current and future technology landscape, evaluate its functional requirements, and use one or more of the integration approaches described in this section to achieve its desired goals and objectives.

Having discussed the different integration approaches in detail in this section, we will now focus attention on describing a methodology that can be used to integrate ECM processes and systems within and beyond an organization.

## 9.5  TEN STEPS TO INTEGRATE ECM SOLUTIONS

It is often said that when a system is working at peak performance, the whole is greater than the sum of the parts. Nowhere is this saying more true than when applied to integration of ECM solutions. It is one thing to go through the individual steps of implementing an ECM solution—and to be sure, there are advantages to this level of effort, but it is quite another matter to thoroughly integrate an ECM solution, taking care at each step to ensure that the solution is designed to maximize return at every level within and beyond the organization. Given the level of effort and resources invested in an ECM solution, it is well worth being sure that the engine is hitting on all cylinders.

The challenge of integrating an ECM solution is not an uncommon one in modern business. CIOs across the world struggle with issues of integrating a spectrum of new applications with their current technology landscape, including ERP systems, BI systems, portals, content management systems, and other legacy systems. In a recent study, AMR Research found that large companies spent, on average, about $3 million on integration projects alone in 2005, while mid-size organizations invested approximately $1.1 million in similar types of products and services.

Great investment and effort are required to plan, schedule, and execute an integration project successfully, and there is significant opportunity for great benefits. It makes sense to discuss the steps that must be kept in mind to maximize the potential of success when integrating an ECM solution within—and between—the technology landscape of an organization and its business partners. By way of an overview, there are ten essential steps in integrating an ECM solution within a mid- to large-size organization (see Figure 9.11):

Step 1:   Understand business goals and objectives
Step 2:   Align resources and organization with enterprise integration strategy
Step 3:   Define scope of effort and outline metrics
Step 4:   Establish clear lines of ownership and accountability
Step 5:   Develop functional specifications
Step 6:   Develop technical specifications
Step 7:   Configure and construct
Step 8:   Test integration and perform cutover tasks
Step 9:   Deploy pilot integration
Step 10: Measure success and support continuous improvement

## 9.5.1 Step 1. Understand Business Goals and Objectives

Although integration with internal and external applications can have a substantial impact on the overall success of an enterprise, technology alone does

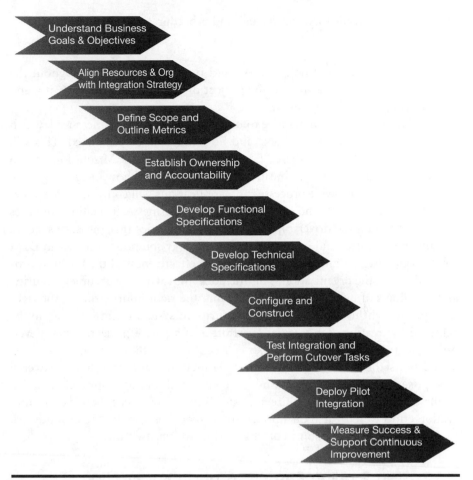

**FIGURE 9.11.  Ten Steps in ECM Solution Integration**

not add value. It is essential to understand business goals and objectives and to align the ECM solution integration initiative with them early in the project. Typical business goals and objectives that relate to integration of ECM solutions include:

- Increase visibility into contracts executed worldwide by all groups/ divisions/business units of the organization
- Improve accuracy and efficiency of the contract management processes by reducing total time required from contract authoring to contract execution

- Enhance regulatory, contractual, and procedural compliance throughout the organization

These business goals and objectives should be revisited often throughout the integration project to ensure that the project direction is still aligned with, and contributing to, achieving them.

In addition, it is also imperative to understand what will be measured, which metrics are critical to the business, and how they will be calculated. This will help the team understand where ECM processes and the ECM solution fit into the short-term and long-term business strategy, as well as how integrating these with other enterprise-wide processes and applications will contribute to achieving the company's goals and objectives. Meeting business expectations requires correctly defining the drivers, intent, scope, and metrics that measure success.

Integrating intra- and intercompany technology solutions (such as an ECM solution) focuses on improving efficiency and effectiveness of the business processes that run the organization. This includes improving the accuracy, security, and timeliness of information (i.e., providing the right information at the right time to the right users). This level of maturity in system integration cannot be achieved by treating each integration effort as a separate project. When developing an approach for integrating an ECM solution with other enterprise-wide applications, the technology landscape, the functional landscape, and the overall enterprise integration strategy must be considered and appropriately aligned. While this approach may require a greater initial investment than if each integration effort were treated on a project-by-project basis, it lays the groundwork to support the organization's current and future needs.

## 9.5.2  Step 2. Align Resources and Organization with Enterprise Integration Strategy

The goal of an enterprise integration strategy is to reduce the long-term TCO, to increase business agility, and to establish a competitive advantage by providing a mapping between business requirements and initiatives with enterprise-wide integration. Such a strategy delivers high ROI by maximizing reuse of existing systems, process models, and data definitions. A typical enterprise integration strategy involves extensive resource alignment and provides the following details.[*]

---

[*] Beth Gold-Bernstein and William Ruh, *Enterprise Integration: The Essential Guide to Integration Solutions,* Addison-Wesley, Boston, 2005.

### 9.5.2.1 Overview

This section typically indicates how the enterprise-wide integration strategy ties back to business strategy and initiatives. It presents the organization's current and to-be technology landscape as well as discusses any major constraints (for example, a legacy system's limitations or the need for high security due to regulatory requirements). The ECM solution integration approach should consider all such organization-wide constraints, initiatives, and requirements and should leverage any technology, knowledge, and expertise that exist in-house from past integration efforts.

### 9.5.2.2 Scope

The scope of a true enterprise integration strategy should be enterprise-wide. However, due to the significant amount of time, money, and effort that may have been invested in past technology solutions, an organization may choose to have different integration strategies at the business unit level or based on geography. The ECM solution integration approach should be aligned with this strategy in terms of scope for maximum ROI and long-term agility. This will ensure alignment in terms of strategy and deployment of data synchronization, legacy system integration, desktop integration, and business-to-business integration.

### 9.5.2.3 Stakeholders

The enterprise integration strategy typically identifies all key stakeholders in the organization who are involved in setting the direction, deploying technology solutions, ensuring that standards are adhered to, and maintaining enterprise infrastructure. These tasks are usually decentralized in most organizations, but without a common enterprise integration strategy, the cost of deploying and maintaining interfaces between applications can be very high. When an ECM solution integration approach and methodology are being developed, it is critical to ensure participation from these key stakeholders. They can ensure that the plan developed is in alignment with other business initiatives, policies, standards, and guidelines, as well as leverage any investment that the organization might have made in a central technology competence center or group.

### 9.5.2.4 Integration Strategies

The enterprise integration strategy typically defines best practices and provides guidelines for the following:

- Redundancy management strategy
- Skill set management strategy
- Reusability strategy
- Process-driven integration strategy
- Services-oriented architecture strategy
- Implementation strategy

The ECM solution integration effort should consider the skills and knowledge that exist within the organization, as well as leverage the procedures, guidelines, and experience that the organization may have developed while integrating other applications. Managing redundancy in technology and skills lowers the cost of ECM integration in the long run and helps maximize ROI. For example, if an organization has invested heavily in an enterprise application integration tool such as webMethods, it would be logical to integrate the ECM solution with other enterprise-wide applications that use webMethods as well. In addition, while the business-process-driven integration approach and the services-oriented architecture approach have the potential to deliver a very high ROI, true business value is only achieved when these strategies are implemented across functional areas, across geographies, and across organizations.

### 9.5.2.5 Standards

The standards section of an enterprise integration strategy is probably most useful when developing an approach and methodology for integrating an ECM solution into an organization's technology and process landscape. Standards reduce costs, increase reusability and business agility, prevent dependence on specific vendors or technologies, and therefore help preserve an organization's IT investments. An enterprise integration strategy typically defines the following standards for an organization:

- **Standard communication protocol and technology**: Most organizations have standardized on TCP/IP or other similar network protocols for integration between internal applications. When an ECM solution is being integrated with an ERP, SCM, SRM, CRM, portal, or BI application, an organization should choose its standard communication protocol/technology for this initiative as well. For business-to-business integration, most organizations have standardized on electronic data interchange and SOAP (Simple Object Access Protocol). Since most best-of-breed ECM solutions today are already

Web-enabled, many forward-thinking organizations choose SOAP for communicating with vendors over the Internet.

- **Standard application interface**: Until recently, software vendors developed and provided prepackaged (and popular) adapters for rapid integration deployment with other applications such as ERP, SCM, and CRM systems. Today, many forward-thinking organizations are choosing to create Web Service interfaces between applications in an attempt to develop a standards-based, services-oriented architecture. It is no surprise to note that most best-of-breed ECM solution vendors have recently added hundreds of prepackaged Web Services to transfer data to and from ECM solutions.

- **Standard message format**: While TCP/IP used to be the standard message format of choice, today XML (Extensible Markup Language) is taking over as the de facto message standard for both internal and external communications. XML has been embraced enthusiastically by all major IT solution vendors (including ECM solution vendors) and user groups. Unfortunately, not just one XML-based standard is emerging. There are many different ones—for different industry sectors and sometimes even within the same industry sector. A challenge that most organizations are facing today, and will continue to face over the next few years, is not only to integrate a wide array of applications but also to interface to multiple XML message formats.

- **Standard process model**: A process model enables organizations to retain and reuse business knowledge (agnostic of the technology solution), including the business process flow, business rules, internal control checkpoints, and metrics. A contract management process model should be developed prior to embarking on the journey of integrating the ECM solution within an organization. This model should follow the process modeling standards defined within the enterprise integration strategy. Such a process model enables organizations to manage and optimize ECM processes, integrate them with other business processes, and implement changes rapidly across the organization.

- **Standard for meta-data**: Data mapping between source and target applications in an interface is a tremendously time-consuming task. This involves identifying the data elements in each application that represent the same entity and defining data translation rules to convert data from the source system's format to that of the target system. For example, a vendor may be called vendor in one application, supplier in another application, and company in yet another application. Organizations that develop and maintain an enterprise-wide data dictionary that identifies all data elements and their mapping to each other save time, effort, and cost in the long term. Organizations have an opportunity to use this data dictionary when integrating an ECM solution with other applications and should make sure that the data elements from the ECM solution are appended to the enterprise data dictionary for use on future integration projects.

### 9.5.2.6 Risks

This section of the enterprise integration strategy defines potential risks to technology deployment and maintenance within the organization. It is essential to understand all risks associated with an ECM solution integration effort, which range from program-level risks to project and functional risks, those associated with resource allocation and business processes, and last but not least, technical risks. Factors influencing the potential severity of any given risk include the size and scope of the ECM solution integration initiative, the current state of contract life cycle management practices and data within the enterprise, the experience and skill sets of the project team, system integration partners and vendors, the depth and breadth of management's commitment to the effort, and the impact of other initiatives competing for limited time and resources. The process of risk management plays a vital role in ensuring that an ECM solution integration is successfully accomplished.

## 9.5.3 Step 3. Define Scope of Effort and Outline Metrics

The scope of the integration effort needs to be defined before any development work begins. This is to ensure that the efforts of all individuals involved are aligned and coordinated for success. It is also important to note that scope should be as detailed as is possible. For example, the scope of a typical buy-side ECM solution integration project would include the following:

1. **Process scope:** The following business processes are candidates for consideration:
   - RFx to procurement of stock materials
   - RFx to procurement of nonstock materials
   - RFx to procurement of specified services
   - RFx to procurement of unspecified services

- Contract creation and authoring (including use of contract and clause templates)
- Contract collaboration (internal and external)
- Contract approval (internally based on dollar value or any other criteria chosen)
- Contract execution (including recording of signatures and setting validity dates)
- Contract administration (including analysis, reporting, and termination/renewal)

2. **Applications scope:** The following technology solutions are typically candidates for consideration in a buy-side ECM solution integration project:
   - RFx/sourcing application
   - ERP application
   - SCM application
   - SRM/spend analysis/spend management application
   - Supplier portal
   - Employee portal
   - Data warehouse/BI application
   - Legacy applications

3. **Data scope:** As illustrated in Figure 9.12, the following data elements are typical candidates for consideration in a buy-side ECM solution integration project:
   - *Configuration data elements:* Company codes, purchasing organizations, plant codes, purchase groups, material groups, payment terms, shipping terms, incoterms, units of measure, currency codes, tax codes, and addresses
   - *Master data elements:* Materials, suppliers, users, purchasing information records, and source lists
   - *Transactional data elements:* Bids, contracts, purchase orders, goods receipt, and service entry sheets and invoice receipts

### 9.5.3.1 Key Metrics in Scope

Metrics employed in ECM solution integration initiatives are not much different than the ones employed in ECM solution implementation initiatives. Such metrics usually consist of averages, total cycles, and percentages of key criteria. Well-defined and documented metrics help set the direction, focus, and scope of an integration effort. Since an ECM solution integration initiative contributes to these metrics directly or indirectly, they can also be used to evaluate the success

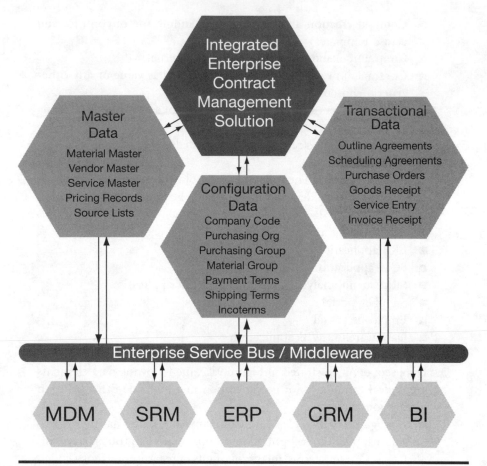

**FIGURE 9.12.** **Typical Data Elements in Scope for an ECM Solution Integration Initiative**

of the initiative, monitor the integration, and develop/deploy future enhancements for optimizing the processes further. For a detailed description of which metrics to use, how many metrics to use, and how to implement a metrics-based ECM solution integration or implementation initiative, refer to Chapter 10.

### 9.5.4  Step 4. Establish Clear Lines of Ownership and Accountability

The ultimate responsibility for an ECM solution within an organization may lie with one or more C-level executives. However, the day-to-day ownership and accountability for the ECM solution, as well as its integration with other enterprise-wide solutions, need to be established early in the process. This should include program and project management for the initial design, development, and implementation of the ECM solution and its integration, as well as ongoing management of the solution and its interfaces after go-live. Most organizations recognize the need for a team effort in initial implementation and integration of an ECM solution, but fail to anticipate (or accurately estimate) the effort associated with maintaining and sustaining the solution and its interfaces in the long term. If this accountability is not defined early in the deployment process, even a great ECM solution may fail to deliver the expected benefits and promised ROI. Planning for the maintenance and support required after deployment of an ECM solution and its interfaces should acknowledge the necessity of using functional and technical resources that work at a global, as well as local, level. Only when such a support structure is put in place proactively and supported by top management will an ECM solution deliver in accordance with the initial design principles and vision.

## 9.5.5  Step 5. Develop Functional Specifications

The content of a functional specification document is intended to provide the "what"—or the exact functional/business requirement. In the next step, a corresponding technical specification or configuration document is developed to document the "how"—how a specific functional or business requirement will be addressed. Some of the key sections in a functional specification document are:

- **Purpose of the interface**: Define the purpose or business requirements behind creating the interface.
- **Business process**: Describe the business process, along with the people, subprocesses, and technology involved. This section usually includes process flows along with roles/responsibilities and internal control checkpoints.
- **Source and target system**: For each interface, the source and target systems need to be identified. The source of configuration data and master data is usually an ERP application or SCM application, and the ECM solution is one of the target systems. Since contracts are created and executed inside the ECM solution, it is the default choice as the system of record for contracts and thus acts as the source system. The target system for contracts is usually an ERP application, SCM application, legacy system, data warehouse system, or a

supplier portal. For other transactional data elements (such as purchase orders, goods receipts, and invoices), the source system is usually the ERP application, and the ECM solution is a target system that aggregates and presents follow-on transactions against a contract, actual quantity received to date, quantity and amount invoiced to date, and performance of supplier against contractual terms and conditions.

- **Volume:** What is the volume of data (structured and/or unstructured) that will be exchanged? The volume of data that is expected to be transferred between the ECM solution and another enterprise-wide application is a key factor in determining how an interface will be built. For example, a vendor interface may be designed to transfer only changed/deleted vendor records from the source system to the ECM solution, while a purchasing group interface may be designed to transfer all records from the source system to the ECM solution. This is because, while a mid- to large-size organization usually has hundreds of thousands of vendor records, the number of purchasing group records usually is from just a handful to a few hundred.

- **Frequency and latency:** How quickly and how often are data to be transferred? For example, do data need to be exchanged in a synchronous manner or asynchronously? Consider, for example, the interfaces between an ERP application and the ECM solution for configuration data. Configuration data elements such as company code, purchasing organization, purchasing groups, and material groups are fairly static data elements. Interfaces that transfer configuration data elements are good candidates for batch processing, for example once a week. Transactional data elements (such as contracts, purchase orders, and goods receipts and invoices), on the other hand, are fairly dynamic in nature. These data elements are good candidates for real-time exchange via interfaces between the ECM solution and the ERP application. Real-time interfaces are ideal since they transfer data from the source system to the target system instantaneously. However, such interfaces are a big drain on the performance of any application or suite of applications. The need for real-time data integration always must be balanced with its impact on system performance. Master data elements (such as vendor master, material master, and pricing records) are not as static as configuration data elements and not as dynamic as transactional data elements. Thus, hourly or daily updates in batch from the system of record (such as SAP) to the ECM solution may be sufficient to meet business requirements. It is important to involve key business users in making this decision.

■ **Translation and transformation:** How complex is the data translation and/or transformation involved, and what business rules should be used? For example, the United States may be listed as USA in one application, US in another application, and U.S.A. in yet another application. Business rules can be coded in a middleware application that can translate the value of country code from US in the source application to USA in the target application. In addition, data transformation rules (such as transforming the customer master data object from the ERP application to a ship-to- or bill-to-address data object in the ECM solution) need to be clearly outlined in the functional specification.

■ **Security requirements:** Key security requirements around interfaces should be described in detail in the functional specification documents. Defining the user ID and user profile that should be used to post data in an ERP application, based on contract data pushed from an ECM solution, is an example of such a requirement.

■ **Events and/or schedule that trigger the interface:** As an example, when a user clicks on the "execute" button in order to execute a contract in the ECM solution, a contract-push interface should be executed to push the contract number and associated details from the ECM solution to an ERP application. When the contract is created successfully in the ERP application, it should trigger another push to the ECM solution that pushes the contract number from the ERP application to the ECM solution for cross-reference purposes. There may also be some interfaces that are not triggered by an event. For example, updates to vendors, materials, customers, and price records may be grouped together in a batch and moved from the source system to the ECM solution every hour or every two hours. It is important to define this schedule for every interface in its functional specification document, as the technical design of an interface could vary significantly based on such requirements.

■ **Selection criteria:** When a new vendor is created in the ERP application, for example, the vendor number, vendor address, and other relevant details may need to be pushed to the ECM solution. All vendor records that could be used to execute a contract in the future are good candidates to be pushed to the ECM solution. However, a vendor record set up in the ERP application for payment purposes only need not be pushed to the ECM solution. In this case, selection criteria should be established (using vendor account group or some other similar classification) so that the vendor interface moves only relevant records to the ECM solution.

- **Dependencies**: Predecessors and successors must be defined for each interface. For example, consider the scenario where the details of an executed contract are to be published from the ECM solution to all appropriate enterprise solutions, such as the ERP, SCM, SRM, CRM, master data management (MDM), and BI applications. In this case, before a contract can be pushed out to these applications, the master data (such as vendor and materials) needed to support the contract data must exist in the target systems. However, configuration data elements (such as company code, purchasing organization, and plant codes) are needed to support master data records. Therefore, interfaces responsible for creating and updating configuration data elements must be executed first, followed by the interfaces for master data, which in turn should be followed by the interfaces for transactional data. This sequence/interdependency should be systematically imposed and ensured or numerous errors may need to be manually resolved on a repeated basis.

  Another group of dependencies that deserves mention here relates to the status of data elements in different applications being integrated. For example, checks should be in place in the ECM solution to ensure that a contract is not executed against a vendor that may have been blocked or flagged for deletion in a source system due to quality issues, compliance issues, or other performance-related issues. Similarly, if an invoice is blocked in the ERP application, the corresponding contract in the ECM solution should not be updated with the actual invoiced quantity or value until the block is removed and the invoice is posted in the ERP system.

- **Accompanying changes**: All configuration changes, business process changes, manual tasks, and reports needed to support normal business operations once the ECM solution is integrated should be summarized, reviewed, and approved. End users and super-users may need formal training. Arrangements should be made to provide the training and tool set to help users succeed in their changed or new roles.

- **Exception/error handling and recovery/restart procedures**: The functional specification should define business requirements around exception and error processing, as well as around recovery and restart procedures. Such requirements need to be kept in mind during development so that maintenance of the ECM solution and its interfaces can be effective and efficient. It is critical to identify specific process flows for support, support roles, associated security profiles, training requirements, and the supporting documentation necessary to sustain and ensure high-quality technical and functional support.

- **Reporting requirements**: All ECM solution interface-related reporting requirements, such as total number of transactions, percentage of successful transactions, types of errors, and reasons for errors, should be identified. In addition, reports should be designed to clearly indicate the records created/updated, date and time when a record was created or updated, and any system success/error messages that were recorded in each transaction.

## 9.5.6  Step 6. Develop Technical Specifications

Technical specification documents build upon the functional specifications prepared in the previous step. These documents provide technical information to developers/programmers to either develop new or modify existing code, interfaces, adapters, and Web Services to fulfill the business requirements captured in the functional specifications. At a high level, these specifications must include the following:

- **Architecture design**: Key items to be included in this section are an architecture and component-level diagram, interface description, algorithm or pseudocode, restrictions/limitations (the external environment and/or infrastructure required for the interface to work as expected), performance issues (information on topics that may impact the run time performance, security, or accuracy of the interface), and any design constraints (attributes of overall software design that constrain the design of the interface).
- **Data design**: A description of all data structures, including internal (data structures that are passed among components of the ECM solution), global (data structures that are available to multiple applications within the technology architecture), and temporary (files created for interim use), should be included in this section.
- **Services design**: This section should include a detailed description of the services that should be invoked when a transaction is posted or some other similar business event occurs. Pseudocode should be provided to describe the logic as well as input data, expected results, and error handling.

- **User interface design:** This section should include a description of the impacts to user interface, by adding, for example, a new menu item, menu bar, tool bar, or a button to trigger an event that invokes a remote function call or a service.
- **Testing:** Test strategy and preliminary test case specification should be included in this section. Further detail should be provided relating to unit test cases, data and steps required to execute the test, and expected results, including performance expectations as well as error handling expectations.

## 9.5.7 Step 7. Configure and Construct

Defining the specifications of an ECM solution would be of little value without ensuring that the solution is completely and correctly configured and integrated in a manner that satisfies all levels of business requirements. The functional and technical specification documents described in the previous sections guide this configuration and construction process, a process which varies depending upon the particular approach and technology solutions used. In all cases however, configuration and construction should include the following tasks:

- Configuring or customizing the ECM solution selected
- Developing custom code, adapter, interface, or Web Service
- Documenting the configuration/customization changes made to the ECM solution as well as the logic that has been coded into the adapters and interfaces
- Conducting internal or unit tests

Documentation of configuration and construction is critical to guarantee the knowledge transfer of the integration from the implementation team to the support team. It should typically include:

- Lists of assumptions and prerequisites necessary to ensure execution of successful transactions using the configuration/construction
- List of mandatory, optional, and informational fields
- Appropriate values expected in different fields
- Dependencies between different fields
- Description of any new screens and/or reports designed
- Description of error messages, including what they mean and what actions should be taken to resolve corresponding errors
- User roles, profiles, and permission/authorization requirements

Unit testing—a continuous process throughout the interface construction process—involves testing a particular module of code with the goal of validating that the individual modules of the overall program are correct. For example, creating a material or updating an existing material in an ECM solution based on data derived from the ERP application is a unit test. Unit testing helps eliminate uncertainty in the modules themselves and can be used in a bottom-up testing approach. By first testing the component parts (i.e., the various interfaces or modules) and then testing the combined components, follow-on testing becomes much easier. This is discussed in the next section.

## 9.5.8 Step 8. Test Integration and Perform Cutover Tasks

The main objective of testing the integration developed between an ECM solution and other enterprise-wide applications is to ensure that the solution (i.e., adapter, Web Service, portal) developed meets the business requirements defined in the functional specification. A group of key stakeholders should be selected to:

- Identify defects as early as possible in the testing process
- Ensure that defects are fixed per the business requirements

In addition to ensuring a defect-free integrated ECM solution, testing should also address the following objectives:

- Validate that existing functionality in the ECM solution—and in the other enterprise applications that are being integrated—is not negatively impacted
- Validate the roles and responsibilities as well as the security profiles of all users who will be either directly or indirectly executing the interfaces, as well as those of users who will be maintaining the interfaces on an ongoing basis
- Validate the training material for both the deployment of the integration and the ongoing support after go-live
- Validate the dependencies, triggers, and performance estimates against the business requirements documented in the functional specification documents

A process-oriented testing approach is recommended to ensure that the ECM solution integration effort improves the contracting business processes by making them more efficient and effective. Test cycles, test cases, and test scripts should be developed based on the different business and technical requirements captured in the functional and technical specifications. At a high level, the process-oriented testing approach includes the following tasks:

- Define test requirements
- Define test cases per test requirement
- Define test script for each test case
- Define test data, expected results, and security profiles to be used per test script
- Execute test scripts
- Record and analyze test results
- Register test problems and issues
- Solve issues and reexecute scripts
- Assess test sign-off criteria

The following are the primary types of tests that must be performed to validate that an integrated ECM solution is defect-free.

### 9.5.8.1 Integration Testing

In integration testing, the individual interfaces are combined and tested as a group. Integration testing follows unit testing and precedes system testing. The purpose of integration testing is to verify the functional, performance, and reliability requirements placed on major design items. An example of an integration test would include testing the push of vendor data from the ERP application, testing the data mapping done by the middleware, and testing the creation of the corresponding vendor data in the ECM solution.

### 9.5.8.2 System Testing

System testing includes a series of tests conducted on a complete, integrated ECM solution to evaluate its compliance with specified functional and technical requirements. System testing takes as its input all of the integrated ECM solution components that have successfully passed integration testing, as well as the ECM solution itself integrated with any enterprise-wide hardware and software systems. The purpose of this testing is to detect any inconsistencies between the software solutions that are integrated or between any of the software solutions and the hardware.

It is a more limiting type of testing; it seeks to detect defects both within the ECM solution and also within the integrated set of technology solutions as a whole. For example, the process of creating, negotiating, approving, and executing a contract within an ECM solution is an example of a system test. At the same time, the process of entering a requisition, converting the requisition to a bid, converting the bid response to a contract, authoring a contract through to executing it, using a contract to create a purchase order and send it to the supplier, verifying goods receipt against the purchase order, and posting an invoice against the purchase order is also an example of a system test. In this case, business processes span multiple applications, and the goal of the test is to make sure that the configured solutions, processes, and interfaces work as desired and documented in the functional specifications.

### 9.5.8.3  Regression Testing

Regression testing involves reexecuting tests that have been previously run to ensure that configuration or code changes made to the ECM solution to enable integration with other applications have not had a negative impact on functionality that was already working. Experience has shown that reemergence of faults is fairly common in such efforts, due to the complexity involved in revision control, fixing code in multiple applications using multiple programming languages and database management systems, or repeating mistakes in rewriting a piece of code that were made in the previous version of the code. For example, let's assume that an organization maintains the DUNS number for all its suppliers in the vendor record of its ERP application. This field can then be added to the vendor interface that pushes vendor data from the ERP application to the ECM solution. However, such a change must be followed by regression testing of the interface to ensure that addition of a new field to the interface has not caused any new problems or recreated any errors that were originally fixed in the previous version of the interface. Regression testing is a best practice in ECM solution integration projects.

### 9.5.8.4  User Acceptance Testing

User acceptance testing (UAT) is a common testing cycle used in most IT implementation projects to obtain confirmation from a group of key stakeholders or subject matter experts that an object, interface, or functionality meets mutually agreed upon requirements. This step is of critical importance in ECM solution integration projects since it ensures that the flow of data and communications across multiple technology solutions is in place prior to going live. The focus of UAT is more on the flow of transactions executed rather than the technical processing aspects of the systems. It, therefore, involves testing the configuration of the ECM solution and other enterprise-wide solutions along with the security, reports, interfaces, conversions, enhancements, and forms that may have been added to enable the integration. UAT is a key tool for gaining buy-in from end users prior to rolling out a new system or an existing system with enhanced functionality such as an integrated ECM solution.

### 9.5.8.5 Performance Testing

Performance testing is the process of engaging in a carefully controlled process of measurement and analysis with the goal of ensuring that any application-level, database-level, operating-system-level, or network-level bottlenecks are eliminated and to set a baseline for future regression tests. Such testing within an ECM solution integration effort helps ensure prior to go-live that the re-sponse time from the designed interfaces is acceptable.

### 9.5.8.6 Load Testing

Load testing (also called volume testing) is the process of exercising the inte-grated set of technology solutions, including the ECM solution, by feeding them the largest tasks they can handle. An example of this is testing a mail server by triggering thousands of e-mail notifications from the ECM solution. The goal of load testing is to expose bugs that do not surface in cursory testing, such as memory management bugs, memory leaks, or buffer overflows, and to make sure that the interfaces developed meet the performance baseline established during performance testing.

### 9.5.8.7 Stress Testing

Stress testing (also called negative testing) attempts to break the system under test (i.e., the integrated ECM solution) by either overloading its resources or by taking away resources. The primary objective behind this type of testing is to ensure that the system fails and recovers gracefully. For example, if the network switches/routers shut down unexpectedly, if the connection to the database is lost, or if the number of concurrent users doubles unexpectedly, how does the integrated ECM solution react? Does the system just hang, does it freeze, or does it fail gracefully? Is it possible to recover the system from its last good state, and are meaningful error messages sent to the error log or connection log? Is the security of the system compromised due to the unexpected failure?

### 9.5.8.8 Cutover Tasks

Once all test cases have been successfully executed, cutover tasks can be initiated. A formal plan is sometimes needed to manage the transition from stand-alone to an integrated ECM solution. The primary objective behind developing such a cutover plan is to ensure that all tasks are performed in an organized manner, in the correct sequence, and result in minimal disruption to the production environments of the applications being integrated, including the ECM solution. Cutover tasks vary from one ECM integration initiative to the next, as these tasks depend on the ECM solution and the applications being integrated, the technology and integration approach used, the functionality and business processes that are being integrated, and the database systems and data elements involved. One of the key cutover tasks in ECM solution integration initiatives is to make a backup of the ECM solution and other applications involved in order to have a fast fallback option in case the transition does not go as planned.

## 9.5.9 Step 9. Deploy Pilot Integration

The process of integrating an ECM solution into the fabric of an organization is not a sprint to the finish line. It is a journey that, depending on the scope, availability of resources, and several other factors, could take a long time. It is, therefore, important to build short-term victories into the deployment plan of an ECM solution integration effort.

## 9.5.10 Step 10. Measure Success and Support Continuous Improvement

In the absence of the commitment and ability to measure key performance indicators critical to success of the initiative, there is literally no baseline against which to determine the value added by integrating an ECM solution in the organization. Far more than a requirement to fulfill minimum standards, measurement is crucial to the successful deployment of sound integration approaches and methodologies—it is an inherent component of an ECM solution integration effort. Moreover, without adequate measurement systems in place, further refinement of the ECM solution and its integration with other applications is virtually impossible; any suggested enhancements would, at best, be hunches.

Much like a compass without a needle, an ECM solution integration initiative without measurement is of little real use or value. Because of the critical role of metrics in ensuring success in ECM solution implementation and integration initiatives, this topic is dealt with separately in more detail in Chapter 10.

As the ECM solution integration process begins to bear fruit, gain momentum, and become part of the organizational technology and functional landscape, it will become possible for the organization to consolidate its progress, focus upon areas where true gains have been made, and refocus efforts on those areas yet to be addressed. For example, an organization can choose to implement integration between the ECM and other enterprise-wide applications only at the configuration and master data level initially. This scope can be expanded to include transactional data in the next phase, followed by integration with the BI application, single sign-on, e-mail system, and enterprise portal in yet another phase. Of course, the sequence of these phased rollouts can be different for different organizations, depending on organizational priorities. While some organizations may structure their ECM solution integration rollout based on data hierarchy, others may choose to do so by geographic regions (for example, first in North America, then in Europe, and so on), by organizational structure (for example, first at a business-unit level, then at a global level), or by organizational functional groups (for example, first integrate the ECM solution on the buy side, then on the sales side, then on the financial side, and so on).

Obviously, this level of dynamic adjustment in the ECM solution integration process is only possible when an organization employs a system of monitoring progress and rapidly adjusting its strategies, approaches, and resources to address areas of greatest need. In some respects, the stakes get higher as ECM solution integration approaches completion. Much time and effort have already been invested in the dynamically changing technology and functional landscape; therefore, even more is now expected. This is all the more reason why, as an ECM solution integration initiative approaches the initial vision, management must be even more responsive to change, more willing to assist those areas of the project in need, and more willing to solicit support from senior management and from the "boots on the ground." At this stage of ECM solution integration, it is crucial that the organizational engine be in top running condition, with as few unnecessary interdependencies as possible.

## 9.6 VISION OF A FULLY INTEGRATED ECM SOLUTION

Over the past few decades, virtually all large organizations have made substantial investments of time, money, and manpower in the deployment of enterprise technologies. The original intent behind the implementation and deployment of these technology solutions was to simplify, streamline, standardize, and enhance core business processes that support an organization, in order to dramatically improve productivity, enable real-time decision making, and ensure compliance. Outcomes have largely been favorable: line employees are more productive than ever, managers are equipped with real-time decision support tools, and compliance administrators are better able to navigate through the maze of legal, regulatory, and contractual obligations within their purview.

However, some key challenges remain. As the number of technology solutions deployed within an organization increases significantly, new requirements are placed on end users; for example:

- Mastering and implementing new applications on a day-to-day basis
- Understanding and using the delta functionality every time an application is upgraded
- Understanding how to enable integration between numerous disjointed applications
- Using new technology solutions to collaborate and communicate in as close to real time as is possible
- Remaining effective and efficient in one's "real" job while keeping up with the pace of technology advancements

Beyond these specific challenges and limitations, organizations involved in deploying new technology solutions invest significant time, effort, and resources in their implementation and support, yet they often realize only a fraction of the potential ROI originally envisioned. Part of the solution to this ROI dilemma may lie in the overall approach of implementation managers to new technology applications. Instead of viewing individual technology solutions as stopgaps to meet a specific need in an organization's technical landscape, perhaps the solution lies in looking at the functional and technical landscape of an organization in terms of its core end-to-end business processes. Perhaps the goal of maximizing ROI might better be accomplished if technology solution implementations enabled business processes end to end via seamlessly integrated technology solutions in a manner that promotes standardized and compliant business processes, efficiency, effectiveness and ease of use for the end user.

For example, a business-to-employee (B2E) portal might best be used to present an internal, role-based view to an employee. The B2E portal could provide a guided experience to end users, (e.g., a contract author), so that contracting processes are invoked, related tasks executed, and corresponding data moved in the correct and proper sequence, both in and between applications, permitting internal or external interface to an organization from a single user. With reference to ECM, this is possible only when an ECM solution is integrated with a B2E portal that is in turn integrated with the organization's ERP, SRM, CRM, MDM, finance, business warehouse, and other applications (see Figure 9.13). In such an environment, a contract author would log in to the enterprise portal daily and view all tasks assigned to him or her. If one of the tasks is to execute a contract based on a bid that was selected and saved in

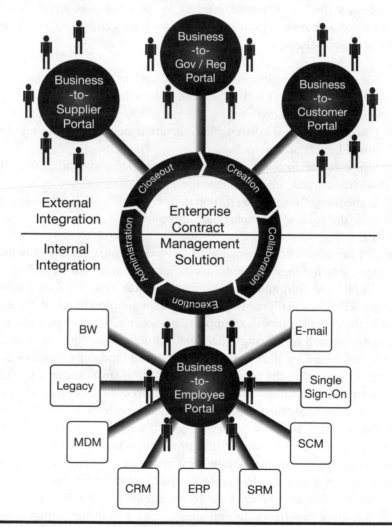

**FIGURE 9.13. Vision of a Fully Integrated ECM Solution**

the SRM application, the contract author should be able to access the bid and copy appropriate data from it into a new contract without switching applications. The B2E portal should provide a single interface to seamlessly integrated applications, including the ECM solution, so that routine tasks associated with contracting processes (such as executing a contract) should automatically trigger follow-on tasks or notifications within the ECM solution or in other applications (such as sending an e-mail notification to procurement personnel to inform them about the executed contract).

Similarly, a business-to-business (B2B) portal should be used by an organization to exchange information with suppliers during the RFx processes, collaborate with suppliers during contract authoring and negotiation steps, exchange information with suppliers regarding status of approval and execution of pertinent contracts, and monitor supplier performance against negotiated terms and conditions. An ECM solution could be integrated with a B2B portal (as shown in Figure 9.13), which could in turn be integrated with the organization's ERP, SRM, procurement, receiving, invoicing, and other similar applications. A contract author from the supplier's organization could then log in to the ECM solution via the B2B portal, retrieve contracts forwarded to him or her, make changes to clauses where appropriate, and enter comments and attach documents, if necessary. A contract author would also be able to retrieve all contracts executed by the supplier with the organization in the past and verify/validate that his or her organization's performance is recorded accurately within the system for future reference. Scanned copies of executed contracts and any related amendments would also be available to both parties through such an ECM solution integrated with a B2B portal.

The vision for integration of ECM solutions into the broader fabric of an extended enterprise also applies to an organization's relationship with its customers/consumers. In addition to providing a consumer with information about an enterprise's products, services, and organization, a business-to-consumer (B2C) portal could also be used to provide access to contracts executed with that consumer. In this manner, a customer could log in to the ECM solution via the B2C portal and collaborate with the organization's representatives during the contract authoring, collaboration, execution, and administration phases of the contract life cycle. All historical information associated with such contracts, including scanned copies of executed documents, file attachments, e-mail message trails, and bills due, as well as calls received by the customer service department, could be linked to such contracts and shared with the consumer as well as others when appropriate. This would require that the ECM solution be integrated with the B2C portal, which in turn would be integrated with the ERP, sales and distribution, warehouse management, accounts receivable, and business warehouse applications.

Last but not least, if an organization uses a business-to-government (B2G) portal, it should consider integrating its ECM solution to this portal as well. Such a portal could be used to publish critical information about an organization to appropriate government agencies, regulatory bodies, and even to organizations responsible for maintaining standards, such as ISO. For example, Sarbanes-Oxley Section 409 requires organizations to disclose to the public, on a *rapid* and *current* basis, any information concerning material changes in their financial condition or operations (which may include trend information, qualitative information, and graphical presentations) which may be deemed as useful to protect the investors or in the public interest. An ECM solution is best suited to address this and many other similar regulatory compliance requirements and therefore should be one of the technology solutions that is integrated with the B2G portal.

This vision of an ECM solution—fully integrated internally with other business processes and technology solutions via the B2E portal and integrated externally with suppliers via a B2B portal, with customers via a B2C portal, and with government, regulatory, and standards organizations via a B2G portal—is depicted in Figure 9.13. While there is no doubt that the journey to design, implement, deploy, and support a fully integrated ECM solution is extremely challenging, the benefits far outweigh the costs and the risks involved with such an initiative. ECM solutions—when integrated internally and externally—result in reduced costs, increased revenues, diminished financial and legal risk, improved working relationships, and averted misunderstandings for all organizations involved.

## 9.7 SUMMARY

As today's modern organizations face new and greater challenges to their survival and success, the need for fully integrated contract management systems becomes increasingly obvious. The point no longer needs to be debated that victory in today's modern business environment will go to the organization that can best conceive, craft, negotiate, administer, monitor, and enforce its legal agreements—both internally and externally. Ultimately, the challenge of ECM is not about the component parts of a process; it is not about the nuts and bolts as much as it is about the whole machine—the entire organization, functioning as a coherent, integrated unit. Logically, if contracts provide the structural and informational connectivity between the component parts of an organization, the efficiency, effectiveness, and agility of contract integration becomes a key element in the ultimate benefit an enterprise offers to its customers, partners, employees, and stakeholders.

In the opinion of this author, the importance of ECM solution integration cannot be stressed enough. It lies at the core of the entire ECM solution implementation process and as such deserves the attention devoted to it in this chapter. Integration must be viewed from the outset of ECM solution implementation—at virtually every stage of the contract life cycle, from conception and creation to closeout and analysis. Only then will the forces that confront and challenge the integrity and efficacy of the contract life cycle be sufficiently addressed to ensure a truly functional ECM application.

The many benefits of an ECM solution—whether enhanced visibility of contracts, increased revenue, decreased costs, or streamlined processes—remain concepts or words on paper unless the ECM solution is truly integrated within, throughout, and beyond the organization. In short, there is a fundamental business imperative for an integrated ECM solution, as opposed to a technology solution that is viewed as a stand-alone or stopgap application. Integrating an ECM solution offers an organization the opportunity to maximize its ROI by fulfilling its role as an extended enterprise, one with optimal agility and capacity to operate in a global and technologically dynamic environment. Full use of outsourcing opportunities exists for an organization with an integrated ECM solution, and such an organization has the best possible opportunity to proactively conduct its affairs in this era of compliance.

The business case for ECM solution integration is compelling on both the revenue and cost side of the equation. While there are admitted risks and costs associated with ECM solution integration, they are quantifiable, capable of being mitigated, and far outweighed by the numerous and lasting benefits of full-scale integration. In point of fact, the depth of benefits of a well-designed ECM solution integration reaches far beyond the surface elements of cost savings, speed, and accuracy—the benefits have actually been proven to have a profound influence on the components of latency at critical stages in the life cycle of virtually all major business decisions within an organization. The net result of this benefit is to dramatically accelerate the value realization of an organization's business decisions as they migrate to tangible relationships and transactions in the world of commerce.

Once the decision has been made to integrate an ECM solution, the specific approach to such a process deserves careful consideration. The four major heuristic approaches—information oriented, business process oriented, services oriented, and portal oriented—offer a spectrum of opportunities and challenges that should be considered at the outset of this initiative. Regardless of the approach taken in ECM solution integration, there are ten major steps in the process, beginning with a comprehensive understanding of a company's overall business goals and objectives. Alignment of resources, definition of scope and effort, and outlining of metrics comprise the next steps in the process, followed by establishing clear lines of ownership and authority on the part of integration team members, development of specifications, and actual configuration of the integration program. Lastly, testing, deployment, and measurement complete the ten major steps in the process.

Certainly, integration of an ECM solution is a major undertaking for any organization, one which increases with the size and complexity of the subject organization itself. But, in like manner, the potential benefits also increase, and it is the conclusion of this author that mid- to large-size enterprises are more than well advised to integrate their ECM solutions and to treat the integration process as one that deserves its own priorities, resources, plan, and team.

Once an organization has successfully integrated its ECM solution—and done so with the long-range view in mind, it is positioned to achieve maximum benefits from its current and future contractual relationships. Ultimately, a fully integrated ECM solution will permit a seamless flow of information and resources that are aligned with the mission and plans of management and designed to accrue benefits for the organization's present and future stakeholders.

# METRICS:
# THE CATALYST TO
# ACHIEVE AND
# MAINTAIN SUCCESS

## IN THIS CHAPTER:

- Metrics
- Metrics in ECM

## 10.1 OVERVIEW

No single aspect in an Enterprise Contract Management (ECM) solution implementation is more critical than ensuring that desired results and benefits are
obtained and are being sustained. Every stage preceding this step is potentially
of no value to a contracting organization unless there is an objective system for
measuring the success of the ECM solution implementation. This success is
measured in terms of the effect of the solution on the enhancement of revenues,
minimization of costs, and risk reduction.

This chapter provides some key metrics that can be used by an organization
before, during, and after ECM solution implementations. However, before embarking on this discussion, it is worthwhile to provide background information
for the following key questions:

- What are metrics?
- Which metrics work best?
- How many metrics should be used?
- When should these metrics be used?
- How can a metrics-based program be implemented?

## 10.2  METRICS

### 10.2.1  Defining Metrics

A metric is an auditable and verifiable measurement made over a specific time period that communicates vital information about a process or an activity. Metrics can be specialized (so that they cannot be benchmarked or interpreted outside a specific organization, division, or group) or generic (so that they can be benchmarked against or aggregated across divisions, groups, business units, etc.). They are typically used to indicate progress or achievement.

### 10.2.2  Choosing Metrics

The concept of metrics is compelling, yet many struggle to identify and use metrics consistently and effectively. This is because the process of defining what to measure, how to measure it, and how to report it is daunting. Metrics can be qualitative or quantitative, diagnostic or predictive, and financial or behavioral. The selection of the right type, number, and combination of metrics is a fundamental step of critical importance in setting up a successful ECM system via the implementation of an ECM solution. Metrics should be SMART—that is, **S**pecific, **M**easurable, **A**chievable, **R**elevant, and **T**imed. In addition, some of the other key attributes of the metrics selected should be as follows:

- Metrics should be linked to an organization's vision, values, and key business drivers.
- It is better to focus on fewer but more vital metrics rather than more but trivial metrics.
- Metrics should be selected so as to address the needs of all, internal as well as external, stakeholders.
- Metrics should flow down to all levels within an organization and should be consistent.
- Metrics should focus on the past, present, and future.

- Multiple metrics can be combined into a single metric to give a better overall assessment of performance.
- Metrics should be continuously monitored, analyzed, and adjusted when required as the business environment and/or strategies change.
- Baseline, goals, and targets should be established based on research rather than arbitrary numbers.

Chosen well, these metrics can lend visibility to and control over the entire life cycle of a business process and can deliver value to the stakeholders and customers of the organization.

## 10.2.3  Implementing a Metrics-Based Program

Establishing a system of metrics for use in any business process improvement initiative, such as an ECM improvement initiative within an organization, is as important to the overall process and outcomes as the creation of any system of weights and measures. Such a system, once in place, serves as the common language that all parties use to design, measure, assess, and refine the business processes and systems in question. When establishing metrics at the outset of such a program, the following questions should be asked:

- What are the key metrics for this process?
- Are these metrics valid?
- Are these metrics reliable?
- Does everyone involved understand these metrics?
- Are adequate and accurate data available?
- What is the baseline for each metric?
- What is the goal for each metric?

Beyond the quantitative aspects of the metrics themselves, there are underlying guiding principles that should be adhered to. These principles form the underpinning for the values that are being employed; much like an underlying theme to a musical composition or its rhythm, such principles give the individual notes their context. For each metric, serious consideration should be given to consistency, ease of communication, and flexibility of use. Basic guidelines that should be employed in setting up a metrics-based program are as follows:

- Start with the customers.
- Establish key and consistent measures.

- Determine baselines.
- Benchmark processes.
- Set goals.
- Involve everyone using a top-down as well as a bottom-up approach.
- Represent metrics visually.
- Focus on a small set of key but critical metrics.
- Establish a process to interpret results and take prompt action where required.

## 10.3 METRICS IN ECM

As mentioned earlier, a combination of metrics and subjective surveys is essential in measuring the results of ECM implementation, including the value added to the core contracting group, to business functions such as procurement and sales, and to the organization as a whole. By defining, quantifying, and measuring key elements in each of these areas, coupled with subjective surveys to learn the "human effect," an ECM solution can routinely be evaluated for its value to the organization.

### 10.3.1 Adding Value to the Contracting Group

At the heart of the value of an ECM solution is its daily use in the hands of the organization's contracting professionals. Here is where "the rubber meets the road"—there are no indirect risks or impacts here, but instead either the clear realization of tangible benefits from a successful project or the headaches and costs of a suboptimal implementation. Nowhere are objective measures of the effectiveness of an ECM solution more critical than in the contracting group. Consequently, a number of metrics could be employed with systematic discipline in monitoring the results of the implementation, including:

- Average number of active contracts managed per contracting professional
- Average number of new contracts executed per contracting professional
- Average number of amendments executed per contracting professional
- Average time to author a new contract
- Average time to negotiate a contract
- Average time to get approval internally to execute a contract
- Average time to execute a contract

- Total cycle time from contract creation to contract execution
- Percentage of contracts that have nonstandard terms or language
- Percentage of nonstandard contracts that were not formally approved
- Percentage of contracts that have penalties associated with non-compliance
- Percentage of contracts that have auto-renewal clauses
- Percentage of activities missed on contracts that have auto-renewal clauses
- Percentage of contracts that are based on standard and approved contract templates
- Percentage of contractual obligations that are fulfilled per the terms of the contract

In addition to the above objective measures of the effectiveness of an ECM solution, there are several subjective measures that can significantly enhance the assessment, including surveying contract authors, approving authorities, and administrators regarding their assessment of the efficiency, user friendliness, and accessibility of contracts with the newly implemented solution.

## 10.3.2  Adding Value to Business Functions

As the contracting process moves from authoring and approval and begins to impact the sourcing and procurement functions, there are a number of important measures of effectiveness that should be employed, including the following objective metrics:

- Percentage of the total spend under contracts
- Percentage of the total spend under contracts by vendor, by region, by commodity, etc.
- Percentage of the contracted spend that was approved
- Percentage of the contracted spend that was approved by vendor, by region, by commodity, etc.
- Average time from initiation of negotiations to execution of a contract with a supplier
- Number of suppliers with which one or more contracts exist

In addition, and as with the contracting group, sourcing and procurement staff and management should be surveyed regarding the efficiency of the contract life cycle management processes and ECM solutions, both within the organization (e.g., buyers, procurement managers, commodity managers) and beyond, including interactions with vendors, intermediaries, and regulatory entities.

## 10.3.3  Adding Value to the Organization as a Whole

Ultimately, the entire organization should benefit from a successful ECM implementation. It is incumbent upon the ECM implementation manager to anticipate the method by which such organization-wide impact might be gauged. Logical metrics at the organizational level include:

- **Reduction of costs**
  - ☐ Total spend over a specific period of time
  - ☐ Total spend against contracts over a specific period of time
  - ☐ Percentage of spend against percentage of partners (using Pareto analysis) over a specific period of time
- **Reduction of risks**
  - ☐ Number of contractual litigations that were brought against the organization over a specific period of time
  - ☐ Number of violations of applicable local, national, or global regulations over a specific period of time
  - ☐ Number and severity of issues identified in audits over a specific period of time
- **Improve efficiency**
  - ☐ Average cycle time for the entire supply chain (i.e., make/buy to sell)

Ideally, key members of the organization's major divisions should be queried regarding the impact of ECM implementation on their operations and on their perception of the organization's overall operations. At the very least, this process should include participation from operations, legal, finance, risk management, audit, human resources, and regulatory affairs.

It is obvious that several metrics, though listed as relevant for one group or level, are critical to multiple groups and levels of an organization. Also depending on the organization, some measures are more important than others. Therefore, each organization should develop a "balanced scorecard" by applying appropriate weights to different performance measures. This will enable specific calculation of an overall performance score for the effectiveness of the ECM solution in reducing costs, improving efficiency, enhancing visibility, and reducing risks.

In order to ensure that an organization is deriving good value from its ECM processes and systems, an ongoing process should be established that does the following:

- Defines what the "critical-to-success" factors are and specifies how they will be measured
- Establishes specific metrics based upon business requirements and organizational goals
- Performs regular post-implementation audits
- Analyzes the performance of the contracting group, procurement and sourcing group, and the organization as a whole on a regular basis
- Creates an environment for continuous improvement and control

This ongoing process can be established within a larger Six Sigma initiative as described in Chapter 6. In situations where an organization does not use Six Sigma principles to guide business process and system improvement initiatives, the ongoing process described above should be established within the ECM solution implementation effort or within the ECM improvement initiative, if one exists.

It should be noted that as an organization gains higher ECM maturity levels via implementation of an ECM solution and adoption of ECM best practices, its capabilities—and therefore its business requirements and focus—will change over time. Therefore, metrics that were identified as key before an ECM solution implementation may not be as critical to the organization post-ECM solution implementation. This may occur due to many factors, such as elimination of manual tasks due to automation offered by the ECM solution, changes to roles (new roles may be added or existing roles may be assigned different permissions within the ECM solution), etc. Thus the set of metrics selected should be reviewed often to ensure alignment between the metrics and the organization's current goals, objectives, and strategy.

## 10.4  SUMMARY

For any organization striving to achieve excellence in ECM processes and systems, robust metrics are critical. Good metrics provide vital information about the health of a process or an activity. When properly selected, measured, analyzed, and reported, metrics can help in the design and building of a comprehensive and dynamic ECM system for any organization. However, structuring and sustaining such a system requires a comprehensive, honest, and routine evaluation of the current ECM maturity level of the organization, as well as commitment to collecting the data and disseminating the metrics to those who can truly act upon them. In the next and final chapter of this book, key success factors and lessons learned from past ECM solution implementations will be presented, along with suggestions for sustaining excellence in ECM systems and processes after an ECM solution implementation.

# SUSTAINING EXCELLENCE BEYOND THE IMPLEMENTATION

## IN THIS CHAPTER:

- Top Ten Success Factors and Pitfalls in ECM Solution Implementations
- Sustaining Success Beyond Implementation

## 11.1 OVERVIEW

So far in this book, we have discussed in detail the current state of Enterprise Contract Management (ECM) and the common challenges faced by contracting professionals in managing the thousands of contracts that form the foundation of all business-to-business relationships and transactions in today's business environment. Information was presented about new and powerful technologies called ECM solutions, which have been designed and developed specifically to assist contracting professionals across industry sectors and geographies in managing all phases in the life cycle of contracts. The highly complex topics of the relationship between ECM and compliance management and the ECM Maturity Model were discussed, as they are of critical importance to understanding the context of ECM solutions before embarking on the initiative to install, implement, and roll out a solution across an enterprise.

Different topics related to implementing and integrating an ECM solution, within and beyond an organization, were then presented. Tried, tested, and proven implementation methodologies, based on the author's experience in implementing ECM solutions in over twenty-five organizations, were presented, along with change management and risk management considerations. In this final chapter of the book, the top ten success factors and pitfalls observed in past ECM implementations are summarized, and the book closes with a discussion of how to sustain success and continuous improvement in ECM.

## 11.2 TOP TEN SUCCESS FACTORS AND PITFALLS IN ECM SOLUTION IMPLEMENTATIONS

Similar to most technology solution implementations, an ECM solution implementation presents challenges in project management, change management, and risk management. Most of these challenges are not unique to ECM solution implementations. For example, lack of alignment with business strategy and goals, lack of end-user involvement during the solution design and configuration, lack of communication from the top down or the bottom up, etc. are challenges that have been experienced in technology projects for the last several decades. However, since an ECM solution exerts its influence directly, or indirectly, on almost all functional groups within an organization, the process of implementing an ECM solution presents a few unique project management and change management challenges, which are not typically observed in technology projects of similar size and effort.

As was discussed in earlier chapters of this book, ECM solutions are fairly new. These best-of-breed solutions did not exist in the twentieth century. Most ECM solution vendors are still adding new functionality at a rapid pace, and the market has not matured completely. Implementation of such new technology solutions presents some unique challenges, such as the lack of a good knowledge base, lack of experienced consultants, and a lack of standard training and certification. It is, therefore, critical for the success of an ECM solution implementation that senior managers, project managers, contract administrators, and everyone else involved in the initiative understand the key success factors and pitfalls listed in Table 11.1.

## 11.3 SUSTAINING SUCCESS BEYOND IMPLEMENTATION

In the past, delivery of a project on time and under budget was used as the key measure of success of a project. However, this narrow view often disregards the critical aspect of the quality of the results and the ability of an organization to sustain the changes implemented by the project. Many organizations have unsuccessfully treated an ECM solution implementation as a project with a finite start and finish. Key resources are put together on the team tasked with implementation of the ECM solution, and at the end of the implementation, these resources are reassigned to their old jobs. Such organizations fail to capitalize on the knowledge and experience gained by these key resources and lose the momentum which helped them successfully implement the ECM solution in the first place. Other organizations utilize Six Sigma methodology during the implementation process, but do not retain the project team's resources past the project finish to drive continuous improvement via the Six Sigma DMAIC approach described in Chapter 6 of this book. In this final section, therefore, some tips are presented for organizations to sustain excellence beyond their initial ECM solution implementation.

A successful ECM solution implementation is one that brings about sustained change within the ECM process and drives a ripple effect of continuous improvement throughout all aspects of the organization. However, sustaining excellence beyond the initial implementation does not occur on its own. Suffice it to say that once an ECM solution has been implemented, there are a number of key points to bear in mind—"maintenance tips," as a mechanic might term them—to ensure that the long-term benefits of the ECM solution are fully realized. The following are a few key points:

1. **After initial implementation**: Be on guard against complacency. Take proactive steps to be sure that DMAIC is a continuous cycle, focusing on *continuous improvement, continuous change,* and *continuous learning.* Stay close to the metrics and related reports to be sure the system is performing as expected and being adopted as planned. Reach beyond the ECM solution itself and integrate it with other company-wide applications to keep improving efficiency and effectiveness, adding value at each stage in the user experience. Continuously improve the accuracy and quality of your incoming and outgoing data.

2. **Retain the capability**: Establish and support appropriate control measures to ensure sustained levels of performance. Monitor performance with discipline, and communicate results objectively and routinely. Keep watch for variations, errors, and unpredicted outcomes, and address and deal with them using a Six Sigma team approach to sustain the success that has been achieved to date.

3. **Keep the customers in mind and involved**: Never take your eye off of the customer. To the contrary, encourage customer input, and

**TABLE 11.1. Top Ten Success Factors and Pitfalls in ECM Implementations**

| No. | Success Factor | Pitfall | Observations |
|---|---|---|---|
| 1 | ECM implementation effort should be aligned with organization's strategy, priorities, and goals and with other enterprise initiatives | Program mentality and technology road map do not exist; also, ECM implementation is not aligned with organization's strategy and goals | Whether the ultimate goal is higher customer satisfaction (in the case of sales contracts), effective supplier relationship management (in the case of procurement contracts), or better compliance and risk management, alignment of ECM solution implementation and its integration with other applications within an organization and with the organization's business strategies, priorities, and goals are a must. This is critical for effective change management, buy-in from end users of the solution, and sustaining excellence in ECM process management. It is also important to view the ECM solution implementation initiative as a part of overall governance, risk management, and compliance management strategy, as this helps in minimizing the total cost of ownership, maximizing the ROI, and leveraging technology, skills, knowledge, and expertise already existing within the organization. |
| 2 | Strong partnership between business and IT exists and forms the foundation of the ECM implementation initiative | ECM solution implementation initiative is viewed as a primarily technology-driven project with little to no participation needed from functional groups | An ECM solution, by its very nature, influences many groups, divisions, and organizational strata within an organization. Virtually anywhere the contracts in question have potential impact is fair game for an ECM solution to exert its effect. Thus, the real users of an ECM solution are spread out across an organization. These are the users who work in the system on a daily basis and understand the shortcomings of the application. These users know what data they have to pull on a routine basis from which system and reenter into the ECM solution or vice versa. Therefore, their input should be sought proactively to define and confirm the scope of ECM solution implementation and its integration within and beyond the organization. A representative group of these users should be involved in key decisions throughout the project and especially in user acceptance testing. It is critical to obtain buy-in from these business users or else no amount of training at the end of the project will overcome the obstacle of users not accepting or not using the system as intended. Many IT projects have failed due to the general perception of the end users that the project was driven by the IT group and shoved down the throats of the business users. |

| 3 | Top-down as well as grass roots support is gathered in the initial phases of the initiative | Either the top-down support or the grass roots support, or both, is missing | An ECM solution implementation is as much a change management initiative as it is a software implementation effort. Therefore, an initiative of this magnitude is successful only when an organization's leadership is passionate and committed to excellence and fully willing to change in order to achieve excellence. Leaders should challenge the processes and scope of the implementation effort at all levels, inspiring others with a shared vision. They should establish goals at the highest levels within the organization, empowering others to act and serving as role models while offering encouragement to stay the course.<br><br>At the same time, the real users of an ECM application are the people in the purchasing, maintenance, operations, customer service, human resources, finance, and accounting departments who need access to contracts and related data on a daily basis. It is critical to seek their buy-in up front in such an initiative that is bound to impact their day-to-day functions. |
| 4 | Resources used have domain expertise and a clear understanding of business processes, objectives, and technical objectives | The team composition lacks resources with an understanding of the underlying processes and/or is inexperienced in implementing the ECM solution | For the newly initiated, ECM solution implementation and its integration with internal and external applications can seem like a daunting task, one that requires an experienced guide and partner in the process. No single decision in the implementation process can have a greater impact than the ECM consulting partner chosen for this purpose. The right consulting partner not only should have a proven track record when it comes to standard ECM implementation, but also should be able to demonstrate knowledge of how to handle the unexpected events that will certainly arise and potentially derail the process. The ECM consulting partner should offer ample evidence of having implemented and integrated ECM solutions with a variety of back-end systems, relevant and current training, certification, and expertise at all levels in the ECM processes, as well as related business processes, from the implications of reengineering to the impact on supplier relationships. The ECM consulting partner should complement the skill sets of the internal implementation team, from planning to creation of the blueprint to final realization of the implemented ECM solution and post-go-live support. |

**TABLE 11.1.** Top Ten Success Factors and Pitfalls in ECM Implementations (continued)

| No. | Success Factor | Pitfall | Observations |
|---|---|---|---|
| 5 | Business-process-driven implementation approach is used | A tactical approach to implementation is used; technology solutions are implemented and integrated on a one-by-one basis, with the primary focus being integration at the data level | As described in Chapter 9, business-process-driven implementation and integration provides organizations with the ability to interact with any number of systems, inside or outside the organization, by integrating entire business processes both within and between enterprises. Thus, business-process-driven implementation and integration is a holistic approach toward implementing and integrating a technology solution such as an ECM solution. In addition to its focus on enabling efficient and effective business processes, it takes into account meta-data, technology platforms, and the people involved in these business processes. It therefore provides another complete layer on the stack, over and above more traditional application integration approaches such as the information-oriented and services-oriented approaches.<br><br>This is not to say that the other integration approaches should never be used. There are situations when other approaches may be just as useful/effective. However, the approach that best meets the requirements of an ECM solution integration initiative is the business-process-driven approach. This approach should lay the foundation on which the integration design is built, and other integration approaches should be used as and where appropriate. |
| 6 | A proven implementation and integration methodology is used to drive the different phases of the initiative | No methodology is used; at the end or near the end of each task, the team decides what is most appropriate to do next | A methodology is a structured set of principles, practices, and procedures for effective and efficient project management, including appropriate documentation and control mechanisms for the organization and management of an initiative such as an ECM solution implementation and its integration within, and beyond, the organization. If no specific methodology is used for each phase of the project, critical steps, dependencies between tasks, and associated documentation may be missed, which can have serious consequences in subsequent steps. This usually results in significant rework, which consumes resources and wastes precious time, effort, and momentum on the project. |

| # | Factor | Symptom | Discussion |
|---|--------|---------|------------|
| 7 | The problem statement/scope is well defined | Scope of the ECM implementation initiative is either too narrow or too wide | If the scope of the ECM implementation initiative has not been appropriately assessed, it can lead to either over- or underutilizing the team and its resources. Moreover, results may be out of sync with expectations. If the scope of the project is too small, for example, the organization may not see savings that are significant. If the scope is too wide, the project is doomed to fail from the beginning. |
| 8 | The ECM solution integration initiative is driven by metrics at every phase/decision point | Metrics are either not used or used inconsistently; when they are used, the results cannot be trusted | In the words of W. Edwards Deming, "In God we trust; all others, must bring data!" Data represent the ultimate level playing field in terms of ECM solution integration implementation. Agreed-upon metrics applied to objective results enable the capture, tracking, analysis, and explanation of results that can point toward true and lasting improvements in the process under investigation. Obviously, care must be taken not to rely on data for its own sake, and precautions must be taken to ensure that there is neither deliberate not inadvertent skewing of data. Solid adherence to the principles of quantitative inquiry and experimental design is essential; this is, in many respects, a process of science tempered by art and not vice versa. |
| 9 | Clear lines of responsibility and accountability beyond initial rollout are established early in the project | No clear definition of who is responsible and who is accountable for the ECM solution being implemented, both during the project and after go-live | As mentioned earlier, the ultimate responsibility for the ECM solution may lie with one or more C-level executives. However, the day-to-day ownership and accountability for the ECM solution, as well as its integration with other enterprise-wide solutions, need to be established early in the process. Most organizations fail to anticipate (or accurately estimate) the effort associated with maintaining and sustaining the solution and its interfaces in the long term. If this accountability is not defined early in the deployment process, even the best ECM solution may fail to deliver the expected benefits and promised ROI. Only when a detailed integration design, good integration development, and thorough testing effort are supplemented with a strong support structure will an ECM solution deliver in accordance with its initial vision, goals, and expectations. |

**TABLE 11.1. Top Ten Success Factors and Pitfalls in ECM Implementations (continued)**

| No. | Success Factor | Pitfall | Observations |
|---|---|---|---|
| 10 | Detailed training and knowledge transfer plan is developed and executed | Training of support personnel and knowledge transfer from project team members are afterthoughts | Training improves staff performance and makes an organization more productive and competitive. It is critical to look ahead during the ECM implementation development phases and identify specific training requirements. Developing a training plan and executing it correctly are of utmost importance in ensuring that the technology solution deployed as part of the ECM solution improvement initiative will be successfully supported and sustained in the long run. Such training should include not only details of the functionality of the application, what interfaces have been developed, what they are designed to accomplish, and how they work, but also how to troubleshoot when issues arise.<br><br>It is said that "a little learning is a dangerous thing," but it might also be argued that "more knowledge is not always better." Expediency in learning and in application is the key. Train the right people at the right time and on the right topics! |

obtain frank and constructive complaints, criticisms, and suggestions. Use surveys, focus groups, and similar tools to continuously gain insight into your customers' expectations, needs, and reactions to changes in your processes.

4. **Make the most of what you know**: Take full advantage of your growing knowledge base, and transfer relevant data and conclusions to team members and end users as appropriate and constructive for continued progress. Provide ongoing coaching, training, e-learning, and systems training. Create and maintain a database of lessons learned. Encourage tips and tricks; use frequently asked questions and internal feedback loops. Share successes rapidly and be generous with recognition and praise when due.

5. **Vision and leadership**: Maintain continuity of leadership and vision beyond the project's completion date. Instill a culture of excellence.

6. **Infrastructure, reinforcement, and control**: Ensure that you have created and support an architecture for success, to reinforce the depth and breadth of the Six Sigma commitment. Maintain the involvement of senior management, instilling across the enterprise the ECM goals and strategies that have been implemented. Host quarterly reviews with senior management, and identify actual and projected benefits, savings, and mitigated risks. Fully use the metrics that have been created to measure and monitor the project well beyond its launch date.

7. **Organizational culture**: Recognize that the success of ECM solution implementation is neither static nor strictly a technological phenomenon—it is largely based in the culture of the organization in which it functions. By embracing this cultural dimension, it is possible to utilize communications, training, reward, and recognition to further solidify the role that an ECM solution implementation plays in an organization's long-term success.

8. **Expanding ECM beyond the organization**: Actively involve suppliers, customers, outsourcing partners, and distributors in the ECM solution implementation and its subsequent daily use in the organization. Build bridges of language, metrics, and reporting systems that promote shared goals and attitudes between and among individuals, teams, and divisions throughout the value chain.

## 11.4  SUMMARY

In today's highly competitive and global business environment, ECM solutions have emerged as a powerful new tool in the arsenal of top management, offering enhanced negotiating and pricing perspectives, superior visibility and compliance controls, and an overall increase in competitiveness both within and beyond the organization. However, the prospect of implementing an ECM solution can be daunting. It is understandable that a number of issues, concerns, and risks arise during an ECM solution implementation. Through a combination of sound planning, careful team building, good consultative support, clear understanding of key success factors as well as pitfalls to avoid, and periodic evaluation of value added, the process of ECM solution implementation can be achieved with minimal risk and disruption to operations and a near-seamless conversion to superior control over this critical area of informational management systems.

Last, but not least, steps must be taken to ensure that gains made during an ECM solution implementation will be sustained within and throughout the organization. Only then can the true benefits of an ECM solution be fully realized by producing tangible benefits in all aspects of an organization's contractual life cycle and management, for customers and the stakeholders who are both beneficiaries and stewards of the organization's future.

# APPENDICES

## REGULATIONS AT A GLANCE

| Standard/ Regulation | Brief Description | Industries/ Institutions Impacted |
|---|---|---|
| Sarbanes-Oxley Act Section 302 | The CEO and CFO must certify that (a) internal control system provides them with all material information and (b) they have evaluated internal control system and reported its effectiveness based on their evaluation | All publicly traded companies, public accounting firms, auditors, brokers, etc. |
| Sarbanes-Oxley Act Section 401 | Mandates disclosure requirements for off-balance-sheet transactions and other agreements that may have material effect on the financial performance and statements of a company | All publicly traded companies, public accounting firms, auditors, brokers, etc. |
| Sarbanes-Oxley Act Section 404 | Requires that an organization's 10-K include an "internal control report" containing an assessment of the organization's internal control system | All publicly traded companies, public accounting firms, auditors, brokers, etc. |
| Sarbanes-Oxley Act Section 409 | Issuers must disclose information on material changes in their financial condition or operations on a rapid and current basis | All publicly traded companies, public accounting firms, auditors, brokers, etc. |
| Sarbanes-Oxley Act Section 802 | Intentional alteration, destruction, mutilation, concealment, or falsification of records, documents, or any tangible object shall have serious consequences | All publicly traded companies, public accounting firms, auditors, brokers, etc. |
| Sarbanes-Oxley Act Section 906 | CEOs and CFOs need to ensure that all financial reporting, including annual and periodic reports, accurately presents in all material respects the financial condition and results of the operations of the issuer and conforms and complies with the act | All publicly traded companies, public accounting firms, auditors, brokers, etc. |

**REGULATIONS AT A GLANCE (continued)**

| Highlight | More Information |
|---|---|
| Provides requirements for audit committees, financial reporting, insider trading, change disclosure, and assessment of control by top management | http://www.sarbanes-oxley.com |
| Specifies that each annual and quarterly financial report shall disclose all material off-balance-sheet transactions, arrangements, agreements, and other obligations that an issuer may have with suppliers or customers with which there may be some conflict | http://www.sarbanes-oxley.com |
| The internal control report must confirm that management is responsible for establishing and maintaining an adequate internal control system and procedures for financial reporting; this assessment must in turn be reported on by the organization's external auditors | http://www.sarbanes-oxley.com |
| Does not specify what "real-time" disclosure means; similarly, specifies that "material" changes need to be disclosed, but no definition of what is considered to be a "material" change is provided; specifies that the information disclosed should be "necessary or useful" to investors and in the public interest; the regulation leads to a lot of ambiguity | http://www.sarbanes-oxley.com |
| Specifies that financial documents of all types be preserved for three years and audit-related documents should be preserved for seven years; also, the Public Company Accounting Oversight Board has recently ruled that all forms of electronic documents are subject to the law, including e-mails, instant messages, and even chat sessions | http://www.sarbanes-oxley.com |
| Adds a provision to U.S. criminal laws that contains a separate certification requirement; this provision expressly created new criminal penalties for a knowingly or willfully false certification | http://www.sarbanes-oxley.com |

**REGULATIONS AT A GLANCE (continued)**

| Standard/ Regulation | Brief Description | Industries/ Institutions Impacted |
| --- | --- | --- |
| **HIPAA** (Health Insurance Portability and Accountability Act of 1996) | Protects "individually identifiable health information," that is, any data identified by name, Social Security number, address, or birth date, whether electronic, paper, or oral, and requires patient notification of privacy policies | Healthcare, pharmaceuticals, insurance |
| **PIPEDA** (Personal Information Protection and Electronic Documents Act) | Prohibits collection, storage, and disclosure of personal information related to an individual without that person's explicit consent | All businesses in Canada; interestingly, U.S. and U.K. businesses may also be bound by the rules protecting Canadian citizens' personal information |
| **Gramm-Leach-Bliley Act** | Requires financial services companies to implement safeguards for customers' current and legacy information | Banks and other financial institutions such as securities firms, insurance agencies, lending firms, brokerages, credit counseling firms, etc. |
| **EUDPD** (European Union Data Protection Directive) | Protects the "fundamental rights and freedoms of natural persons, and in particular, their right to privacy with respect to the processing of personal data" | All local and international organizations doing any business with an organization in the member states of the European Union regardless of industry, shape, or size |
| **FDA 21 CFR 11**: **Electronic Records, Electronic Signatures** | Defines the recommendations for managing audit trails, access control, and electronic records retrieval | All industry segments regulated by the FDA including but not limited to biopharmaceuticals, personal care products, medical devices, and food and beverage |

## REGULATIONS AT A GLANCE (continued)

| Highlight | More Information |
|---|---|
| Security rule, effective April 21, 2005, requires best practices for ensuring that electronic patient data are confidential, available as needed, and maintained with integrity intact | http://www.hhs.gov/news/press/2002pres/hipaa.html |
| Establishes the principles of accountability, identifying the purposes for the collection of personal information, obtaining consent, limiting collection and use, disclosure and retention, ensuring accuracy, providing security, and making information management policies readily available to govern the collection, use, and disclosure of personal information | http://www.privcom.gc.ca/legislation/02_06_01_01_e.asp |
| Makes it illegal for a financial institution to share customers' "nonpublic personal information" with third parties unless the organization first discloses its privacy policy to consumers and allows them to opt out of that disclosure | http://www.ftc.gov/privacy/glbact |
| Specifies that user data must be collected for a specific purpose, must be processed lawfully, and cannot be retained any longer than required; companies that fail to comply with the directive face fines or even shutdowns | http://www.cdt.org/privacy/eudirective/EUDirective.html |
| Establishes requirements to ensure that electronic records and signatures are trustworthy, reliable, and generally equivalent substitutes for paper records and traditional hand-written signatures | http://www.21cfrpart11.com |

**REGULATIONS AT A GLANCE (continued)**

| Standard/ Regulation | Brief Description | Industries/ Institutions Impacted |
|---|---|---|
| **SEC 17a-4** (Securities Exchange Act of 1934) | Store electronic records in nonrewritable, nonerasable format; records retention; ability to capture, store, and manage correspondence/communications regarding business transactions | Broker-dealers, banks, securities firms, any financial institution involved in trading of securities of any type |
| **FISMA** (Federal Information Security Management Act) | Requires all federal agencies to develop, document, and implement an agency-wide information security program to ensure the information systems of the agency are protected | All federal agencies |
| **FSA** (Financial Services Authority) | Abolishes the existing polarizing regime for advice and introduces new enhanced disclosures to consumers; strengthens the standing of independent advice in that firms presenting themselves as independent advisers will have to operate only on a "defined payment" system to remove the potential for commission bias | Banks, insurance agencies, financial services agencies |
| **Basel II**: **Capital Framework for Banking Institutions** | Impacts the identification, measurement, and monitoring of risks and may require banks, depending on each bank's starting point, to enhance and standardize processes related to credit risks, including commercial policy and organization, and to identify and measure operational risks in a comprehensive and consistent manner | Banking institutions |
| **DOD 5015.2**: **Department of Defense Records Management Application Design Criteria Standard** | Provides implementation and procedural guidance on the management of records in the Department of Defense; this standard sets forth mandatory baseline functional requirements for records management application software used by Department of Defense components in the implementation of their records management programs | All federal agencies |

## REGULATIONS AT A GLANCE (continued)

| Highlight | More Information |
|---|---|
| Gives retention periods for securities broker/dealer records; stipulates requirements if electronic record-keeping systems are used | http://www.sec.gov/ rules/final/34-38245.txt |
| Requirements apply to any agencies and contractors whose information systems support the operations of a federal agency | http://csrc.nist.gov/sec-cert |
| Aims to reduce financial crime and create a milieu of trust within the financial services sector; attempts to prevent fraud, dishonesty, and criminal market misconduct such as insider dealing | http://www.fsa.gov.uk/ Pages/Doing/Info/MGI |
| The new agreement contains, within the framework of capital adequacy regulation and in connection with the assessment of risk, a number of review procedures as a basis for capital calculations; furthermore, the supervisory review arranges for strengthening qualitative and individualized supervision; detailed transparency rules are intended to cause a regulatory reaction of the market | http://www.bis.org/ publ/bcbsca.htm |
| This standard also defines required system interfaces and search criteria to be supported by the record management applications and describes the minimum records management requirements that must be met, based on current National Archives and Records Administration regulations | http://jitc.fhu.disa.mil/ recmgt/standards.html |

## REGULATIONS AT A GLANCE (continued)

| Standard/ Regulation | Brief Description | Industries/ Institutions Impacted |
|---|---|---|
| **USAPA** (U.S. Patriot Act) | Requires businesses to provide customer information to law enforcement agencies with greatly relaxed restrictions on warrants; in addition, for financial services firms, modifications to the Bank Secrecy Act and new provisions create increased demands to detect and report suspected money-laundering activities | All businesses |
| **FOIA** (Electronic Freedom of Information Act) | Amended and updated the Freedom of Information Act (5 USC 552) to include access to public information held in electronic form; all U.S. federal agencies are authorized to delete identifying details when their inclusion would constitute a "clearly unwarranted invasion of personal privacy" provided justification for that deletion is given in writing | All federal agencies |

**REGULATIONS AT A GLANCE (continued)**

| Highlight | More Information |
|---|---|
| The net result of this act is that activities deemed suspicious by law enforcement, ranging from book selections in public libraries to unusual cash transactions, may be subject to investigations that require IT to track, interpret, and report on customer data | http://www.epic.org/ privacy/terrorism/ hr3162.html |
| Like all federal agencies, the Department of Justice generally is required under the Freedom of Information Act to disclose records requested in writing by any person; however, agencies may withhold information pursuant to nine exemptions and three exclusions contained in the statute; the Freedom of Information Act applies only to federal agencies and does not create a right of access to records held by Congress, the courts, or state or local government agencies; each state has its own public access laws that should be consulted for access to state and local records | http://www.usdoj.gov/ oip/ |

# LIST OF
# ABBREVIATIONS

| Abbreviation | Definition |
|---|---|
| API | Application programming interface |
| B2B | Business to business |
| B2C | Business to consumer |
| B2E | Business to employee |
| B2G | Business to government |
| BA | Business analytics |
| BAM | Business activity monitoring |
| BI | Business intelligence |
| BPM | Business performance management |
| CEO | Chief executive officer |
| CFO | Chief financial officer |
| CIO | Chief information officer |
| CM | Enterprise content management |
| CMM | Capability Maturity Model |
| CRM | Customer relationship management |
| CTQ | Critical to quality |
| CTS | Critical to success |
| DFSS | Design for Six Sigma |
| DMAIC | Define, Measure, Analyze, Improve, and Control |
| ECM | Enterprise Contract Management |
| ECM-MAM | Enterprise Contract Management Maturity Appraisal Method |
| ECM-MM | Enterprise Contract Management Maturity Model |

| Abbreviation | Definition |
|---|---|
| ERM | Enterprise risk management |
| ERP | Enterprise resource planning |
| EUDPD | European Union Data Protection Directive |
| FCM | Financial control management |
| FDA | U.S. Food and Drug Administration |
| FISMA | Federal Information Security Management Act |
| FMEA | Failure Mode and Effects Analysis |
| GLBA | Gramm-Leach-Bliley Act |
| GRC | Governance, risk, and compliance management |
| GUI | Graphical user interface |
| HIPAA | Health Insurance Portability and Accountability Act |
| IDEAL | Initiate, Diagnose, Establish, Act, and Learn |
| IDOV | Identify, Design, Optimize, and Validate |
| IP | Internet Protocol |
| ISO | International Organization for Standardization |
| IT | Information technology |
| KPI | Key performance indicator |
| MDM | Master data management |
| OCM | Organizational change management |
| OSHA | Occupational Safety and Health Administration |
| OTC | Order to cash |
| P2P | Procure to pay |
| PIPEDA | Personal Information Protection and Electronic Documents Act |
| RFx | Request for... (for example, RFI = request for information, RFQ = request for quotation, RFP = request for proposal) |
| ROI | Return on investment |
| SCM | Supply chain management |
| SEC | Securities and Exchange Commission |
| SEI | Software Engineering Institute |
| SOAP | Simple Object Access Protocol |
| SOX | Sarbanes-Oxley Act |
| SRM | Supplier relationship management |
| TCO | Total cost of ownership |
| TCP/IP | Transmission Control Protocol/Internet Protocol |
| TQM | Total Quality Management |
| UAT | User acceptance testing |
| XML | Extensible Markup Language |

# BIBLIOGRAPHY

"The BI Watch: Real-Time to Real-Value," Richard Hackathorn, *DM Review,* January 2004.

"The Capability Maturity Model for Software: Version 1.1," Mark Paulk, Bill Curtis, Mary Beth Chrissis, and Charles Weber, *IEEE Software,* vol. 10, no. 4, pp. 18–27, July/August 1993.

The Compelling ROI of Contract Management, AMR Research, Boston, February 2003.

The Contract Management Benchmark Report: Procurement Contracts: Maximizing Compliance and Supply Performance, Aberdeen Group, Boston, March 2006.

"Contract Management Is the Next Step in Smart Supply Strategy," Susan Avery, *Purchasing Magazine,* vol. 133, no. 12, pp. 60–64, July 2004.

The Contract Management Solution Selection Report, Aberdeen Group, Boston, June 2005.

Contract Optimization: A Recession-Proof Strategy for Maximizing Performance and Minimizing Risks, Aberdeen Group, Boston, May 2003.

*Design for Six Sigma,* Greg Brue and Robert G. Launsby, McGraw-Hill, New York, 2003.

*Design for Six Sigma in Technology and Product Development,* C.M. Creveling, J.L. Slutsky, and D. Antis, Jr., Prentice Hall PTR, Upper Saddle River, NJ, 2003.

"The Development of a Supply Chain Management Maturity Model Using the Concepts of Business Process Orientation," Kevin McCormack, and Archie Lockamy III, *Supply Chain Management,* vol. 19, no. 4, pp. 272–278, 2004.

"An Enterprise Approach to Compliance Management," Steve Lindseth and Ted Frank, *CFO Project,* vol. 2, October 2003.

Enterprise Architecture Maturity Model, NASCIO, Lexington, KY, December 2003.

Enterprise Data Management Maturity Model, DataFlux Corporation, Cary, NC, June 2004.

*Enterprise Integration: The Essential Guide to Integration Solutions,* Beth Gold-Bernstein and William Ruh, Addison-Wesley, Boston, 2005.

Examining Contract Management Software, Mike Kaul, diCarta/Emptoris, Burlington, MA, November 2003.

*The Extended Enterprise: Gaining Competitive Advantage Through Collaborative Supply Chains,* Edward Davis, Financial Times Prentice Hall, Upper Saddle River, NJ, 2003.

The Future for Compliance—Using Technology to Deliver Value, Pricewaterhouse-Coopers, New York, 2003.

"Governance, Risk Management, and Compliance—The Value of Integrated GRC in Highly Regulated Industries," *80–20 Leaders Online,* November 2004.

A Holistic Approach to Realizing Sustained Results, Christopher Brousseau, Scott Sparks, and Robert Shecterle, *ASCET,* vol. 5, July 26, 2003.

How Information Technology and Business Organizations Can Meet Global Compliance Mandates, Meta Group, Stamford, CT, 2004.

How to Move Your Company to Sustainable Sarbanes-Oxley Compliance: From Project to Process, PricewaterhouseCoopers, New York, 2005.

*IDEAL*<sup>SM</sup>: *A User's Guide for Software Process Improvement,* Bob McFeely, Carnegie Mellon University, Pittsburgh, 1996.

*Implementing Six Sigma: Smarter Solutions Using Statistical Methods,* Forrest W. Breyfogle III, John Wiley & Sons, Hoboken, NJ, 1999.

Information Security Management Maturity Model, Vicente Aceituno Canal, 2006 (http://www.ism3.com/).

Integrity-Driven Performance: A New Strategy for Success Through Integrated Governance, Risk and Compliance Management, PricewaterhouseCoopers, New York, 2004.

Key Practices of the Capability Maturity Model: Version 1.1, Mark Paulk, Bill Curtis, Mary Beth Chrissis, and Charles Weber, Software Engineering Institute, Carnegie Mellon University, Pittsburgh, February 1993.

*Leading Change,* John P. Kotter, Harvard Business School Press, Boston, 1996.

Leveraging Six Sigma: An IT Perspective, Kristen Softley, Info-Tech Research Group, Ontario, Canada, 2005.

*Managing Change and Transition,* Richard Luecke, Harvard Business School Press, Boston, 2003.

*Next Generation Application Integration: From Simple Information to Web Services,* David S. Linthicum, Addison-Wesley, Boston, 2004.

On Demand Supply Management Benchmark, Aberdeen Group, Boston, March 2005.

"Project Management Process Maturity Model," Young Hoon Kwak and C. William Ibbs, *Journal of Management Engineering,* pp. 150–155, July 2002.

Sarbanes-Oxley Compliance—A Bridge to Excellence, Deloitte & Touche USA LLP, New York, 2004.

Six Keys to Better Procurement Contract Management, Gartner Research, Stamford, CT, October 2003.

*Six Sigma: The Breakthrough Management Strategy Revolutionizing the World's Top Corporations,* Mikel Harry and Richard Schroeder, Currency Doubleday, New York, 2000.

*Six Sigma for Dummies,* Craig Gygi, Neil DeCarlo, and Bruce Williams, Wiley, Hoboken, NJ, 2005.

*The Six Sigma Handbook: A Complete Guide for Green Belts, Black Belts, and Managers at All Levels,* Thomas Pyzdek, McGraw-Hill, New York, 2003.

*The Six Sigma Way: How GE, Motorola, and Other Top Companies Are Honing Their Performance,* Peter S. Pande, Robert P. Neuman, and Roland R. Cavanagh, McGraw-Hill, New York, 2000.

Sustainable Compliance—Industry Regulation and the Role of IT Governance, Mercury Interactive Corporation, Mountain View, CA, 2004.

Systems Security Engineering Capability Maturity Model, Software Engineering Institute, Pittsburgh, June 2003.

Systems Security Engineering Capability Maturity Model, Appraisal Method, Software Engineering Institute, Pittsburgh, April 1999.

Under Control: Sustaining Compliance with Sarbanes-Oxley in Year Two and Beyond, Deloitte Consulting, New York, 2005.

The Use of Maturity Models/Grids as a Tool in Assessing Product Development Capability, P. Fraser, J. Moultrie, and M. Gregory, IEEE International Engineering Management Conference, Cambridge, August 2002.

Using the Design for Six Sigma Approach to Design, Test, and Evaluate to Reduce Program Risk, Mark J. Kiemele, Air Academy Associates, Colorado Springs, CO, 2003.

# INDEX

## A

Aberdeen Group, 141
Ability to perform, 95
Acceptability, 167
Access, 65, 75
Access control, 68, 284
Accountability, 184, 277
 compliance and, 81
 of employees, 59
 establish, 236, 237, 244–245
 of management, 45
Accounting firms, 282
Accounting management, 62, 66
Accounting scandals, 48
Accounts payable, 37, 222
Accounts receivable, 37, 222
Accruent, 36, 71
Achievement, measuring, see Metrics
ACL Services, 69
Active Reasoning, 69
Activities performed, 94, 95
Actuate, 69
Adherence, ensuring, 141
Ad Hoc maturity level, 100, 101, 108–109, 112,
 130, 140
Adjustment contracts, 7
Administrative support, 205
After-sale service, 166
Agile enterprise, 210, 213–214
Agility, 238, 239, 240
Akonix, 69
Alerts, 39, 40, 65, 73, 75, 76
Alignment, 90, 91, 205
Allied Signal, 150
Amendments, 14, 27, 118, 214
AMR Research, 141
Analysis, 26, 96
 contract, 15, see also Contract closeout/renewal
 and analysis

Analysis latency, 222–224
Annual reports, 48, 282, 283
API, see Application programming interface
Application interface, 241
Application programming interface (API), 226, 228
Application scope, 243
Application services, shared, 231
Application support liaison, 186
Approva, 69
Approval rules, 102
Architecture, 34, 182
 costs, 219, 220
 design, 249
Archives, 64
Ariba, 71
As-is process, 161, 162, 170
Audit, 19, 40, 62, 75, 222, 269
Audit committee, 283
Auditors, 48, 60, 282, 283
Audit trail, 25, 26, 40, 65, 69, 75, 76, 77, 81, 215, 284
Authority, 65
Automated notifications, 39, 65, 213, 215, 222
Automation, 24, 41, 140
AutoTask, 70

## B

B2B portal, see Business-to-business portal
B2C portal, see Business-to-consumer portal
B2eMarkets, 36
B2E portal, see Business-to-employee portal
B2G portal, see Business-to-government portal
BA, see Business analytics
Balanced scorecard, 268
Baldrige National Quality Award, 149
BAM, see Business activity monitoring
Bank of America, 150
Bank records, 51, 286–287
Bankruptcies, 48
Banks, 49, 284, 286–287